CHILDREN'S VIEWS OF FOREIGN PEOPLES

THE CENTURY PSYCHOLOGY SERIES

Richard M. Elliott, Gardner Lindzey, and
Kenneth MacCorquodale

Editors

Children's Views of Foreign Peoples
A Cross-National Study

Wallace E. Lambert
McGill University

Otto Klineberg
Université de Paris

New York
APPLETON-CENTURY-CROFTS
Division of Meredith Publishing Company

Supplementary tables to this book have been deposited as Document number 8863 with the ADI Auxiliary Publications Project, Photoduplication Service, Library of Congress, Washington, D.C. 20540. A copy may be secured by citing the Document number and by remitting $47.50 for photoprints, or $12.25 for 35 mm. microfilm. Advance payment is required. Make checks or money orders payable to: Chief, Photoduplication Service, Library of Congress.

BF
7 2 3
.R 3
L 3

Preface

We take great pleasure in thanking a large number of people and organizations for the assistance they offered us at various stages of this investigation. None of these, of course, are responsible for the content of the study or the way it is presented.

First, the International Union of Psychological Sciences made it possible for a group of behavioral scientists to get together with us on several occasions and discuss ways of studying the development of stereotyped thinking in children. We want to thank, in particular, G. W. Allport, J. Blackburn, G. Dubreuil, G. A. Ferguson, A. Inkeles, Marie Jahoda, W. W. Lambert, H. Levin, D. Levinson, N. Mailloux, J. Nuttin, H. Paul, R. Ribiero, Vera Rubin, M. Sherif, and D. Solomon. Their ideas and suggestions at the planning stage were especially helpful.

Then, the directors of UNESCO's Department of Social Sciences provided a subvention for a pilot study of the origins and development of national stereotypes in children; the experience we derived from this preliminary survey was of great value to us.

Dr. Vera Rubin, representing the Research Institute for The Study of Man, saw some promise in the project and arranged to support the large international investigation of stereotyped thinking that constitutes the empirical basis of this volume.

As the research and analyses started, we became indebted to many others. First, to the research associates in the different national settings who supervised the collection of data for the study, and the school principals who permitted the interviewing to be carried out in their schools. Next, to the children, over three thousand of them, who gave us some insight into their ways of thinking about them-

selves and foreign peoples. Then, to several research assistants at McGill University, Judith Sandiford, Grace Yeni-Komshian, H. Barik, Hannah Frankel, and Lucie Butler, who verified and checked the details of the research findings.

Those who read early drafts of the manuscript suggested important improvements; in particular, we thank G. W. Allport, A. Baldwin, F. Greenstein, A. Inkeles, W. W. Lambert, Estelle Leontief, M. B. Smith, H. Triandis, R. Tyler, and Judith Wallerstein. Some of their reactions were, at first, a source of concern because we realized that certain questions asked could not be satisfactorily answered with the data at our disposal. Through discussions, however, we came to realize that most of their questions and suggestions were meant to be taken as indications of what further steps in this research domain might be particularly profitable.

The directors and staff of the Center for Advanced Study in the Behavioral Sciences made it possible for one of us (Lambert) to finish the manuscript in the most incredibly peaceful yet stimulating circumstances. At the Center, Miss Miriam Gallaher was of special help, asking essential questions about our first-level conclusions, editing, and helping us to integrate the results.

Finally, Janine Lambert listened patiently to many versions of the story presented here and offered invaluable suggestions, so that, in most cases, overly enthusiastic statements were appropriately tempered and common sense was not sacrificed to technical smoothness.

Thus, many people expended a considerable amount of time and effort in the various phases of the work, permitting us to solicit much new information from children in many parts of the world. The total study presented here, however, is really only a start, a first step in the investigation of children's thinking about foreign peoples. It was not meant to answer theoretical questions about the development of national awareness or about ethnocentric and prejudiced thinking so much as it was to provide basic information and research procedures to serve as source material and guides for others, including ourselves, who will want to look more deeply into certain more circumscribed questions about children's views of foreign peoples. In this regard, we hope the research will be helpful.

More than that, however, the study has opened up a whole series of new questions, many of which were not fully anticipated at its start. Some of these we have been able to answer in part, while others brought to light here can now be thought about and examined. To take one example, we were not able to appreciate fully, in advance, the potential power of a cross-national approach to such a topic as children's ways of looking at their own national group in contrast with others. As social scientists, we were acquainted with the feelings and thoughts of members of minority and majority groups within particular nations. But in this work we encountered patterns of results which suggest that children in certain cultural settings consider themselves as minority or majority members of a *world* community. The best we have been able to do here is to bring this and a number of other ideas of the same sort into view and, with some satisfaction, point to them in the hope that others will then wish to examine them and test their implications. This has been an exciting venture in international scientific cooperation, and we hope it will be followed by many more.

W.E.L.
O.K.

Contents

Part 1

Introduction, Methodology, and National Profiles

In the first chapter we set the stage for our own investigation of children's conceptions of foreign peoples by discussing previous research on the matter. The ideas coming from these earlier approaches constitute the foundation for the present study, and the methods used by others suggested the form our study should take. In the second chapter we describe in some detail the procedures used and their rationale. We also briefly introduce the eleven national settings in which the investigation was conducted and describe how each study was carried out. In Chapter 3, we present overall summaries of the most noteworthy results obtained in each of the national studies. These profiles convey the culturally distinctive ways of reacting to foreign peoples and at the same time reveal interesting cross-national uniformities. Discussions of cross-national comparisons, however, are reserved for Part II.

1

1

Introduction

The extensive investigation described in the following pages is the direct result of a suggestion made at a meeting of UNESCO in Paris about ten years ago. On that occasion a number of aspects of UNESCO's program in the social sciences were critically examined, and special attention was given to the proposal that inquiries be conducted into "the ideas which the people of one nation hold concerning their own and other nations." UNESCO had received instructions along these lines in 1947 in connection with the project on "Tensions Affecting International Understanding," and had as a consequence conducted a number of studies on such topics as the nature and distribution of national stereotypes, their prevalence in the mass media, and methods by which they might be modified. In the meantime, investigations on these and similar subjects were being carried out by psychologists and sociologists in many countries, and the relevant literature had assumed extensive proportions. It was felt, however, that one very important issue had been almost completely neglected, namely, the origin and development of national stereotypes in the minds of children.

The stereotypes being considered here take the form of generalizations concerning the members of a particular national group. They are usually regarded as applying to all or nearly all of those who constitute such a group. These generalizations are revealed in the frequently expressed judgments or opinions about the character of *the* Germans, *the* French, *the* Americans, or *the* Russians. Unlike many other generalizations, they are based not on an objective and inductive collection of data, but on hearsay, rumor, anecdotes, or in short, on evidence that is insufficient to justify the generalization.

There has been considerable discussion as to whether the word *stereotype* adequately applies to the relevant phenomena. One writer[1] prefers the expression "the images of peoples" on the ground that this is wider and more inclusive. Another writer[2] distinguishes between stereotypes, categorizations, evaluations, and behavioral intentions, all of which relate to what may be called the "image" of our own and other groups. Still others[3] define a stereotype as a relatively stable opinion of a generalizing and evaluative nature, thus combining in one concept stereotype, opinion, generalization, and evaluation. In this volume we will refer to children's *views* of other peoples, as well as of their own, in the belief that this expression is broad enough in meaning to symbolize the various phenomena investigated.

The research in this field, particularly as it relates to stereotypes, has been reviewed in detail in a number of publications.[4] It may be sufficient at this point, therefore, to refer briefly to some of the major trends which can be identified. The early study by Katz and Braly[5] set the pattern for the use of checklists from which the subjects, usually college students, chose those adjectives they felt could properly be attributed to various ethnic groups. A slight modification of this technique was used with representative samples of one thousand subjects in each of nine countries in a survey conducted under UNESCO's auspices.[6] The method is easy to apply, and the statistical treatment of the results is relatively simple. It is not sur-

[1] S. Marandon. Les images des peuples. *Rev. Psychol. Peuples*, 1964, *19*, 8-21.

[2] H. C. Triandis. The influence of culture on cognitive processes. In L. Berkowitz, (Ed.), *Advances in experimental social psychology*. New York: Academic, 1964.

[3] H. C. J. Duijker and N. H. Frijda. *National character and national stereotypes*. Amsterdam: North-Holland, 1960.

[4] Duijker and Frijda, *op. cit.*; Triandis, *op. cit.*; O. Klineberg. Tensions affecting international understanding: a survey of research. *Soc. Sci. Res. Council Bull.*, 1950, No. 62.

[5] D. Katz and K. W. Braly. Racial stereotypes of one hundred college students. *J. abnorm. soc. Psychol.*, 1933, *28*, 280-290.

[6] W. Buchanan and H. Cantril. *How nations see each other*. Urbana: Univer. of Illinois Press, 1953.

prising, therefore, that this technique found an echo in other studies conducted in other countries. The stereotyping tendency was seen to be widespread. In fact, Duijker and Frijda seem to regard it as universal and inevitable.

Various other techniques have emerged as social scientists with different backgrounds and training became interested in the stereotyping process. Subjects have been asked to write stories about foreigners, or to complete in their own words an incomplete sentence designed so as to evoke stereotyped views. Various forms of structured and unstructured interviews have been used, and controlled experiments have been conducted to examine how stereotypes affect perception and judgment. All these approaches furnish proof of the important role stereotypes play in the views individuals have of their own and other nations.

A second major approach deals with what might be called "collective" as contrasted with "individual" stereotypes, employing the methods of content analysis to investigate the nature of stereotypes presented in the mass media. Perhaps the best known among these studies is that by Berelson and Salter on American magazine fiction.[7] This technique, too, in one form or another, has been widely applied to such areas as the content of motion pictures, the press, literature in general, textbooks used in the teaching of history and geography, books and articles written by visitors from abroad or by members of different ethnic groups within the same nation, and historical changes in the content of specific stereotypes. The results taken together suggest that the mass media may play a subtle but nonetheless important part in determining, or at least in reinforcing, the development of national stereotypes in individuals. Although it is also possible that the causal connection is in the reverse direction, with individual stereotypes being responsible for the content of the mass media, it is actually most probable that there is a reciprocal relation between the two.

A third research effort is directed toward discovering some of the concomitants of stereotypes and the stereotyping tendency, either in personality characteristics, as in the classic study of the authori-

[7] B. Berelson and P. J. Salter. Majority and minority Americans; an analysis of magazine fiction. *Publ. Opin. Quart.*, 1946, *10*, 168-190.

tarian personality,[8] or in the general political situation.[9] In the latter case we encounter again the problem of cause and effect. Do national stereotypes contribute to the pattern of international relations, or do they merely reflect the preexisting, politically-determined friendliness or hostility? One clear fact seems to emerge, namely, that once the stereotypes have developed, for whatever reason, they do help shape our expectations regarding the behavior of members of other nations, as well as our perception of their characteristics and motivations. Here, too, the conclusion appears to be justified that the notion of a reciprocal causal relation comes closest to the true picture.

In the fourth place there have been a number of studies in which stereotypes and attitudes have been experimentally manipulated. The investigation which first comes to mind is that by Sherif *et al*,[10] in which two groups of boys in a summer camp were placed in a series of frustrating situations that encouraged the development of considerable mutual hostility, and as a consequence, well-defined negative stereotypes of a reciprocal nature. Avigdor[11] also conducted an experiment in which stereotypes developed according to plan.

Several investigators have come close to the subject matter of this volume through research on the development of ethnic self-identification of children, as well as on the views held by children of different ages toward members of other ethnic groups. With a starting point similar to our own, although the general course of the investigation was quite different, Hartley *et al*[12] asked numbers of New York children such questions as "What are you? What is Daddy?" The results indicate that with increasing age children gradually substitute ethnic for personal terms in designating themselves and other members of their families. The use of ethnic self-identification precedes the ethnic recognition of other groups. Children who were

[8] T. W. Adorno, E. Frenkel-Brunswik, D. J. Levinson, and R. N. Sanford. *The authoritarian personality*. New York: Harper & Row, 1950.

[9] Buchanan and Cantril, *op. cit.*; see also R. Aron. *Paix et guerre entre les nations*. Paris: Calmann-Levy, 1962.

[10] M. Sherif, O. J. Harvey, B. J. White, W. R. Hood, and C. W. Sherif. *Intergroup conflict and cooperation: the Robbers Cave experiment*. Norman: Univer. of Oklahoma Press, 1961.

[11] R. Avigdor. Etudes experimentales de la genèse des stéréotypes. *C. int. Sociol.*, 1953, *8*, 154-169.

[12] E. L. Hartley, M. Rosenbaum, and S. Schwartz. Children's perception of ethnic group membership. *J. Psychol.*, 1948, *26*, 387-398.

themselves members of a minority usually developed an ethnic awareness at an earlier age than others. This finding was corroborated in a
number of subsequent studies. Furthermore, ethnic distinctions for
both minority and majority group members appear to develop very
early in life. For example, considerable awareness of racial characteristics was noted among Negro and white children even in nursery
school,[13] and this awareness increased markedly with age. These
studies suggested to us that we should examine children's views of
themselves as a basis for understanding their views of foreign
peoples.

As far as changes in the content of stereotypes are concerned,
there is considerable evidence that perceptual and learning processes
are involved, especially with regard to a developing capacity among
children to make differentiations.[14] The stereotypes of young children
are typically very general ones, completely positive or negative. With
increasing age they become more specific, as well as more similar to
those held by adults. A study of the attitudes and stereotypes of
southern white children showed, for example, that whereas the
younger children ascribed only bad traits to Negroes, those in the
upper grades indicated considerably more variation in their responses, and agreed, in closer correspondence with the adults from
that region, that Negroes also possessed some good qualities. There
was at least some degree of differentiation in the stereotypes held by
these older children.

Becoming more mature may, in some circumstances, retard
or disrupt stereotyped thinking, according to some of the findings
of a study by Piaget and Weil.[15] A series of interviews with Swiss
children of different ages gave some striking results. One interview
with a girl of 8 ran in part as follows:

Have you heard of foreigners?
Yes, there are Germans and French.
Are there any differences between these foreigners?

[13] M. E. Goodman. *Race awareness in young children.* Cambridge, Mass.:
Addison-Wesley, 1952.

[14] R. Blake and W. Dennis. The development of stereotypes concerning the
Negro. *J. abnorm. soc. Psychol.*, 1954, *38*, 525-531.

[15] J. Piaget and A. M. Weil. The development in children of the idea of
the homeland and of relations with other countries. *Int. soc. sci. Bull.*, 1951, *3*,
561-578.

Yes, the Germans are bad, they are always making war. The French are poor and everything is dirty there. Then I have heard of Russians, but they are not at all nice.

How do you know?

Everyone says so.

On the other hand, a boy of 13, after mentioning a large number of foreign countries he had heard about, was asked,

Are there any differences between all those countries?

His answer was, in part,

You find all types of people everywhere.

Unfortunately, just growing older does not always have this effect, but sometimes the process can be helped by providing the child with certain specific experiences from which he can learn. In a study conducted in London,[16] school children were questioned concerning their opinions of other ethnic groups, particularly of Africans; they were then brought into contact with two able African women teachers, who spent a few weeks in the schools. The difference between before and after is very instructive. One child, for example, stated before the experience, "I do not like black people; they are different in nature to us, more savage and cruel sometimes, so you don't trust them ever." The same child afterwards said, "There does not seem to be any difference between them and us except the colour. I like them. They are nice people."

These findings touch on a central aspect of our own research: Where do the stereotypes—favorable or unfavorable, general or specific—come from? How do they originate? How do they develop? A good many years ago, American children were asked what they thought were the reasons for the attitudes and opinions they held with regard to various racial and national groups.[17] The list of such reasons as given by the children is extensive, and includes references to differences in customs, physical appearance, language, and religion; the degree of similarity or dissimilarity in comparison with one's own group; certain behavioral characteristics such as

16 H. E. O. James and C. Tenen. *The teacher was black*. London: Heinemann, 1953.

17 R. Zeligs and G. Hendrickson. Factors regarded by children as the basis of their racial attitudes. *Socio. soc. Res.*, 1935, *19*, 225-233.

thrift, degree of education, and success in sports; and the number of famous citizens which that group had produced. This list is of interest because it indicates what, *at the conscious level,* is responsible for the ethnic attitudes and opinions held by these children.

We have emphasized the words *at the conscious level.* We, too, have remained at that level, and this may be regarded by certain specialists with different research proclivities as a serious limitation of our study. Our aim was not, however, to give a complete account of the origin of stereotypes or views about other peoples. We are aware that stereotypes develop out of a variety of causes, only some of which are immediately accessible to consciousness.[18] Children can tell us nothing of the manner in which stereotypes can be used as a rationalization for keeping others "in their place" or for preparing the way for hostile action against an "enemy," or for giving status and security to individuals whose ego requires the feeling of superiority over others. We are convinced, however, that whatever the origin of stereotypes, learning and perceptual processes are involved; there is transmission from generation to generation, from adults and their world to children and theirs. That is what we have asked these children to help us understand.

Although the original purpose of our inquiry was to examine the origins and development of stereotypes, we encountered a number of other issues that we have tried to bring to light and examine. These include the development and significance of ethnic identification, attitudes of friendliness and unfriendliness to other groups, feelings of similarity to and difference from others, the stereotyping process itself, and the interrelations among these various phenomena. Fortunately, an easily integrated series of findings emerges from our study, permitting us to conclude with a theoretical statement about the development of stereotyped thinking in children. In the process we hope we may have made a contribution also to the complex methodology of cross-national research and to discovering some of the ways in which children resemble one another or differ according to their national origins.

---

[18] The complexity of this matter is carefully shown in the work of Harold R. Isaacs. *Scratches on our minds: American images of China and India.* New York: John Day, 1958.

2

Purpose and Methodological Approach

Man's thinking is often marked by tendencies to generalize about all members of a class of events, objects, or people from direct or merely indirect experience with only a few examples. For instance, references of a very general nature are often made to such events as New England summers, women's ways of behaving, or Irishmen's habits, as though there were few variations, if any, worth mentioning within each class. Typically, these highly simplified sketches about classes of things or people become more than convenient summaries. Since these mental schemata are usually incomplete and biased, they give those who hold them a false reference point for perceiving and reacting to new instances of a class of events or people. That is, when new instances are encountered they are often too readily categorized without being carefully examined for their individuality. It is this psychological process of *over*generalizing that is called *stereotyping*. Stereotyped thinking about a whole group of people in terms of their national, ethnic, or religious background can and often does become the basis for all forms of prejudice; prejudice that most people, even the most sophisticated, fail to recognize in themselves or others.

Many of the more durable stereotypes are formed and develop during the early periods of life, and once established they tend to distort new perceptions of people and social events. And yet most research on stereotyped thinking, as we have pointed out, has been

10

conducted with college students or young adults who have already formed a great number of stereotypes. Furthermore, these studies have been mainly demonstrational in nature and have been carried out in one national setting or another, notably in the United States. The purpose of the present research was to fill a gap in our understanding of the genesis of stereotyped thinking of this sort by examining the conceptions children from various parts of the world have of foreign peoples and by studying how thinking about others develops from the early years on.

GENERAL PROCEDURE AND METHOD

This is a large and complex study. It is based on information received from 3,300 children of three age levels from eleven parts of the world. In order to avoid confusion and to keep the study orderly, many important decisions had to be made.[1]

The Age Levels of Children Studied

The first decision concerned the age of children to be examined. Certain guides were available in the technical literature on children's thinking. The study by J. Piaget and Anne-Marie Weil[2] in 1951 suggested that not until the age of 8 or 10 did Swiss children fully comprehend what national group they belonged to and demonstrate that they could express well their ideas about foreign peoples. Piaget and Weil also noted that some Swiss children between 12 and 14 years of age presented the view that foreign peoples with their different ways of life are nonetheless just as important and valuable as any other group, including the Swiss people. These findings suggested that the age of children selected for this study should extend below 8 and above 12 years.

There was other evidence that this age range would be of par-

[1] Many of these decisions were made in light of the results of a pilot study: W. E. Lambert and O. Klineberg. A pilot study of the origin and development of national stereotypes. *Int. soc. sci. J.*, 1959, *11*, 221-238.

[2] J. Piaget and A. M. Weil. The development in children of the idea of the homeland and of relations with other countries. *Int. soc. sci. Bull.*, 1951, *3*, 561-578.

ticular interest. G. W. Allport in his survey and analysis of prejudice[3] concluded that the first stage in learning prejudice from others presumably starts, for American children at least, around age 6, and that by the age of 10 many southern white children in the United States had learned to totally reject Negroes. When the social atmosphere stresses democratic ideals, Allport argues, the American 12-year-old often shows *verbal* acceptance but *behavioral* rejection of minority groups. By 15 years American youngsters often have great skill in imitating the adult modes of switching their prejudiced or democratic talk and action according to the situation.

With these considerations in mind, it was decided to choose three age samples of 100 children from each country included in the study: 100 6-year-olds (i.e., those who were between 6 and 7 years of age), 100 10-year-olds, and 100 14-year-olds.

The Interviewing Procedure

The next matter to be decided was the method for soliciting information. Because we believed strongly that the procedure should be open-ended, particularly for the young children involved, the decision was made to use an interview which while structured would remain flexible enough to elicit whatever ideas, descriptions, and expressions of feeling children had about foreign peoples, and yet not so structured that certain comments would be forced to emerge. In addition, a maximum spontaneity of response was to be provided for, even though certain questions would be asked of all children in order that various cross-national comparisons could be made. It was planned in advance that the child would be free to spontaneously mention various foreign groups before being asked about a number of standard reference peoples, and that in either case he should be allowed to describe and evaluate these peoples in his own terms and indicate from where he thought he got his information about them.

[3] G. W. Allport. *The nature of prejudice.* Boston: Beacon Press, 1954, 307-311. The very interesting recent work on the development of children's ideas about nationality by Gustav Jahoda in Scotland also makes it clear that we had decided on the most appropriate age range; see G. Jahoda. The development of children's ideas about country and nationality. *Brit. J. educ. Psychol.*, 1963, *33*, 47-60 and 143-153.

Then he would be asked to discuss his own national group, and, finally, through his imagination, he would describe what countries in particular he would most and least like to live in if he were not living where he was. (A sample of the standard interview is given in Appendix A.)

As it worked out in most cases, each child was seen individually in a room set aside for interviewing in the school. The teacher usually introduced the interviewers to the class and the children were permitted to leave one at a time for the interview. At the end of the interview the child was asked not to discuss what took place with the others in his school until the interviewing for the whole school was completed. Interviewers spent several minutes gaining a friendly and interested attitude before commencing. It was explained to the youngest children that they were to play a question-and-answer game, while the older children were told they were to discuss certain matters that would interest them. It was made clear to them that there were no right or wrong answers, and that their personal views and opinions were of special interest. In general, the children appeared to enjoy the experience, even after the 45 or more minutes often taken in questioning and discussion.

First the children were asked: What are you? What else are you? What else are you? Anything else? In response to these four questions, some mentioned their national background spontaneously; those who did not were asked what country they lived in. They were then encouraged to name some other peoples from foreign countries who were "like" and some who were "not like" themselves. Next, they considered seven standard reference peoples (Americans, Brazilians, Chinese, Germans, Indians from India, Negroes from Africa, and Russians) and decided in each case if these people were "like" or "not like" themselves. A series of standard questions was asked about each foreign group, those referred to spontaneously as well as those brought to the children's attention. In what way are the Brazilians, for example, like us? Tell me what else you know about Brazilian people. (When multiple responses were given to these two questions, we analyzed only first responses.) Do you like the Brazilians? Why do you say that? (Only first responses to this question were analyzed.) How do you know about Brazilians? Later, the child answered the same questions about the people of his own country.

After all eight peoples had been referred to, the child was asked: What country would you *most like* to be from if you weren't (for example) Japanese? And: What country would you *least like* to be from if you weren't Japanese? The 14-year-olds also responded to questions taken from an "Ethnocentric Questionnaire" designed by Else Frenkel-Brunswik[4] to measure children's suspicion of foreigners and people outside one's own group. Since her description of this prejudice scale appeared to be appropriate for cross-cultural research, we made use of it in all eleven countries. (A sample of this questionnaire is given in Appendix A.)

Coding of Responses

Because of the amazing diversity of responses one receives to such questions from children of various nationalities, it was impossible to work with the verbatim responses of each child. However, we learned that coded categories of response could be developed that maintain a good deal of the original meaning of the response. The protocols of the pilot study mentioned earlier were of great value in drawing up code categories. Detailed directions for coding responses were sent to the social scientist in charge of each of the eleven national studies. Questions that arose about certain cases were settled by the McGill team and the decision transmitted to all other national teams. (The directions given each national research director for using the five major codes are presented in Appendix B.)

The two codes of particular importance dealt with the *evaluative* features (Code 2) and the specific *content* of responses (Code 3). If a child said that the Chinese "are different from us because they eat with chop sticks," this response would be coded first as a "non-evaluative statement about differences" in Code 2 and also as a "statement about habits of living" in Code 3. Another child might say that the Chinese "sit on the floor, not on chairs," which would be coded in the same fashion as the first child's description. This example illustrates the loss of specific information introduced by coding, a loss that is particularly apparent when non-evaluative statements are involved. In such cases the general content of the

[4] Else Frenkel-Brunswik. A study of prejudice in children. *Hum. Relat.*, 1948, *1*, 295-306.

response, that categorized in Code 3, would be the main information retained. We were, of course, mainly concerned with evaluative rather than non-evaluative responses, and the codes were designed with this in mind. Thus, responses such as "they are mean and warlike people" or "they want the whole world" would be categorized as "aggressive" in Code 2 and as a reference to a "personality trait or description" in Code 3. From the information coded in both Codes 2 and 3, then, one can reconstruct fairly accurately the general meaning of the original responses, especially those of an evaluative nature. Thus, the codes permit one to synthesize the common features of large numbers of apparently idiosyncratic statements.

The Selection of National Groups

Another major decision had to be taken as to how many and which national groups should be included in the study. We turned to a group of specialists in psychology, social psychology, sociology, and cultural anthropology for help with this decision. The idea was to choose as varied and representative a sample of nations of the world as possible within manageable time and financial limits. It became apparent that no generally accepted criteria for drawing a random sample of children of the world were yet available, and that if we were to limit our choice to about ten nations, we should only refer to it as "a small, varied, and interesting sample." The eleven nations finally chosen were: (1) The United States of America, (2) South Africa, Bantu children only, (3) Brazil, (4) English Canada, (5) French Canada, (6) France, (7) Germany, (8) Israel, (9) Japan, (10) Lebanon, and (11) Turkey. It was urged that the Middle East be well represented and that one or two nations within the Soviet sphere of influence be included. Unfortunately, the Russian social scientists contacted showed no interest in the project, but plans were made to have a Polish group included. However, this plan did not materialize, to our very great disappointment.[5] Because

---

[5] Since then, Dr. Antonina Kloskowska of the University of Lodz in Poland has used a modified form of these procedures to carry out a study along the lines described here. See: A. Kloskowska. The Negroes as seen by Polish children. Int. J. comp. Sociol., 1962, III, No. 2, 189-199.

Gustav Jahoda has also recently conducted a basically similar study in Scotland; see G. Jahoda. Development of Scottish children's ideas and attitudes about other countries. J. soc. Psychol., 1962, 58, 91-108.

an American group had been selected, the inclusion of a Canadian group did not seem necessary. But since the overall study would be directed from Montreal, where two major ethnic-linguistic groups live in close proximity, it was decided to include groups of English-speaking and French-speaking Canadian children.

Each research director chose the children in his or her country according to a standard scheme. First, all children had to have at least normal intelligence as determined either by objective test results or by teachers' estimates. Second, an equal number of children from lower and middle socio-economic class levels, defined according to the standards of each nation, were to be included. Third, children from large urban centers only were considered, and, fourth, an equal number of boys and girls were to be included in each age and social class subgroup.

Special care was also to be given to the interviewing itself. Interviewers were to be chosen who were well experienced with children either as interviewers, teachers, or researchers. They were also to be trained and given practice interviews with this particular schedule before commencing. Furthermore, they were to be readily perceived as members of the child's own national group so that the investigation would be regarded as a local one, and in no sense as a North American or foreign inquiry.

The interviewing started in all eleven settings during the first half of 1959. The interview information was coded and carefully checked by each national research director, and summary code sheets were sent to the McGill team where the material was checked again. For several national groups, errors in coding were detected and these were sent back for correction. The data were then transferred to IBM cards and a program was written[6] so that the tabulating could be carried out by an electronic computer. The tables of results compiled in Montreal were sent to each national research director, who then wrote a preliminary report. When these reports were received by the McGill team, they were rewritten according to a standard plan so that cross-national analyses and comparisons could be made.

Although general procedures were followed by the directors of all national studies, still there were important local variations in approach. These are presented in summary form below.

[6] We are particularly grateful to Professor W. D. Thorpe of McGill University for writing this program.

THE AMERICAN STUDY

Staff

The study was directed by Dr. Richard Alpert of the Department of Social Relations at Harvard University and was administered by John P. Hill, a graduate student with experience in field survey and interviewing techniques. Mr. Hill carried out the analysis of data and wrote the summary report. The seven interviewers used were either graduate or advanced undergraduate students in the Department of Social Relations. They all had previous research experience working with children and all seven interviewed both boys and girls of all age levels.

Subjects

The subjects attended schools in Watertown, a suburban community of metropolitan Boston. Four elementary schools and one junior high school were used. Because a large proportion of this community's population is of Armenian extraction, every effort was made to interview children with other, more representative ethnic backgrounds. In this sense, Watertown is not atypical for it would be difficult or impossible to find any section of metropolitan Boston where there was not some such disproportion of one or two ethnic subgroups.

Information regarding the intelligence of the children and the socio-economic status of their families was obtained from the teachers who were asked to rate each child in terms of the other children in his particular grade. Teachers were permitted to choose the children who were to be interviewed, keeping in mind the requirements of social class and sex differences. Thus, there may be a bias in the sample toward children the teachers thought would "do well" or "make a good showing," but because there was a good range in the number and "richness" of responses, it was felt that this bias was not a strong one, if it did in fact exist.

Interview Procedures

The interviewers were trained individually by the project administrator. After familiarizing themselves with the questions, they listened to and criticized samples of taped interviews. They then carried out practice interviews, one of which was taped and later examined carefully by the project administrator and the interviewer. The training stressed establishing of rapport, non-directive probing, and thoroughness in recording responses.

Coding Procedures

Coding was done by two individuals, one coding all protocols for Codes 1, 4, and 5, and the other in charge of Codes 2 and 3. The first five protocols coded for each age level were done in consultation with the project administrator. The background variables (Personal Data) were coded by the project administrator and the ethnocentrism scores were double-checked. Code 3 proved the most difficult to use, and when questions about its use arose, they were answered by the McGill team.

Special Considerations

Because of the variety of ethnic backgrounds found in American communities, it was necessary to emphasize that *foreign* groups were being referred to in the interviews. Accordingly, the following instructions were given to the interviewers: "These are questions which might be confusing to our American children. After the question as phrased on the questionnaire, *emphasize* that you don't mean Chinese (Negroes or Indians) that live in this country by saying something like: 'By this, we *don't* mean the Negroes who live in America but the Negroes who live in Africa.'" Even with this clarification, the responses of some children who obviously had no conception of Chinese, Negroes, or Indians other than those who lived in the United States were not scored.

THE BANTU STUDY

Staff

The Bantu[7] study was directed by Dr. Hazel D. Rosenthal, a social psychologist in Johannesburg. The actual interviewing was done by Bantu men and women who held diplomas in social science,

[7] To avoid confusion, the more general term "Bantu" is used here rather than "African" or "South African Africans," which may be more appropriate ones for inhabitants of South Africa.

and who had extensive experience with children and were fluent in the languages needed for interviewing. They conducted practice interviews under the director's supervision. The completed interview protocols were checked by the director and coded by university graduates with training in psychology and statistics.

Because of other commitments Dr. Rosenthal was unable to complete a final report of the results, so that the analyses of results and the final report were completed by Miss Judith Sandiford and W. E. Lambert at McGill University.

Subjects

The Negro people of South Africa are divided into various subgroups, each with its own language. The children chosen as subjects for this study were drawn from two of these language groups, the Zulu and the Sesotho, the final samples containing half of each. The interviewing of the two younger groups of children, the 6- and 10-year-olds, was conducted in their particular language, while both English and the vernacular were used with the 14-year-olds, who had studied English extensively at school by this age. Accordingly, the English form of the interview schedule was "back-translated"[8] into both Zulu and Sesotho.

The Bantu children receive publically supported education under the Bantu Education Act. However, children do not commence school until age 7. Thus, for the 6-year age-group, nursery school and kindergarten children were selected from the Bantu townships in the Johannesburg area. The two older age-groups were chosen from the regular Bantu schools in the same area. Approximately twenty schools were used and great care was taken to explain the purpose of the study to school principals, who were very cooperative.

Estimates of intelligence and socio-economic backgrounds were made by the teachers and principals on the basis of information about each child's standing and progress in school and about the occupational level of the parents.

---

[8] This procedure makes use of two bilinguals who work independently. One translates the English version, say, into Zulu and the second translates the Zulu version *back* into English. When the two English copies differ in any respect, the case is discussed until a translation is decided upon that both agree most accurately matches the original.

Special Considerations

Since a number of Chinese and Indian people live in South Africa, the questionnaire was modified to specify Chinese "from the land of China" or Indians "from the land of India" whenever questions were asked about the Chinese or Indians. The same procedure was followed when referring to Americans ("from the United States") and Russians since "Americans" and "Russians" were names of local adolescent gangs.

THE BRAZILIAN STUDY

Staff

This study was directed by Dr. Réné Ribeiro, a psychiatrist and behavioral scientist from the Universidade do Recife, in Recife, Brazil. The interviews were conducted by an experienced social worker and a graduate student in the social sciences at the University of Recife. These two assistants were thoroughly trained by Dr. Ribeiro, who also checked and coded all the interview protocols.

Special care was taken in the translation of the interview questionnaire, starting from the English and French versions that were available. The first translation was pre-tested on a small group so that the most appropriate idioms could be found, making the final versions a good translation and one readily understood by the children of both social classes at all three age levels.

Subjects

The study was conducted in Recife, the third largest city in Brazil (population 750,000). The city is a major port, and an industrial and commercial center for the northeast region of the country. The basic cultural patterns of Brazil are well represented in Recife since the socio-cultural unity of the country cuts across regional differences.[9] The results of this study are believed to be representative of the basic orientations of Brazilian culture and society except for the recent deviant patterns found in the very large metropolitan centers of Rio and São Paulo. Even in these cities, however, distinc-

[9] See G. Freyre. Interpretacion del Brasil. *Fondo de Cultura*, Mexico, 1945, 71-96.

tive Brazilian cultural values are believed to exist in spite of the unbalanced growth that has affected them.[10]

The age-groups of children were selected with the full cooperation of school authorities in both publicly financed and private schools. The two types of schools were used in order to have unambiguous social class differences. Schools were selected in lower- or middle-class sections of the city, and information about the occupation of each child's father was made available, since occupation is a particularly important determiner of social status in Brazil.[11] In the samples used, 67 percent of the middle-class children had parents in managerial or professional positions in comparison to 13 percent of the lower-class children. Only 4 percent of the middle-class children had parents who were artisans or skilled laborers as against 18 percent of the lower-class children. None of the middle-class children had parents who were unskilled laborers, in comparison to 41 percent of the lower-class children.

Because Brazil is a multiracial society, it was important to choose subjects according to their ethnic backgrounds. The middle-class samples were made up of 91 percent white, 8 percent mestizo, and 1 percent Negro children. Although the general population proportions are 51 percent white, 34 percent mestizo, and 15 percent Negro, social stratification in Brazil follows the color line to a great extent.[12] Thus the samples of children used in the present study are felt to be representative of the general distribution of ethnic groups among the social classes considered.

THE ENGLISH-CANADIAN STUDY

Staff

This study was directed by Dr. Wallace E. Lambert, a social psychologist at McGill University. The interviewing and coding were carried out by David Matheson, a graduate student, and Mrs. Clifford Anderson, an advanced undergraduate. Both had extensive training and professional experience in dealing with young children and

[10] See M. Diegues, Jr. Regiões culturais do Brasil. CBPE, Rio, 1960, 496-510.

[11] B. Hutchinson. Mobilidade e trabalho. CBPE, Rio, 1960, 19-51.

[12] R. Ribeiro, Religião e relações raciais. Ministerio de Educacão, Rio, 1956, 104 ff.

adolescents. They conducted several practice interviews with children before starting the study proper. The interview protocols and the coding were checked by the director and his assistant.

Subjects

Montreal was chosen because it has two major linguistic subgroups, the French-speaking population with historical ties to France, and the English-speaking community with historical ties to Great Britain. It was decided to carry out two separate studies, one with "English" Canadians, the other with "French" Canadians. However, like most large Canadian cities, Montreal has received a large number of British and European immigrant families since World War II.[13] In many cases, regardless of linguistic background, immigrant children attend English-speaking public schools. Accordingly, there was no convenient way to define "English" Canadian children other than as those who spoke English well enough to be included in the normal educational program. The subjects, therefore, were either children of English-speaking parents whose families had been in Canada for generations, or children of immigrant parents who had settled in Canada and decided to send their children to schools where English is the spoken language.

Furthermore, none of the children were of the Catholic religion. In Montreal, there are two independent public school systems, one Catholic and the other "Protestant." Actually the latter is a "non-Catholic" system since children from Jewish, Greek, or Russian Orthodox families, for example, would attend the Protestant schools. The school systems are subdivided further since there are separate schools for French- and English-speaking Catholic students and for English- and French-speaking non-Catholic children. For convenience, it was decided to choose the English samples from non-Catholic schools. Thus, the samples are not representative of the English-Canadian population since no Catholic English-speaking families are included. As non-Catholic English-speaking Canadians, they do make a clearer contrast with the French-speaking Catholic subjects of the French-Canadian study to be described below.

[13] F. E. Jones and W. E. Lambert. Attitudes toward immigrants in a Canadian community. *Publ. Opin. Quart.*, 1959, *23*, 537-546.

Two high schools and four elementary schools from the greater Montreal Protestant School System were used for interviewing. Intelligence test scores or teachers' estimates of intelligence were available for all students. The school principals and teachers collaborated to categorize children as lower or middle social class. Information about the father's occupation was also obtained from each child, which served as a double check, especially for the two older age groups who could give more complete details.

The children to be interviewed were chosen by the teachers with the general specifications of social class background, normal intelligence, and an equal number of boys and girls in mind. There was no apparent bias in this selection.

THE FRENCH-CANADIAN STUDY

Staff

Dr. W. E. Lambert of McGill also directed the French-Canadian study. The interviewing was conducted by a group of graduate students from the Université de Montréal and a French woman who had been a teacher in French-Canadian schools. The interviewers, after being instructed in the use of the interview questionnaire, were given opportunities to practice before commencing the study. The interview information was checked and coded by the director and his assistants.

Subjects

The administrators of the French section of the Catholic School Board of Montreal were generous in granting permission to interview in the schools and in helping to select schools from lower- and middle-class districts. Social class was determined, however, by selecting children whose parents had occupations that placed the family in lower or middle social classes, according to Montreal standards. Care was taken to insure that all children interviewed had at least normal intelligence as determined either by standard test results or by the judgment of teachers.

The large majority of the French-Canadian children were natives in the sense that their families had been in Canada for generations and use French as their daily language. However, a small proportion of the children had parents who had come to Canada since World War II from various European countries and chose to have their children attend French Catholic schools. Thus, all of the children were of the Catholic faith.

The English form of the interview questionnaire was translated into French and then, as a check, back into English by a panel of Canadian French- and English-speaking bilinguals.

THE FRENCH STUDY

Staff

At its start, this study was directed by Dr. Rosette Avigdor-Coryell, a social psychologist working in Paris. Dr. Avigdor-Coryell selected and trained a small group of interviewers, all of whom had previous training in the social sciences or in education. The data were checked and coded by Mrs. Coryell and an assistant. Unfortunately, the analysis and write-up could not be completed by the Paris group. Instead these aspects of the study were carried out by Dr. W. E. Lambert at McGill.

Subjects

Permission was granted by the Ministère de l'Education Nationale to interview students in the French public school system in Paris. The educational authorities, teachers, and the Paris group of social scientists collaborated in deciding which children were to be considered as coming from middle- and lower-class homes. For the French study, as for the others, middle class means that the children belonged to families where the fathers were in the professions, or in managerial or highly paid salary positions, whereas the lower-class children primarily came from families where the fathers were semi-skilled or unskilled laborers. The Paris team felt that the samples finally chosen were representative of French children of middle- and lower-class background, with at least normal intelligence, who live in large cities in France.

The English questionnaire was translated into French and back into English, as a check, by two European French-English bilinguals.

THE GERMAN STUDY

Staff

The late Dr. Kripal S. Sodhi directed the German study, and Wolfgang Manz, of the Freie Universität in Berlin, administered the testing and became director after Dr. Sodhi's death. Twenty advanced students of psychology were trained to do the interviewing, and three additional people, all with previous experience in coding procedures, coded the interview data and helped with the analysis.

Subjects

The German children attended public schools in all sections of West Berlin. The schools were selected with the cooperation and advice of the Berlin school authorities. In order to avoid "neighborhood effects," that is, discussion among students, only two children were taken from any one schoolroom. It was felt that children might talk to their classmates about the interview even though they were asked not to. Social class was determined by the father's occupation and the neighborhood of residence.

It was felt that the children included in the study were representative of Berlin children in general who come from lower- or middle-class homes and who are of at least average intelligence. However, since in Berlin there was an unusual number of military personnel from various nations, these children very likely had much more experience with foreign peoples than would be the case for children living in other large German cities.

The English version of the interview form was back-translated by two English-German bilinguals.

THE ISRAELI STUDY

Staff

The Israeli study was directed by Professor S. N. Eisenstadt of the Department of Sociology of The Hebrew University in Jerusalem. The investigation was administered by Erling Schild with the assistance of Miss B. Samuels, both of the Hebrew University. Three other students in the Sociology Department worked as interviewers and coders.

Subjects

Because of the composition of the Israel population, problems arose in choosing samples of children at the three age levels. First, if the sampling had been carried out according to social status only, the proportion of respondents of Oriental origin would have been much higher in the "lower-class group," while the "middle-class group" would have been predominantly of European background. Thus, any differences found between the two classes might have been due to ethnic rather than social status differences. Second, if no precautionary measures were taken, a considerable part of the sample might have been children who had been in Israel for a relatively brief period, and their views might then be ascribed to the society of birth (Morocco or Poland, for example) rather than to experiences in Israel. Third, the criteria of stratification in Israeli society are far from clear. Thus it could be expected that many cases would arise where the classifications "lower class" and "middle class" would be doubtful. With these problems in mind, the following procedures were adhered to.

A list of children attending various community-sponsored summer camps was obtained. Then information on each child's age, name, and address was gathered. Judging by the family name and the place of residence, the children on the list were divided into four groups for each age level: European, middle class; European, lower class; Oriental, middle class; Oriental, lower class. Family name was used as an index of ethnic background and place of residence as an index of status. (This procedure was for sampling purposes only. In the final sample further information about ethnic origin and father's occupation was obtained.) The number of children in the group with fewest subjects (Oriental, middle class) was used as the number to be taken from each of the three remaining groups, and these subjects were selected randomly.

At the initiation of each interview the interviewer asked how long the child had lived in Israel. If the period was five years or more, the child remained in the sample. If the period was less than five years, the interviewer interrupted the interview as soon as possible without offending the child. The older children were told in advance that "we'll talk to some of you for some time, to others briefly, and to others not at all. We've drawn lots to see who'll be who."

For the rest of the subjects, the team turned to the public schools. The elementary schools in Jerusalem and Tel Aviv were classified according to the presumed ethnic and status composition of the children, and within each stratum a random sample of schools was selected. The interviewers were instructed in the sampling problems of the study and a quota of children, equal for each of the four ethnic-status groups, was assigned to each. The interviewer kept a running score of the number of children interviewed who actually belonged to one of the four groups. If one group was underrepresented, the interviewer turned to an additional school in the stratum which was presumed to cover the underrepresented group. Concurrently, a check on the representation of the groups was kept by the coordinator and the interviewers were accordingly guided in the choice of schools. Here again children residing less than five years in Israel were excluded from the sample.

The questionnaire was translated into Hebrew and then back into English by a different translator. The few discrepancies that turned up were resolved by the two bilinguals and the project director.

One problem arose in the interviewing: the children of families of Oriental origin gave much less extensive responses and were much more inclined to reply "I don't know." It was decided to probe more deeply with these subjects than with the European children. This proved effective, although it prolonged the duration of the interview.

THE JAPANESE STUDY

Staff

The Japanese study was directed by Dr. Koji Sato, assisted by Dr. Sei Nakazima and Tadao Kambe, all of the Department of Psychology at Kyoto University. The interviewing was carried out by five graduates and one advanced undergraduate student of psychology, three women and three men. They were carefully trained in interviewing children, and each conducted practice interviews under supervision.

Subjects

The city of Kyoto was considered to be a representative urban Japanese setting, and the Taiken school area was selected, after consultation with the Board of Education and the Educational Research Institute of Kyoto City, as a region which included both lower and middle socio-economic classes.

Subjects were taken from a kindergarten, a primary school, and a junior high school, all in the Taiken school area, and from one nursery school in a suburb. All of these schools are coeducational. In Japan, primary and junior high schooling are compulsory, and graduates of primary schools in a school area are required to enter a junior high school in the same area. Thus random sampling among primary and junior high school children should include random samples of the population of that area.

Intelligence was determined by test results or by teachers' ratings, and socio-economic class was decided in consultation with the teachers and the Educational Research Institute.

The English questionnaire was translated by the director and his staff with the consultation of American English-Japanese bilinguals. The interviews were conducted in the Kyoto dialect.

THE LEBANESE STUDY

Staff

Dr. E. Terry Prothro, a social psychologist at the American University of Beirut, directed the Lebanese study. The interviews were conducted by three graduate students at the University, all of whom were born in Lebanon and held B.A. degrees in Education or Psychology. They were experienced teachers with some previous training in the testing or interviewing of children.

Subjects

Three hundred Lebanese school children were interviewed, all from the city of Beirut. Half of them were judged by their teachers to be from middle-class homes and half from lower-class homes. In the sample selected, there were 171 boys and 129 girls, 128 of them Christians and 172 Moslems or Druzes.

Since so large a proportion of Lebanese children attend private schools, children from those schools as well as from government schools were included in the sample. An effort was made to draw from the schools in all sections of the city, because in Beirut, as in many Middle Eastern cities, there are sharp ethnic and religious differences between the inhabitants of one quarter and those of another. In general, the interviewers felt that the children included were reasonably representative of the Arabic-speaking Beirut children of the middle and lower socio-economic classes. No children were drawn from Armenian, Jewish, foreign, or refugee schools.

This study was conducted in the early months of 1959, less than a year after the civil insurrection of 1958, when questions of national attitudes were matters of life and death. It therefore required great skill on the part of the interviewers to obtain the teachers' permission to ask these questions. The standard interviewing procedure followed in all countries was adhered to in Beirut. The schedule was translated into Arabic and checked by back-translation.

THE TURKISH STUDY

Staff

This study was directed by Dr. Refia Semin, a child psychologist at the University of Istanbul. Two staff members of the University, one in Child Psychology and the other in Experimental Teaching, were assistants. Ten advanced students familiar with clinical methods conducted the interviews.

Subjects

Three groups of children were drawn from the primary and secondary schools of Istanbul. The subjects were chosen so that they were, in the opinion of their teachers, at least of normal intelligence. In certain doubtful cases, standardized intelligence tests were administered to the 6- and 10-year-olds.

To establish the social class of the children's families, it was decided after consultation with local experts, to use information about the number of rooms in the child's home and the number of people with whom he lived as indices of socio-economic class. Following this plan, children of workers, taxi-drivers, policemen, and domestic servants, for example, constituted the lower class, while children of state employees, officers, merchants, doctors, and engineers, were included in the middle-class samples.

The questionnaire was translated by the back-translation method, and no discrepancies were encountered.

3

Summary of Findings: National Profiles

In this chapter we shall present brief summaries of the outstanding[1] findings from each of the eleven national studies. These profiles will give an overall picture of each group's reactions to foreign peoples and will make the cross-national comparisons which are reserved for subsequent chapters more meaningful. A standard format will be used so that for each group the following topics will be considered in order: (1) self-conceptions and descriptions of own group; (2) foreign peoples considered as similar and as different; (3) children's views of desirable and undesirable nationalities; (4) their conceptions of the standard reference peoples; (5) their affective tendencies; and (6) sources of information for their views.

Because we are presenting the major trends from eleven separate studies in this format, the style is necessarily very compact and repetitive. This serves our purpose, however, since Chapter 3 is meant to be primarily a reference source for the basic findings, and the format will aid in cross-national comparisons. The reader will find it most profitable, however, to select only two or three of the national

[1] The statistical tables of the national reports were examined for age trends and various subgroup differences. We tested the statistical significance of all sex group and social class differences and some of the age trends, using significance tests for percentage differences. (When there was more than one response per child, the number of children rather than the number of responses was used to calculate significance, making the tests conservative estimates of significance.) The findings included in the profiles, therefore, are in most cases statistically reliable subgroup differences. However, some potentially interesting but not necessarily significant age trends are included as well.

profiles for careful examination, thereby getting a sense of the children's reactions and thus preparing himself for the cross-national comparisons that follow in Part II. Later, he may wish to return to various profiles for purposes of clarification or to make more detailed comparisons.

The summaries are based on much more complete national reports. The reports were compiled from a set of statistical tables that summarize the array of responses given by particular subgroups of children, but because the tables themselves are so numerous (nearly 40 for each study) they have been omitted here.[2] However, selected informational tables for each of the studies are placed in Appendix C.

THE AMERICAN STUDY

1.   Most American children do not think of themselves in terms of national background. In fact, national or regional references in response to the "What are you?" questions account for only 2 percent of responses at the 6-year-old level, 4 percent at the 10, and 8 percent at the 14. A small number of these referred to themselves as Italian, Irish, English, or Syrian, for example, reflecting their ancestral ethnic origins. The most popular type of response was reference to one's sex. The only other notable self-description is the rather common reference to being "a person." No-response rates for the three age levels 6, 10, and 14 were 51 percent, 42 percent, and 40 percent respectively—unexpectedly high for the older groups.[3]

In describing their national group the American children stressed factual statements and good evaluations, with special emphasis on "wealthy" and "free." Content descriptions at the 6-year-old level concentrate on presumed personality traits (e.g., kind, generous, proud) and habits of Americans. The 10-year-olds also emphasized personality characteristics and habits but considered material posses-

[2] All the tables, however, have been deposited as Document number 8863 with the ADI Auxiliary Publication Project, Photoduplication Service, Library of Congress, Washington, D.C., 20540. Copies of all eleven sets of tables can be secured by citing the Document number and remitting $47.50 for photoprints or $12.25 for 35 mm. microfilm. The cost for any one set of tables is $5.00 for photocopy and $2.25 for microfilm; in this case, one should specify the particular set or sets desired (e.g., "Tables for Bantu study").

[3] These rates, however, are based on the responses given to four repeated probings on the one topic.

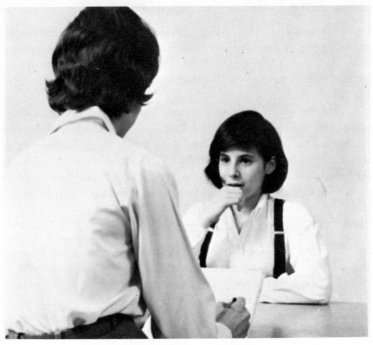

An American Interview.

sions as well, and the 14-year-olds were concerned with political issues as well as personality traits and material possessions.

2. The peoples most frequently considered similar by American children are the British, the Canadians, the French, the Italians, and the Germans (Table C.1). The most important increase with age is the mention of the British. The Africans, Chinese, Japanese, Russians, and Germans are most commonly thought of as different (Table C.2). At age 14, the Russians emerge as the people most different, followed in order by the Chinese, the Africans, and the Japanese.

3. The nationalities that American children would most like to be if they were not American are British, Italian, and Canadian (Table C.3). Within the 6-year-old group there is little favoritism for any one nationality, 26 national groups, including Chinese and German, being named. While the number of peoples mentioned remains fairly constant (27 at age 10, 24 at 14), there is a tendency

with increasing age to focus on the three favorites. At age 14, the proportion of those choosing the British as the people they would most like to be significantly exceeds all other proportions. In general the rationale for choosing is based on non-evaluative statements of fact and similarity, with the children using responses implying alliance (*e.g.*, are friends, friendly, with us in war, are with us) more often than they use evaluative adjectives (good, truthful, brave, or honest). With regard to content descriptions, the criterion for deciding is based on geography and habits of living, and to a lesser extent on personal qualities of the people in question. These kinds of descriptions were not so common when the children described the standard reference peoples, the people they "would least like to be," or even their own national group.

As for least desirable nationalities, at age 6 the American children chose Chinese, German, Indian, Japanese, and Russian, all with approximately equal frequency (Table C.4). At age 10, Russian emerges very strongly, followed by African and German, while at 14 years, the majority of American children would least like to be Russian, with African differentiated from the others as a clear second choice. Comparing Tables C.3 and C.4, it seems that American children, who are taught to view their nation as first in peace and first in war capability, find it difficult to choose to be any other nationality, whereas choosing what *not* to be is far less difficult. The choice of Africans by a fairly large percentage of the children might be interpreted as some sort of generalization from prejudice toward the American Negro. Evaluative descriptions in this case stress the bad, aggressive, different, dominated, and uncultured features of undesirable peoples, with dominated becoming the major theme at age 14, paralleling growth in the political content of their responses. The content descriptions given by children of all ages emphasize political issues, as well as presumed personality traits, habits, geographical location, and physical characteristics. American children appear to be concerned with political domination when choosing the Russian nationality as undesirable, and with cultural and environmental backwardness when choosing the African.

4. The American sample of children perceived the other six standard reference peoples preponderantly as being different from themselves. Four groups were perceived in this way at all age levels:

the Chinese, the Indians from India, the Negroes from Africa, and the Russians. The other two peoples (the Germans and the Brazilians) were perceived as different by the 6- and 10-year-olds, but this trend was reversed at age 14, the majority then seeing Germans and Brazilians as similar. Consistent with this, the evaluative descriptions were primarily in terms of perceived differences. This trend increases with age with regard to the Indians, the Africans, and the Russians; decreases for the Brazilians and the Germans; and remains more or less constant for the Chinese. Non-evaluative descriptions are predominant at all age levels and with regard to most of the reference peoples. In addition to non-evaluative and factual statements, the Chinese, Indians, and Africans were frequently referred to as "different" and as "good." A few children at all ages described the Germans as "good," and at ages 6 and 10 as "aggressive." "Dominated" and "aggressive" were frequent descriptions of the Russians, the former appearing predominantly at 14 years, the latter at 10 years. A subgroup of 14-year-olds described the African Negroes as "uncultured," a response differentiating them from the other standard reference peoples.

The content of the responses varied with age, the younger children more often failing to answer or using only the clothing, physical characteristics, and language categories. In general, at the 10-year level the children tended to add habits and material possessions to their repertoire, and at age 14 to focus on politics and habits. With regard to the Russians, references to politics appear even at the 6-year level, with hardly any physical descriptions at all noted at any age level. For the Africans, on the other hand, descriptions of physical characteristics and habits occur at all three age levels, and there are no references to politics.

5.   American children express a liking for the standard reference peoples far in excess of a disliking. A comparison of the positive and negative reactions shows that, with regard to each of the six nations, positive responses outweigh the rejective. Dislike for the Brazilians, at one extreme, is almost nonexistent, while at the other, dislike of the Russians, although expressed by a strong minority, is not as frequently expressed as liking. There is even a slight increase from 6 to 14 years in the number who express a liking for the Russians, corresponding to a decrease in the number of no-responses.

In all cases, the tendency to like the foreign reference peoples becomes more pronounced with age, although for the Chinese and the Negroes the increase occurs between ages 6 and 10, rather than continuing to age 14. Two groups drew evenly divided responses from the 6-year-olds; the Indians and the Negroes being almost equally liked and disliked. However, the tendency to like the Indians increased strikingly from 6 to 14 years, while the number disliking them diminished noticeably from ages 6 to 14. The percentage reporting dislike for the Negroes decreased from ages 6 to 10.

6. In general, television, movies, and to a lesser extent parents, constitute the major sources of information about foreign peoples for the 6-year-old American children. For the 10-year-olds, television and movies are still important, but school-connected sources such as courses and textbooks begin to be cited while parents become negligible as sources. At the 14-year level, school-connected sources are predominant, along with books, magazines, and other mass media. Personal contact with other peoples is a minor factor. Variants of this general pattern include sources of knowledge concerning the Brazilians, in which case television and movies are not as important as they are for the other reference groups; television and movies predominate as chief sources of information about the Negroes of Africa at all three age levels. The predominant sources of information about the Russians differ considerably from those reported for other national groups. The strong emergence of school-connected sources fails to materialize here, whereas the mass media predominate: over half the children report magazines as their source of information, with a sudden increase in this medium at age 14 making it the major source. Furthermore, radio, a mass medium, is a source unique to the Russians. In contrast, for example, to the Indians, about whom there is a striking increase with age in citation of school-connected sources, information about the Russians and the African Negroes comes predominantly through the mass media. This calls up the question of the extent to which such "information" might reflect propaganda and entertainment stereotypes.

THE BANTU STUDY

1. At ages 6 and 10 the Bantu children referred to themselves primarily in terms of "race" (Code 1, Appendix B). The 10-year-olds

also spoke of themselves as persons, as children, and as boys or girls. At age 14 the number describing themselves in terms of race decreased, although racial characteristics remained an important self-description for the group as a whole. Most important at age 14 was the reference to their sex, followed by "person," and then race. Although the rate of responding increased with age (no-response being 68% at age 6, 40% at age 10, 38% at age 14), at all ages a substantial proportion of the children were unable to answer.

A Bantu Interview.

The Bantu children appeared to have a very limited conception of their own group (Zulu or Sesotho), primarily discussing similarities between themselves and the appropriate superordinate group and offering almost no evaluative adjectives. The similarities mentioned by most children dealt with their physical characteristics, with habits and personality traits being mentioned by a few. Again, an extraordinarily high number were unable to answer, although responsiveness increased with age.

2. The Bantu children in general, and especially the 6-year-olds, had difficulty in naming peoples viewed as similar to themselves (Table C.5). For the most part they placed in this category tribes that, like their own, occupied the area of the Union of South Africa. A small minority of the 10- and 14-year-olds named tribes of the former Federation of Rhodesia and Nyasaland. An increasingly diversified number of peoples were mentioned as age levels progressed, but these responses were not concentrated on any particular people. Except for the youngest children, who had equal difficulty with both types of questions, the Bantu children named peoples considered different from themselves much more readily than peoples considered similar (Table C.6). Moreover, the range of peoples named as dissimilar was much more diversified. A lack of distinction between nationality and race characterized many of the responses, with a number of children naming "Whites" or "Europeans" as different. The 6-year-olds mentioned unspecified "Whites," while the 10- and 14-year-olds named the "Whites," the British (*i.e.*, English-speaking South Africans), the Hindus, the Boers (Afrikaans-speaking South Africans and Dutch), and the Chinese. A few 6-year-olds named Union African tribes, but this tendency disappeared with age. In general, the classification of peoples as similar or dissimilar appeared to follow a racial distinction.

3. As they did in categorizing similar and dissimilar peoples, the Bantu children blurred national and racial characteristics in choosing what nationalities they would most and least like to be. In general, at all age levels they predominantly wished to be unspecified "Whites" if they were not Zulu or Sesotho, although changes from younger to older age levels show a decrease rather than an increase in this tendency (Table C.7). At age 14 there was a slight increase in the number choosing the British, with a few mentioning American. At all ages evaluative descriptions of desirable nationalities specified the qualities "good, wealthy, and cultured," although the order of precedence shifted: at age 6 it was "good" and "wealthy"; at age 10, "wealthy" and "good," with a few mentioning "cultured"; at age 14 the ordering was "wealthy," "cultured," and then "good." Content descriptions followed a somewhat parallel pattern. At age 6 the aspects mentioned were, in order: physical characteristics, personality, clothing; at age 10, personality, material possessions (a jump from

3% to 21%), physical characteristics; and at age 14, personality (28%), material possessions (27%), with minor references to language, politics, and physical characteristics.

Most undesirable at all age levels were other Union African tribes—significantly, the same category named as most similar to themselves (Table C.8). At age 14, while these other tribes still remained the most undesirable, the incidence of their being named decreased along with an increase in naming the Boers as second most undesirable. A large percentage of the children seemed unable to supply a rationale for their choices; 60 percent of the 6-year-olds failed to respond, as did 30 percent at age 10 and 19 percent at age 14. Evaluative descriptions of undesirables stressed "aggressive," "dirty," and "uncultured," with "aggressive" heading the list at all age levels (12% at age 6, 14% at age 10, 21% at age 14). The 14-year-olds also mentioned "unintelligent" and "poor" with greater frequency than did the younger children. Content descriptions were for the most part personality characterizations (*e.g.*, "aggressive"), with a smattering of references to physical characteristics, language, and clothing.

4.   The Bantu children perceived the seven standard reference peoples as being overwhelmingly different from themselves. Six of the seven groups were so perceived at all age levels, the Negroes of Africa being the only exception. Whereas most of the other national groups of children consider Negroes from Africa as one rather well defined group, the Bantu children differentiate among subgroups, seeing some of them as similar and some as different. Thus, in a sense, they responded to questions about "Negroes from Africa" much as French or German children might if asked to describe "Europeans." Designations of their own similarity to African Negroes increased with age, so that at 14 years the opinions of similarity and dissimilarity were equally divided. Perceived similarities with respect to Americans and Brazilians decreased with age, remained essentially stable for the Germans, Russians, and Chinese, increased somewhat for the Indians, and increased significantly, as noted, for the African Negroes. Perceived dissimilarities generally increased with age, except with regard to Negroes. The 10-year-olds showed the greatest tendency to view others as similar; at age 14 there were increases in such responses as "can't decide," "don't know," and

"don't know why" (specifically in reference to the Brazilians and the Chinese).

Evaluative responses at all age levels and in respect to all of the reference peoples center on differences and similarities. Evaluative adjectives were scarce. Americans were occasionally described by the 14-year-olds as "good" and "intelligent," the Germans as "aggressive" and "good," the Indians as "good," the Russians as "intelligent," the Chinese as "aggressive," and a few 14-year-olds regarded some African Negroes as "cultured." At all age levels and in respect to all groups, content descriptions are preponderantly concerned with physical characteristics, but language and personality traits were also occasionally mentioned.

5. At all ages the Bantu children expressed more liking than disliking or indifference for the standard reference peoples, even though, as just noted, they generally considered most of these peoples as different. To be specific, more Bantu children at all age levels liked the Americans than disliked them; almost all had formed an opinion and could answer, and none were indifferent. Also at all age levels they were almost equally divided in expressing like and dislike toward the Brazilians, while toward the Chinese, Germans, and Indians slightly more than half expressed liking and slightly less than half disliking. At age 6, slightly more than half liked the African Negroes, with the tendency to like increasing with age. About two thirds of the Bantu children said they liked the Russians, while one third said they disliked them, and there was no change in this proportion with age.

6. Parents were the main source of information about the standard reference peoples for both the 6- and 10-year-old Bantu children. Some 10-year-olds cited direct contact as a secondary source, particularly with the Chinese and the Indians, and a few also mentioned friends and teachers. At age 14 the influence of parents declined considerably, with no one source dominating; teachers, direct contact, movies, and school texts were mentioned in roughly that order. A large proportion of the 6-year-olds were unable to account for the source of their opinions, especially statements made about the Brazilians and the Negroes. Even at age 14 more than half appeared unable to account for the opinions they had expressed, especially in regard to the Brazilians, the Germans, and the Chinese.

THE BRAZILIAN STUDY

1.   For all three age groups of Brazilian children, references to national, regional, religious, and ethnic group identifications are negligible. The 6-year-olds refer to themselves primarily as "boy" or "girl," then as "person." At age 10 sex identification is still the most frequent self-description, followed by "student" and various assumed qualities such as "friendly," "nice," and "obedient." The 14-year-olds identify themselves mainly as students, secondly in terms of assumed qualities, and thirdly by sex. A considerable proportion of the younger Brazilian children had difficulty in describing themselves, the no-response rates at ages 6, 10, and 14 being 53 percent, 31 percent, and 24 percent respectively.

In describing their own national group, the Brazilian children stressed factual aspects and the evaluative adjective "good." A smaller number also described their own people as "intelligent," "cultured," "happy," and "unambitious." Content descriptions referred to physical characteristics and personality traits, with the latter assuming prominence at age 14. A few of the 14-year-olds mentioned habits and religion.

2.   Brazilian lower-class children were strikingly unresponsive to the question asking them to name foreign peoples they viewed as similar (Table C.9). Of those who did respond, the 6-year-olds (with a no-response rate of 95%) did not show a clear preference for any nationality as similar to their own; the 10-year-olds selected mainly the Portuguese and the Americans, and to a lesser degree the Argentines, French, and Germans; the 14-year-olds named these same groups, and also included the Italians. There are no social class differences in the choice of foreign nationalities considered as similar.

The children of Brazil found it somewhat easier to name peoples they viewed as different from themselves (Table C.10). Again very few 6-year-olds were able to respond; the 10-year-olds named the Chinese, Japanese, Americans, Africans, British, and French, in that order; the 14-year-olds viewed in order, the Chinese, Japanese, Russians, Americans, and British as different. Thus, in general, the Brazilian children consider the Asiatic, Anglo-Saxon, and African peoples as different from themselves.

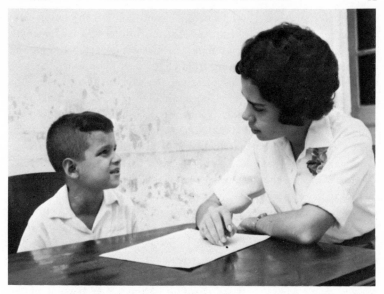

A Brazilian Interview.

3. At age 6 the majority of Brazilian children gave no answer when asked what they would "most like to be" (Table C.11). The 10-year-olds favored the American nationality, then the Portuguese and French, while the 14-year-olds selected American, French, Portuguese, and Italian in that order. Evaluative descriptions of these favorites stress "good" and "wealthy," and factual descriptions increase with age. The content of the descriptions is widely dispersed among the categories of language, habits, material aspects, and personality.

As for "least like to be" (Table C.12), the few 6-year-olds who answered, mainly from the middle class, most often mentioned the Chinese, Japanese, and Russians, describing them as "bad"; at age 10 they named Russians and Africans, followed by Chinese, Americans, and Japanese, describing them primarily as "bad," "aggressive," and "different"; at age 14 the Russians were the preponderant choice, then the Africans, and to a lesser degree the Chinese and Japanese, and the evaluative descriptions stressed "aggressive" and "uncultured." Content descriptions included physical and personality traits, material aspects, habits, religion, and politics, the latter category increasing markedly with age. Again, as in most other instances of the Brazilian study, social class was a factor in rate of response, the bulk of the answers coming from children of the middle class. In this sense, to be sure, social class can be said to affect choices of nationalities as desirable and undesirable.

4.   The Brazilian children perceived the other six standard reference peoples, plus the Argentines,[4] primarily as different from themselves, a tendency that increased with age except in regard to Americans and Argentines, in which cases perceived similarities increased with age and responsiveness. Both age and social class are factors in rates of response, no-response being greatest among the 6-year-olds and the lower-class children of all age groups, although among all groups it remained high with regard to the Indians from India. Social class is also a factor in perceiving similarities and dissimilarities, the middle class in particular stressing the similarities of Americans and Argentines, and the dissimilarities of the Indians, the Negroes from Africa, and the Russians. Although 22 percent of the children interviewed are themselves Negroes (1% of the middle class and 21% of the lower class), only 13 percent of the 10-year-olds and 11 percent of the 14-year-olds perceived African Negroes as similar to themselves. At age 14, about half of those who responded saw the Americans as similar and about half as dissimilar; one third perceived the Germans as similar and more than half as dissimilar; over half saw the Argentines as similar and only a small minority as dissimilar. Perceived dissimilarities in respect to the Chinese, Indians, Negroes, and Russians were pronounced and increased with age, although a minority of 10- and 14-year-olds saw the Russians as similar. Overall, it is mainly the middle-class children who emphasized differences, while the lower-class children more often gave no response or could not decide.

Evaluative descriptions, when expressed, stressed differences along with "good" in reference to all of the standard reference peoples except the Argentines, who were "similar" and "good," and the Indians, whom the children were unable to describe except as "differ-

[4] The Argentine group was included for the Brazilian study only, inasmuch as Dr. Ribiero felt it would be of interest to have Brazilian children's views of one South American group.

ent." The Americans were further described as "intelligent," wealthy,"
"strong," "educated"; the Germans as "intelligent," "aggressive";
the Negroes as "unhappy," "dominated," "uncultured," "unintelligent"; and the Russians as "bad," "aggressive," "intelligent," "cultured." Content descriptions varied primarily with age. The 6-year-
olds who responded stressed physical characteristics and occasionally
language; the 10-year-olds added material possessions and habits,
and, with reference to the Russians, presumed personality traits and
politics; the 14-year-olds mentioned a wider range of categories,
adding religion and especially politics. Politics was stressed in regard
to the Russians, but was not a content category in descriptions of the
Americans, Chinese, nor of any other national group except for some
references to German political tendencies and a few to political issues
in respect to the Negroes.

5. Brazilian children in general did not freely express affection
for the reference peoples. Even though a majority expressed liking
for certain foreign groups, in many instances there were as many
who expressed disaffection or indifference as expressed affection.
Social class differences appear in the tendency for middle-class children to like the Americans and the Argentines especially, and to
dislike the Chinese. A substantial minority of children, particularly
at age 14, refused to generalize about their feelings for the Americans,
Chinese, Negroes, and Russians. Still, the majority of 14-year-old
Brazilian children expressed liking for the American, Argentine, and
German peoples; their affectional attitudes toward the Chinese and
Negroes remained about equally divided as they had been at age 10.
Most 14-year-olds did not respond in regard to Indians, but those
who did divided about equally between liking and disliking. In the
case of the Russians, one third expressed liking, one third disliking,
while the other third refused to generalize.

6. Brazilian 6-year-olds derived the few conceptions they had
about the reference peoples mainly from their parents, although they
cited direct contact in the case of the Chinese, the Americans, and the
Germans. The 10-year-olds, while also mainly influenced by parents
and direct contact, cited other sources as well, the most common
being magazines and movies. Sources of information become increasingly varied at the 14-year level, movies and magazines being mentioned most often, followed by direct contact. School texts and courses

are relatively unimportant, except in the case of the Negroes from Africa. The fact that there is a high incidence of claims of direct contact with Americans, Chinese, and Germans, while no such claims are made as to the other four national groups—even the Argentinian—merits some comment. During World War II a number of American officers and men stationed at Recife became acquainted with Brazilians mainly of the upper and middle classes. Visiting and dating followed, some marriages of American men and Brazilian girls occurred, and lasting friendships were established. At the time of the present study, Americans were returning to Recife to build and operate telemetric stations for U.S. missile projects. Neither is it strange that the children at all age levels gave direct contact as their main source of information or conceptualization about the Chinese, since a small number of immigrants from China came to the area, established laundry businesses, married lower-class Brazilian women, and became Brazilian citizens. The claims of direct contact with Germans, appearing at all age levels and ranking first at ages 10 and 14, is puzzling, however, as the number of Germans in the state of Pernambuco (3,395,185 pop.) is only 1.2 per 10,000 population. Also of interest is the inability at all age levels to indicate sources of information about their fellow Latin Americans, the Argentines; even at age 14 one-half did not respond, and it is the only instance of parents being listed as a source at this age level.

THE ENGLISH-CANADIAN STUDY

1.   A few English-Canadian children mentioned their nationality in response to the question "What are you?" but the percentages are relatively small (2%, 5%, and 7% respectively), indicating that nationality is not a particularly important reference point for them. The most frequent response at all age levels is "boy" or "girl," followed by "person." A substantial proportion of 14-year-olds described themselves as students. Rates of no response at the three age levels 6, 10, and 14 are 63 percent, 43 percent, and 29 percent respectively.

In describing their national group the English-Canadian children gave factual statements and referred to the "good" qualities, the former decreasing and the latter increasing at age 14. A few 10-year-olds said that Canadians were "wealthy," and 14-year-olds described them as "cultured" and "free." The descriptive content deals predominantly with personality traits, a tendency increasing with age until at 14 years personality traits appear in the vast majority of responses. Other categories were, at age 6, physical and language characteristics; at age 10, material possessions, language, occupation, and habits; and at age 14, politics and habits.

An English-Canadian Interview.

2. The Americans and the British were predominantly named as similar peoples by English-Canadian children at all age levels (Table C.13), with the Scots being mentioned by a subgroup of 10-year-olds and the Australians by a subgroup of 14-year-olds. A variety of other peoples were mentioned by a few individuals, including the French (continental) who were named by 1 percent of the 6-year-olds and 4 percent at age 10. The children at all age levels found it easier to name peoples they considered to be dissimilar, responding at a higher rate and scattering their responses over a wider variety of peoples (Table C.14). The 10- and 14-year-olds tended

to view Chinese and Africans in particular as different from themselves; 14-year-olds showed an increased disposition to view the Russians as dissimilar. Other peoples mentioned included Germans, Japanese, and Eskimos.

It is of interest that, with the exception of a few 6- and 10-year-olds who mentioned the continental French as similar, no mention was made of French people (Canadians or continental) as either similar or different by these children living in this bicultural city. It is not clear whether they think of them as "the same as us" or fail to perceive them as a distinctive ethnic or national group. While the French-Canadian children (see the French-Canadian study) frequently mentioned the British as similar, they likewise did not specifically refer to their cohabitants, the English Canadians, as either similar or different.

3. The most desirable nationalities for the English-Canadian children are first the American and second the British (Table C.15). All other responses are scattered over a wide range of peoples with little clustering; a few 6-year-olds said they would like to be Indian, and a few 10-year-olds would choose Scottish. The 6- and 10-year-olds made factual statements in support of their choices, with the 10-year-olds also mentioning "good" qualities and similarities. While 14-year-olds likewise mentioned facts and similarities, the most common reason for their choice is that the desirable group is "good." Descriptive content at the 6-year level was limited to geographical characteristics; at age 10 the categories in order were geography, personality traits, material possessions, and language; while at age 14, personality traits and geography predominated, with minor references to habits and material possessions.

A wide variety of peoples were named as "least like to be," the Germans and Indians appearing as most unattractive to the 6-year-olds (Table C.16). At age 10, the Russians, Germans, Africans, and Indians were almost equally undesirable, middle-class children naming the Russians with considerably greater frequency than did those from the lower class. At the 14-year level, the Russian is clearly the most frequent choice as an undesirable nationality, being named by 50 percent. A few 14-year-olds, particularly those of the lower class, mentioned the German. Descriptive evaluations stressed "bad" and "aggressive" qualities and included factual statements and differences.

The 14-year-olds viewed their unattractive choices as "dominated," and to a lesser degree as "bad," "aggressive," and "poor." The 6-year-olds concentrate on the content categories of personality traits and geography; the 10-year-olds on geography, personality traits, and politics; and the 14-year-olds predominantly on politics, particularly among middle-class children, as well as personality traits and geography.

4. Of the seven standard reference peoples, the English-Canadian children at all age levels viewed the Americans and Germans as essentially similar to themselves; the Chinese, Indians, and Negroes as essentially dissimilar; and the Brazilians and Russians as more dissimilar than similar. Of the two similar peoples, Americans were more often seen to be similar, especially by the middle-class children, with less than one third at age 6 expressing views of dissimilarity and the number becoming practically negligible at older age levels. One half saw the Germans as dissimilar at ages 6 and 10, but by age 14 a majority saw them as similar. The tendency for perceived similarity to increase with age also holds true for the Brazilians and Russians, although here the tendency to perceive dissimilarity likewise increases. Response rates were low with regard to conceptions of Brazilians and Indians, but particularly high for the Chinese, the overwhelming majority seeing the latter as dissimilar. However, in the case of the Chinese, the Indians, and the Negroes, a small minority of children expressed feelings of similarity: at all ages in respect to the Chinese, at ages 10 and 14 in respect to the Indians, and at age 14 in respect to the Negroes.

At all age levels the English-Canadian children's descriptions were mainly non-evaluative, predominantly involving references to similarities and differences. A few children considered the Germans and Russians as "good," "bad," and "aggressive," and the Chinese and Indians as "good" and "poor". At age 14 some children also described the Negroes as "unintelligent" and the Russians as "dominated." Judging from the relatively large number of no-responses, the children had some difficulty in saying why the Americans are similar; only a small percentage of each age group made explicitly favorable statements about the Americans, most of them tending to be objective and descriptive. Descriptive content at the 6- and 10-year levels deals mainly with the physical, language, and geographic characteristics;

at age 14, descriptions are predominantly in terms of personality traits with regard to all the reference peoples. Political characteristics are an important category in describing the Russians but are only infrequently mentioned in describing the Americans and the Chinese.

5.   English-Canadian children in general liked more than half the people they discussed, the older children liking similar peoples much more than those they perceived as dissimilar. Expressions of liking reach a peak at 10 years of age, with regard to both similar and dissimilar peoples. A tendency not to generalize about their feelings increases with age, and at 14 years a few children expressed feelings of indifference toward the various foreign peoples. While in respect to each of the seven reference peoples there were more "like" than "dislike" responses, the age-change patterns were dissimilar. Responses of "like" increased progressively with age for the Americans, the Germans, and the Russians, but decreased at age 14 for the Chinese, the Indians, and the African Negroes. A substantial proportion of 6-year-olds did not respond regarding the Americans but two thirds of those who did, especially from the middle class, said they liked Americans. Also at the 6-year level a small group expressed dislike of the Chinese, and, for a considerable minority, dislike of the Negroes. At age 10 a few said they disliked Negroes, and at age 14 fewer still, with a corresponding increase in those who refused to generalize. Refusal to generalize about the Russians increased with age until, at 14 years, it equaled in frequency the tendency to like Russians. The response rate in respect to Brazilians was low at all age levels, and while there were more expressions of like than of dislike, a substantial proportion of the children refused to generalize.

6.   Television was named as the main source of information for English-Canadian children at all age levels and in respect to all reference peoples. The citing of other sources varied considerably. An important second source was direct contact, particularly for the younger children in respect to the Americans, the Germans, and the Chinese. The high frequency of naming personal contact with the latter is probably due to the younger children's inability to distinguish between second or third generation immigrants and those born in China. School courses, school texts, and books were mentioned by the older children, courses and texts being particularly stressed by the 10-year-olds in respect to the Negroes. At the 14-year level, informa-

tion about the African Negroes came almost solely from television, with only a few children mentioning school texts and courses. In general, television as a source increased in importance with age, in respect to all reference peoples. Radio was mentioned only in connection with information about the Russians. Parents constituted a significant source of information about Americans for the 6-year-olds only, but were mentioned by both 6- and 10-year-olds in respect to the Germans and Russians. Parents, however, were not named as a source of information about the other four peoples.

THE FRENCH STUDY

1. National and regional references played a very minor role in the French children's conceptions of themselves, increasing only from 2 percent to 7 percent through the three age levels. The 6- and 10-year-olds primarily referred to themselves as "boy" or "girl" as did the 10-year-olds who also described themselves as students and in terms of assumed personal qualities. At age 14, personal qualities were most often mentioned, followed by "student" and then by sex, the latter having dropped sharply from the 10-year level. Rates of no response at the age levels 6, 10, and 14 are 58 percent, 33 percent, and 34 percent respectively.

In describing the French as a people, the 6- and 10-year-olds gave mainly factual descriptions or referred to "good" qualities. The 10-year-olds also frequently described the French as "intelligent" and "cultured." At age 14 the predominant description was "good," with somewhat less frequent references made to "cultured," "intelligent," "happy," and "bad." The descriptive content at all age levels centers mainly on personality traits and physical characteristics. The 6-year-olds' frequent reference to personality traits is in sharp contrast to the way they typically describe other peoples, in which case they rarely make references to personality, except, consistently enough, when choosing those peoples they would "most like to be" or "least like to be."

2. The French 6-year-olds were strikingly unwilling or unable to mention other peoples similar to their own group, 86 percent giving no response (Table C.17). The 10- and 14-year-olds, however, responded comparatively easily, most often naming the British and

A French Interview.

Germans as similar, followed by Americans, Belgians, Italians, and Swiss. While the responses are about equally distributed among these popular choices, Belgians were more frequently seen as similar at the 14-year level. Although 6-year-olds found it somewhat easier to name the peoples they viewed as different, still 73 percent failed to answer (Table C.18). The African Negroes and the Chinese were most often seen as dissimilar, followed by the Americans, Japanese, Russians, and Indians from India. The French children apparently think of differences along racial (African and Asian peoples) and political (America and Russia) lines. It is interesting to note that while Russians were not mentioned as similar very frequently, they were named as dissimilar somewhat less often than were Americans. There are no differences in responding attributable to social class.

3. For the French children the most desirable nationalities are the American, British, Spanish, and Swiss (Table C.19). At age 6 the choices were fairly evenly divided among the first three favorites, British having a slight edge, but at age 14 American emerged as the solid choice. Two interesting class differences appear: at age 14 the

middle-class children significantly more than the lower preferred British; the lower-class children somewhat more than the middle preferred Spanish and Italian. The rationale for choosing, at the 6- and 10-year levels, is that these nationalities are "good" or "interesting." The 10-year-olds added "cultured" and "wealthy," and both age groups included factual statements in their descriptions. The 14-year-olds placed less emphasis on facts, stressing instead that the desirable groups are "good," similar, "cultured," and "peaceful." The descriptive content at age 6 is concerned with geographical factors, followed by personality traits. At age 10 the emphasis is on geography, personality, and habits, and at 14, on personality, habits, political aspects, and geography.

The most unattractive nationalities mentioned include African, Chinese, German, Russian, Indian, and American (Table C.20). The 6-year-olds chose African most frequently, and German, Chinese, and American with fairly equal frequency. The 10-year-olds named German, African, and Russian about equally, and Chinese and American less frequently. At age 14 Indian, Chinese, African, and Russian were named with approximately equal frequency, and German and American with less frequency. Leading rationales for the 6- and 10-year-olds were that these people are "aggressive" and "bad," with the 6-year-olds also mentioning "different" and the 10-year-olds "unintelligent." At age 14 the children stressed poverty and "badness," with "aggressive" dropping sharply as a characterizing feature. Personality traits decrease in importance with age, while references to habits and material possessions show the greatest increase. Political aspects are more important at the 10-year level than at ages 6 and 14, with a social class difference appearing at 14 years when the middle-class children express much more interest in this aspect than do those of the lower class.

4. In their perceptions of the seven standard reference peoples, French 6-year-olds, when they responded at all, emphasized the differences between these peoples and their own national group, whereas the 10- and 14-year-olds responded more frequently and mentioned similarities or gave equal emphasis to both. However, the Chinese, the Indians from India, and the Negroes from Africa were seen by all three age groups of French children as being different. Perceptions of Negroes as similar increased slightly among the older chil-

dren at the same time as there were increases in viewing Indians as different. The Brazilians, about whom the French children had no clear conception, were mainly perceived by the few 6-year-olds who responded as dissimilar while the 10- and 14-year-olds were split about evenly between similar and different. Although most of the 6-year-olds who responded also saw Americans, Germans, and Russians as different from themselves, at the 14-year level the trend is markedly reversed, 63 percent seeing Americans as similar to 35 percent as dissimilar, the majority seeing the Germans as similar, and roughly equal proportions seeing the Russians as similar and dissimilar.

Evaluative descriptions were, in addition to factual statements, primarily in terms of perceived differences in respect to the Asian and African peoples, similarities in respect to the Americans and Germans, and similarities and differences in respect to the Russians. There are no major descriptive themes for the Brazilians, minor themes being references to differences, similarities, factual statements, "good," and "happy." In addition, Americans were described as "good" and "intelligent," with a few 6-year-olds mentioning "aggressive" and a few 14-year-olds "wealthy." Germans were described as "good" and "aggressive," and the Russians were seen as "good," "aggressive," and "intelligent." The Chinese, Indians, and Negroes, as well as being seen as different, were perceived as "good," the Chinese and Indians as "poor," and the Indians and Negroes as "unintelligent." Descriptive content concentrated primarily on physical characteristics (appearing at all three age levels), habits, and personality traits, with the 6- and 10-year-olds also mentioning language, geography, and clothing. The major themes at the 14-year level were habits, personality traits, and physical characteristics, with regular but relatively fewer references made to material wealth or poverty, political aspects, and religion, politics being mentioned in respect to the Russians and Germans and religion in respect to the Indians.

5. Except for the 6-year-olds, who either did not respond or divided about equally on expressions of liking or disliking, the French children for the most part said they liked the various reference peoples. The tendency to like increases with age in respect to each of the seven peoples, and expressions of dislike decrease, with the one exception that more 14- than 10-year-olds said they disliked the Chinese. In respect to the Brazilians, middle-class children had a

much stronger tendency to express liking at the 10-year level than at the 14, when they were less prone to like them than were the lower-class children. Response rates are relatively low with regard to the Brazilian, Indian, and Russian peoples. Although the 6-year-olds who responded were about evenly split in their affectional attitudes toward each of the reference peoples, the increase in expressions of liking at the 14-year level is marked.

6. Television and movies were by far the major sources of information and conceptions about the reference peoples, especially at the 10- and 14-year levels. The 6-year-olds, when they responded at all, tended to mention parents as information sources for their views about Americans, Germans, Negroes, and Russians, but not at all for the Brazilians and Indians. Some cited direct contact as their source of conceptions about Negroes. The 10-year-olds also mentioned parents in respect to Americans, Chinese, Germans, and Russians; 14-year-olds cited their parents only in respect to the Germans and Chinese, middle-class 14-year-olds citing them for the latter significantly more often than did lower-class children, although, in general, parents were not important as sources for conceptions about the Chinese. In addition to television and movies, secondary sources for the 10- and 14-year-olds are school courses and texts, books, magazines, and radio. Direct contact also was mentioned as an information source about Americans and Germans. Two highly consistent differences between French boys and girls emerge: (1) 10- and 14-year-old girls consistently give fewer answers when questioned about information sources for six of the seven reference peoples, and (2) in respect to all seven peoples the French girls at both 10- and 14-year levels mention television and movies as sources reliably less often than do boys. There is no immediately obvious reason for this very considerable difference but it might serve as the start of a study of family control of girls in France with regard to attending movies or watching television.

THE FRENCH-CANADIAN STUDY

1. National references are not an important feature of the self-conceptions of the French-Canadian children. Only 2 percent of the 6-year-olds and 4 percent of the 14-year-olds identify themselves in

this manner. The most frequent descriptions are "boy" or "girl"; preponderantly so at age 6 and importantly so at the other age levels. The second most prominent self-description at age 6 is "child" (often stated as *"enfant de Dieu"*), and at age 10, "student." At the 14-year level, "student" takes a very slight precedence over sex (18% and 17%), with all other descriptions trailing by far. Reference to "person" is only of minor importance at all age levels. Rates of no response at the 6-, 10-, and 14-year levels are 58 percent, 35 percent, and 38 percent respectively.

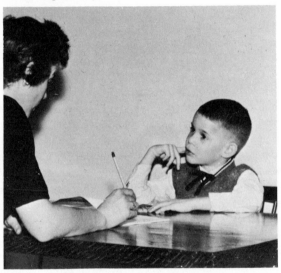

A French-Canadian Interview.

In describing their own national group, the French-Canadian children favored factual descriptions and "good" evaluations and the use of "good" increased regularly through the age levels. Minor descriptive themes are "wealthy" at ages 6 and 10, "intelligent" and "cultured" at ages 10 and 14, and "patriotic" and "peaceful" at age 14. Descriptive content at all age levels deals with personality traits, a tendency that increases with age. This usage is not so noticeable in the French-Canadian children's descriptions of other peoples. Physical descriptions, second in popularity among the 6-year-olds, become insignificant at the 14-year level. Habits appear as a minor theme at all age levels, as do religious and occupational references for the 10- and 14-year-olds.

2. Most of the 10- and 14-year-old French-Canadian children were able to name those foreign peoples they perceived as being "like us," and they popularly chose the French, Americans, and British, and to a lesser extent the Italians and Spanish (Table C.21). They made their choices, in other words, from among two linguistic-ethnic groups, the English-speaking Anglo-Saxons and the Romance-language French, Italians, and Spanish.

The 6- and 10-year-olds apparently found it easier to name dissimilars than similars, and at all ages they most frequently chose the Chinese, the African Negroes, and the Japanese as different from themselves (Table C.22). In the main their view of "different" peoples tends to be based on an Asian and African ethnic dimension, the only exceptions being a growing tendency with age to also view Russians and Germans as dissimilar. At age 14 the peoples most commonly viewed as different are, in order, the Chinese, Japanese, Africans, Russians, Indians and Germans.

3. When asked what nationality they would choose to be if they were not Canadian, a third of the French-Canadian 6-year-olds and a few of the older children stated they preferred to remain as they are (Table C.23).[5] Two nationalities nevertheless clearly emerge as most attractive, the French and American, the latter slightly exceeding the former at the 14-year level. The British and Spanish are minor choices, with the Chinese and African getting a smattering of mention, perhaps indicating some fascination with exotic and different peoples. The frequency of choosing French and American increases with age, while the choice of British declines from the 10- to the 14-year level. The children primarily choose desirable nationalities according to their perception of the peoples' similarity to themselves in personality traits, habits, and language. Their descriptions are primarily in terms of factual statements although the 10- and 14-year-olds also thought of the attractive nations as "good" and

---

[5] It is not clear whether these responses are due to the permissiveness of the French-Canadian interviewers, or to a cultural bias on the part of the children, or perhaps to some language differences in the phrasing or "sound" of the question. The latter does not seem likely, inasmuch as this response does not appear in the French study. In any event, it seems probable that most of them would otherwise have appeared in the no-response row.

"wealthy." One interesting class difference emerges in the tendency of middle-class 14-year-olds to prefer American whereas those from the lower class more often chose French.

The most unattractive nationalities for the French-Canadian children are African, Chinese, and Russian. Russian becomes increasingly more common at each age level, and ranks first at the 14-year level, followed by African and Chinese (Table C.24). Hindu and German were also named, and, though minimally at age 14, Japanese. Evaluative descriptions are in terms of perceived differences and facts, involving physical characteristics, habits, and language. The 10- and 14-year-olds also characterized the undesirable nations as "poor" and "aggressive," and the 14-year-olds as "dominated" and "uncultured." These trends are reflected in the 14-year-olds' concern with personality traits and political life in particular, as well as with the habits, material conditions, and religion of those nationalities considered unattractive. Here, as in several of the other studies, personality traits, habits, and language tend to be stressed in describing the similarities of attractive nationalities, and physical characteristics, habits, and language in describing the differences of unattractive nationalities. However, the frames of reference progressively change; as the children grow older they begin to describe unattractiveness in terms of their perceptions of politics and assumed personal traits. A similar tendency emerges from the children's descriptions of the standard reference peoples (item 4), in the content categories they use in describing similar and dissimilar peoples.

4.   The French-Canadian 6-year-olds, when they responded at all, preponderantly viewed the seven standard reference peoples as different from themselves, being divided even as to the Americans. There is a very pronounced increase, however, from the 6- to 10-year level in viewing some of the reference peoples as similar, but no appreciable change from age 10 to 14. The outstanding increase in perceptions of similarity is in respect to Americans, with some increases regarding the Brazilians, the Germans, and the Russians. Perceptions of dissimilarity, on the other hand, increase with respect to the Chinese, Indians, and Negroes—all of whom were overwhelmingly regarded as dissimilar at all age levels—and in some measure with respect to all other reference peoples except the Americans. A marked class difference appears regarding the Americans, the middle-

class 10-year-olds stressing similarities and the lower-class 10-year-olds stressing differences. At ages 10 and 14, Americans were almost unanimously perceived as similar; the Germans almost equally as similar and dissimilar; the Brazilians slightly as dissimilar; the Russians predominantly as dissimilar; and the Chinese, Indians, and Negroes overwhelmingly as dissimilar.

The 6-year-olds had relatively little information about Brazilians, Indians, and Russians upon which to make evaluations, but when they were able to discuss these foreign peoples, as in the case of the Americans, Chinese, Germans, and Negroes, they used essentially the same descriptive categories as did the older children, including differences, factual statements, similarities, references to "good" qualities, and, in the case of the Germans, "aggressiveness." The 10- and 14-year-olds described most of the peoples as "good," the Russians as "bad," Brazilians, Chinese, Indians, and Negroes mainly as "different," the Russians and Germans as "intelligent" and "aggressive," the Indians as "poor," the Negroes as "uncultured," and the Russians as "dominated." The descriptive content of their responses centers mainly on personality traits and physical characteristics, minor themes being habits of living, language, material aspects, and geography. References to the physical characteristics of the Chinese, Indians, and Negroes are predominant at all age levels but, as a function of age, personality descriptions become a major descriptive theme for these peoples also. Religion appears as a minor theme, and politics is mentioned only in respect to the Russians at the 14-year level.

5.   At all three age levels the French-Canadian children tend to express liking of the reference peoples, even when these peoples are clearly considered to be different from themselves. The 14-year-olds, however, expressed less affection than did the younger children, partly due to a tendency to dislike those they perceived as dissimilar, and partly to increased expressions of indifference. The "most liked" people are the Americans, disliked by a minority of the 6-year-olds but increasingly liked at the older age levels. The Germans and Russians are "least liked," all age groups splitting about equally on like and dislike. Dislike decreases with age for the Germans or becomes indifference, and increases somewhat for the Russians. A minority at all age levels expressed dislike of the Chinese and

Negroes, and at the 10-year level for the Indians as well; at age 14 they either liked the Indians or expressed indifference.

6.   It is a startling finding that French-Canadian children at all age levels do not recall their conceptions of others being shaped to any significant degree by the people they live and interact with—by parents, by friends or teachers, or by direct contact. What information they do have about other peoples comes primarily from television (no children under the age of 16 are allowed to attend movies in Montreal, except for a rare children's program). At the 10-year level, the importance of television reaches its high point as the most important information source, but a trend starts at this age for textbooks and other books to play a minor role. At the 14-year level, textbooks become as important as television in respect to the Chinese, Germans, and Negroes, and almost as important in respect to the Russians. In two cases, those of the Brazilians and Indians, textbooks exceed television as a source of information for 14-year-olds. For conceptions concerning Americans, however, television is the primary source at all age levels. It is noteworthy that Americans are treated as any other foreign peoples by the French-Canadian children; that is, the descriptions given of them are not attributed to firsthand knowledge, such as through direct contact, nor to personal sources such as parents, teachers, and friends. In respect to all of the reference peoples except the Brazilians, magazines are minor but consistent sources for the 10- and 14-year-olds.

THE GERMAN STUDY

1.   While the majority of German children did not describe themselves as being German, the tendency does increase with age— 1 percent at age 6, 3 percent at age 10, and 9 percent at age 14. The two youngest age groups emphasized that they were boys or girls, a tendency which drops into second place behind student for the 14-year-olds. The 6- and 10-year-olds also referred to themselves as persons, students, and children, and a few mentioned various personal qualities. At 14 years the order of precedence in self-description is student at 16 percent, sex 14 percent, person 10 percent, and national identification, child, and personal qualities, all at 9 percent.

A German Interview.

The rate of no-response at ages 6, 10, and 14 is 30 percent, 11 percent, and 18 percent respectively.

The 6- and 10-year-old German children described their own national group primarily through factual statements and in terms of similarities and good qualities. A few described their own people as "good," "ambitious," and "wealthy." At age 14 the pattern changes significantly. These children then view the German people as predominantly "ambitious" and "good" and give very few factual statements and no references to similarities; a small group also described the Germans as "intelligent." Descriptive content deals increasingly with personality traits, which predominate at all three age levels, followed at age 6 by physical characteristics, language, habits, and material possessions; at age 10, by political issues, material possessions, and physical characteristics; and at age 14, by occupation, and political issues. Since there are more evaluative, personality-oriented descriptions given of their own group than of foreign peoples (see below), it is hypothesized that the stereotyping process may start with one's own national group.

2. The peoples that German children most frequently considered similar to themselves are the Americans, British, and French (Table C.25). A few also considered Russians, Austrians, Swiss, and Italians as similar, but with increased age the Russians and Italians were mentioned less frequently and the Swedes somewhat more often. The peculiar situation of Berlin since World War II may affect the generality of these findings for all German children.

Peoples with an African or Asiatic ethnic background were most likely to be named as different (Table C.26). In general the Africans and the Chinese were thought of as different by all three age groups of German children, with less mention of Japanese and Eskimos. A few children also named Russians, Italians, and Americans.

3. German children named Americans, with increasing frequency from 6 to 14 years, as the people they would most like to be if they were not German. Middle-class 6- and 10-year-olds named Americans more often than did lower-class children (Table C.27). The 6-year-olds also named Africans and Chinese, possibly because of their exotic characteristics, as did a few 10-year-olds. At 14 years few peoples other than Americans were mentioned, the exceptions being the Swiss, the Swedes, and the Italians. At age 6 the rationale for choosing included factual statements and descriptions of desirable groups as "good," "wealthy," "cultured," and similar to themselves. At the 10-year level, factual statements were equaled by considerations of wealth, the former being favored by children of the lower class and the latter by those of the middle class. At 14 years the children preponderantly referred to the wealth of the chosen nations. Descriptive content emphasized physical characteristics and geographical location at the 6-year level and material possessions, personality traits, and political issues at ages 10 and 14.

The least desirable nationality at all age levels was the Russian, particularly at age 10, followed by African and Chinese (Table C.28). The only change in the top three from ages 6 to 14 is the replacement of Africans by Chinese for second place. A small number of children at 10 years considered being Eskimo unattractive and at 14 years, being Indian. Evaluative descriptions at age 6 stress the qualities "aggressive" and "bad," with some attention to differences and factual statements, the middle-class children favoring the latter while lower-class children stressed "bad" qualities. The 10-year-olds also emphasized "aggression" but added that the undesirable nations are "poor" and "dominated." At the 14-year level, aggressive characteristics lose their significance and nations are considered unattractive because they are "poor" or "dominated," middle-class children stressing the former and lower-class children the latter. For the 6-year-olds, the descriptive content for unattractive nations focused on physical characteristics, presumed personality traits, and politics; the descriptions of the 10-year-olds dealt with material possessions and habits, and increased the emphasis on politics; at the 14-year level, material possessions and politics became the dominant themes.

4.   With regard to the standard reference peoples, the German children saw two of them practically unanimously as being dissimilar —the Negroes from Africa and the Chinese. In both instances the rate of response was extremely high. Response rates were also high regarding the Americans and the Russians, low at all ages for the Brazilians, and low at 6 years for the Indians from India. In the latter case, response rates increased with age and were accompanied by increased perceptions of dissimilarity. The majority at all ages perceived the Brazilians as dissimilar, especially children of the middle class. At age 6, half of the German children perceived Americans as similar and half as dissimilar, although the similarity view increases with age. They were likewise divided in their perceptions of Russians but with a different pattern: at age 6 a majority saw the Russians as dissimilar, about one third as similar; at 10 years the trend is reversed, two-thirds stating that the Russians are "like us"; at age 14 the trend is again reversed, with the children emphasizing the dissimilarity of Russians in the same proportion as at age 6.

Evaluative responses with regard to the Brazilians, Chinese, Indians, and Negroes are mainly in terms of differences, phrased as statements of facts. In addition, the Chinese were characterized as "good," "bad," and "poor." One gets the impression that the children's picture of China and her inhabitants is a mixture of vague information about the ancient Chinese culture, the invention of paper, the wall of China, Chinese lettering, and her poverty and economic difficulties. There also emerges an admiration of recent efforts to improve the economy. The Indians also were described as "poor" and "good," and the Negroes as "good" by a few at all ages, "poor" and "uncultured" by the 10-year-olds, and as "poor," "uncultured," and "dominated" by the 14-year-olds. The Americans were characterized in terms of differences and similarities at age 6 and similarities at ages 10 and 14 along with references to good qualities and wealth. The evaluation "good" referred specifically to help given ("they helped us after the war," "they flew in goods"); the similarities mentioned referred to ethnic identification ("the Americans were originally Europeans," "there are many German immigrants"), and the evaluation "wealthy" was implied by such statements as "they are as wealthy as we are, maybe somewhat better," or "we are not yet as rich as the Americans generally are." Russians were described in terms of factual statements, differences and similarities, and as "aggressive" and "bad," with "aggressive" referring to perceived threats to Berlin and the division of Germany (which appeared to the children as Communist malevolence), and to all destruction during World War II, for which interestingly enough, they held the Russians responsible. Descriptive content concerned physical characteristics, at all age levels and in respect to all reference peoples with only two exceptions: the 14-year-olds placed presumed personality traits first in describing Americans and political issues first in characterizing Russians. Personality traits are also an important descriptive theme throughout, appearing uniquely (although not predominantly) along with politics even at the 6-year level in descriptions of Russians.

5.   The German children's tendencies to express liking for the other standard reference peoples increase notably from ages 6 to 10, but not from 10 to 14. There are striking increases through all age levels in the tendency to like those foreign peoples considered as similar, that is, the Americans and, for a regular minority, the Russians. Although a substantial minority of German 6-year-olds expressed dislike of Americans, the tendency to like them increased regularly with age. At all age levels many did not respond toward Brazilians; those at age 6 who did were divided equally between like and dislike, while most of the older children who responded said they liked Brazilians. Roughly equal groups of "likers" and "dislikers" of the Chinese emerged at all age levels, with a small increase from ages 10 to 14 of those who did not generalize. A majority at age 6 expressed liking for the Negroes, although a large minority expressed

dislike. With age, however, expressions of liking increased and those of disliking decreased. For the Russians a regular minority expressed affection at all age levels, although at ages 6 and 10 a strong tendency to dislike prevailed. At 14 years, expressions of liking for Russians increased and those of disliking decreased, while a remarkably high percentage preferred not to generalize, perhaps reflecting a generalized distinction between the "good" Russian people and the "bad" government. Thus, from ages 6 to 14, expressions of liking increased and expressions of disliking decreased in all cases except toward the Chinese for whom such expressions remained essentially stable, and toward the Russians for whom an increase in dislike was expressed at age 10.

6. In general, as with other national groups, German 6-year-olds primarily cited parents as sources of information, but this dependence on parents decreased with age as the citation of other sources increased. Television and movies are major sources for German children at all age levels. Direct contact was frequently mentioned by 6- and 10-year-olds with regard to Americans, Negroes, and Russians, but appears to refer to casual encounters such as seeing American soldiers in the streets, or in some cases to be the result of confusing East German police and customs officials with Russians, and Negroes of the U.S. armed forces with Negroes from Africa. References to such contacts decrease with age, probably because of a more refined concept of direct contact, such as friendships, or neighborhood relationships. For information about the Chinese, television and movies are the predominant sources at all age levels. While the children often named these media as sources of information about all reference peoples, it is only in the case of the Chinese that they named a particular film or program, a large number spontaneously mentioning a documentary on the working-camps entitled "The Blue Ants," which had appeared on television shortly before the interviewing took place. Many at all ages could not name any sources of information about the Brazilians and the Indians; those who did primarily cited television and movies, with books assuming increasing importance along with, in regard to Indians, school texts and courses. The Indians are the only standard reference people for whom a distinct influence of school information is evident. Opinion formation about the Russians was greatly influenced by parents as sources at all

age levels, although magazines and especially newspapers were dominant sources for 10- and 14-year-olds. Television and movies were
relatively less important and radio more important as sources of conceptions regarding the Russians.

THE ISRAELI STUDY

1. Only about 5 percent of the Israeli children identified themselves in terms of their nationality, and somewhat fewer in terms of
religion. Ethnic self-identification was practically nonexistent. The
majority of children at all age levels described themselves as "yeled"
(meaning boy as well as child) or "yalda" (meaning girl as well as
child), and these responses were all coded as "child." Thus there is
no means of determining how important sex role differentiations are
in the self-conceptions of the Israeli children. The 6-year-olds also
described themselves in terms of assumed personal qualities, and a
few as "person" or "student," or an "Israeli of the Jewish faith."
The 10- and 14-year-olds also described themselves as a "person" or
a "student," a few referred to personal qualities, and to national and
religious identifications. Rates of no response at the three age levels
6, 10, and 14 are 41 percent, 37 percent, and 26 percent respectively.

In describing the Israelis as a national group, the Israeli children primarily employed factual statements and referred to what they
saw as similarities among themselves. They also perceived their own
people as "good" and "religious." The older children made frequent
use of these same descriptions, the 10-year-olds adding "peaceful"
and "intelligent," and the 14-year-olds further adding "ambitious"
and "educated." The content of the responses dealt mainly with personality traits, a theme that increases with age. Religion and physical
characteristics occur as minor themes. The 10-year-olds mention
habits of living, and the 14-year-olds add material aspects and politics. At the 14-year level, personality traits are overwhelmingly the
most popular category, and physical characteristics show the sharpest
decrease.

2. At all age levels the Israeli children chose as people most
similar to themselves the Americans, British, French, Russians, and
Poles (Table C.29). The large array of foreign peoples considered as
similar is presumably a direct result of the population composition

An Israeli Interview.

of Israel, nearly all children having at least one parent who was born elsewhere in the world. Nevertheless, similarity is predominantly seen with the Americans, the British, and the French, and this is not explainable in terms of the origins of the children's families.

It was somewhat more difficult for these children to name foreign peoples they considered different from themselves, as indicated by the slightly higher proportion of no-answers (Table C.30). In general, they most frequently mentioned the African Negroes, the Chinese, and the Arabs as dissimilar. With age, they increasingly view the Africans and Chinese as dissimilar, and less often so view the Arabs. Other peoples considered dissimilar are the Indians, American Indians, and Japanese, especially by the older children whose response rates are higher.

3. Most Israeli children at all age levels said they would prefer to be American if they were not Israeli (Table C.31). The next most desirable nationalities were the French and the British, and a few

chose Russian and Swiss. A third of the children could not give reasons for their choices, and those who did described the attractive peoples in terms of factual statements, perceived similarities, and "good" qualities. The 10- and 14-year-olds followed this general pattern, the 14-year-olds also referring to the attractive peoples as "wealthy" and "intelligent," while similarities as a theme decreased in proportion. Descriptive content dealt mainly with personality traits, especially at the 10- and 14-year levels. Material aspects showed an important increase between the ages 10 and 14. Neither physical nor political characteristics appear in the descriptions of peoples the children would most like to be.

At all age levels the Israeli children said they would least like to be Arab (Table C.32). In addition, the 6-year-olds mentioned the Egyptian, German, and African nationalities as undesirable. References to Egyptians and Africans increase at the 10-year level, but decrease somewhat at age 14. The tendency to name Germany as undesirable increases considerably at age 14, when there is also some tendency not to want to be Russian. The 14-year-olds thus named the Arab, German, and African nationalities, in that order, with the Russian and Egyptian being mentioned by a minority. Evaluative descriptions of the unattractive peoples, in addition to mention of facts and differences are, at age 6, "bad" and "aggressive." The 10- and 14-year-olds add "uncultured," "unintelligent," and "uneducated" as descriptive themes. As for content of responses, all age groups emphasize personality traits; the 6- and 10-year-olds gave some attention to physical characteristics; the 10- and 14-year-olds spoke of political aspects and living habits.

4. The Israeli children at all age levels generally considered the seven reference peoples to be more different from than similar to themselves. They were practically unanimous in viewing the Chinese and the Negroes from Africa as different, and the majority also saw the Indians from India as different. While most viewed the Germans and Russians as similar to themselves, substantial minorities still viewed them as dissimilar. Approximately equal groups saw the Brazilians as similar and as dissimilar, with the 14-year-olds tending to perceive them as dissimilar. A decisive majority of the Israeli children saw the Americans as similar to themselves. Less than half of the 6-year-olds were able to respond when questioned about any

of the reference peoples, the lowest response being in respect to the Brazilians, and the highest, the Chinese. Response rates increased markedly with age, although they remained comparatively low when the Brazilians were being discussed.

At all three ages the Israeli children primarily described the reference peoples in terms of perceived similarities and differences, and by statements of facts known about them. Few 6-year-olds could describe any but the Americans and Negroes; those who could used the evaluative adjective "good" to describe Americans, and "bad" and "aggressive," the Germans. The 10- and 14-year-olds saw the Americans as "good," "wealthy," and "intelligent"; the Germans as "bad" and "aggressive"; and the Negroes as "unintelligent," "uncultured," and "good." The Russians were seen by 10-year-olds as "bad" and "aggressive," and by 14-year-olds as "bad" and "intelligent." The Chinese appeared as "good" to 10-year-olds and as "interesting" to 14-year-olds. The older children saw the Brazilians and Indians as "good." Content of responses varied according to age level and the nationality being described. In general, physical characteristics are the most common descriptive theme, especially for the younger age groups when describing the Chinese and Negroes. Descriptions of personality become increasingly more frequent at 10 years, and at 14 surpass those of physical characteristics except in the cases of Negroes and Chinese. The 10- and 14-year-olds also stressed habits of living. Politics was mentioned by the two older groups in respect to Germans and Russians, religion in respect to the Indians, and material possessions at all age levels in describing Americans.

5. The Israeli children are generally selective and somewhat cautious about expressing affection for foreign groups. In respect to the African Negroes, about twice as many 6- and 10-year-olds disliked as liked them, but at age 14 the majority said they liked Negroes. Expressions of dislike for two peoples increased with age: (1) slightly more 6-year-olds said they liked the Russians than disliked them, but somewhat more of the older children expressed dislike or refused to generalize; (2) a majority of 6-year-olds said they disliked the Germans, a tendency that increased strikingly at age 10; 14-year-olds increasingly expressed dislike, with a decrease in those who said they liked Germans. Expressions of liking Amer-

icans, Chinese, and Indians increased markedly from 6 years to 10; 14-year-olds showed little change in the proportions, with substantial minorities refusing to generalize. Response rates are low in respect to Brazilians, but most who answered said that they liked them.

6. For Israeli 6-year-olds, parents and friends are important sources of information about the reference peoples. For the 10-year-olds, the major sources are books, friends, and movies; and for the 14-year-olds, books, friends, school courses, magazines, and movies. The 6-year-olds have practically no knowledge about the Brazilians and Indians, and parents—who are to some degree sources at all age levels for conceptions of the Americans and Germans, and at 6 and 10 years for the Russians—are not mentioned at any age level. In general, parents and friends are rather important as sources for the children's conceptions, as are teachers to a less marked degree. Direct contact is mentioned at all age levels in respect to Americans, by the 6- and 10-year-olds in respect to Negroes, and by 10-year-olds in respect to Russians. One interesting aspect is that Israeli children do not name movies as sources of their knowledge of Americans, Germans, and Russians, but they do mention them as sources regarding the Chinese, Indians, and Negroes. Radio as a minor source is mentioned in respect to the Americans and the Russians, probably because of these nations' prominence in newscasts. At the 10- and 14-year levels, books are a major source of information with regard to all the reference peoples.

THE JAPANESE STUDY

1. More than half of the Japanese children in each age group made no response to the "What are you?" questions (at ages 6, 10, and 14, no-response rates are 69%, 54%, and 52% respectively). Aside from a few references to being a person (9%, diminishing to 1% at the older age levels), responses of the 6-year-olds formed no pattern. At 10 and 14 years there was a marked increase in references to national and regional (Kyoto) backgrounds, each category being used by about 15 percent. The two older age groups also made references to their sex (13% at age 10, 14% at age 14), but other than these there were hardly any other common self-references made. No

A Japanese Interview.

references to race were made at any age level, and only about 1 percent referred to religion.

In describing the Japanese as a people, all age groups stressed non-evaluative factual statements, especially the 6- and 10-year-olds. The 10- and 14-year-old children also characterized the Japanese as "good" (3% at age 10, 6% at age 14), "bad" (3%, 13%), "intelligent" (5%, 3%), "unintelligent" (2%, 3%), "poor" (7%, 5%), "aggressive" (2%, 4%), and "uncultured" (1%, 2%). In addition, the 14-year-olds mentioned "unambitious" (3%). A few 10-year-olds (2%) saw the Japanese as "wealthy" but the 14-year-olds did not. It seems that as the Japanese child grows older he becomes increasingly critical of his own people. The content of the descriptions stresses physical characteristics at the 6- and 10-year levels; personality traits were emphasized by the 14-year-olds, with physical characteristics second. Material possessions and habits were also frequently mentioned, with clothing, food, and politics as minor themes.

2. The Japanese 6-year-olds who responded showed some difficulty in naming peoples similar to themselves, but of the few peo-

ples mentioned the Americans are predominant (Table C.33); apparently for the 6-year-olds Americans were somewhat better known than other foreigners. Among the older children an ethnic distinction becomes prominent, the Chinese and Koreans being named as the peoples "most like us," with only a very few naming the Americans or any other foreign nationality.

The response rate is higher for naming dissimilar peoples, indicating that this question was easier for the children (Table C.34). Again, probably due to their being better known, Americans were also chosen by the 6-year-olds as the people most different from themselves, a perception that is maintained as well at the 10- and 14-year levels. The second most frequently mentioned as different are the French for the 6-year-olds, the Hindus for the 10-year-olds, and the British for the 14-year-olds. The frequency of naming Hindus decreases from age 10 to age 14. Other peoples less frequently named as dissimilar, but increasingly mentioned with age, are the Africans, Germans, and Russians.

3. The Japanese children of all three age groups most often wished to be American if they were not Japanese (Table C.35). A few children at ages 6 and 10 also saw the French nationality as attractive, and a small group mentioned the Russian and British. The 14-year-olds gave second preference to the Swiss, followed with equal preference by French, Russian, and German. Lower-class 10- and 14-year-olds in particular wanted to be American, while the middle-class children leaned toward the French and the Swiss. The principal reason given for seeing these nations as desirable was their wealth, this being the predominant response at all three age levels. Desirable nations were described as "wealthy" by more lower-class than middle-class 10- and especially 14-year-olds. The adjective "good" was also used by all three age groups; the 10-year-olds also used the descriptions "cultured," "clean," and "intelligent," while the 14-year-olds mentioned "peaceful," possibly a reflection of their attraction to the politically neutral Swiss. Facts and similarities were sparingly given at all age levels. The descriptive content of most responses refers to the material aspects. Considerably fewer references were made to personality traits, physical characteristics, and politics. Interest in political aspects greatly increases at the 14-year level, accounting at that age for one quarter of all the responses.

Although the American nationality was by far the least desirable for Japanese 6-year-olds, this viewpoint was almost never expressed by the 10- and 14-year-olds (Table C.36). At the 10-year level, African, Indian, and Chinese were named as least desirable, while the 14-year-olds increasingly and overwhelmingly named African, followed by Russian, Indian, Korean, and Chinese (only 1%). Rationales for these choices were, at the 6-year level, "aggressive" and "dirty"; at the 10-year level "dirty," "uncultured," and "aggressive"; and at the 14-year level "uncultured," "dirty," and "dominated." Thus progression from the 10- to the 14-year level shows an increase from 1 percent to 16 percent in the use of "dominated" and a decrease from 35 percent to 20 percent in use of "dirty." Again facts, and especially dissimilarities, were of little importance in descriptions of nationalities mentioned. The content category most used by all age groups is that of physical characteristics. Next in importance for the 6-year-olds are personality traits and language; for the 10-year-olds, geographical and personality aspects; and for the 14-year-olds, political, material, and personality considerations.

4. The seven standard reference peoples were overwhelmingly perceived by the Japanese children as different from themselves. Six of the peoples were seen by all three age groups as dissimilar, a tendency that increases with age, leaving only the Chinese who were perceived by the 10- and 14-year-olds as similar to themselves. Response rates are highest in respect to Americans and Negroes, lowest for Brazilians and Germans, although the rates in all cases increased with age. The Negroes were most decidedly viewed as dissimilar, followed by Americans, Indians from India, Germans, and Russians. A minority, especially among 10-year-olds, saw Americans and Russians as similar to themselves, but an overwhelming majority of 14-year-olds perceived Americans as dissimilar. Perceptions of Brazilians and Indians as similar, though in a minority, increase slightly with age.

All age groups, especially the younger children, described the reference peoples primarily in non-evaluative terms. The 6-year-olds used evaluative adjectives only in referring to two of the peoples, a few describing the Indians as "dirty" and "aggressive" and the Negroes as "dirty." Americans were described by 10- and 14-year-olds as "wealthy" and "good"; Indians as "uncultured" and "dirty";

Negroes as "uncultured" and by a few 10-year-olds as "aggressive"; Russians as "intelligent" and "aggressive"; and a few described the Chinese as "aggressive." In addition, 14-year-olds said the Brazilians, Germans, and Indians are "good"; the Germans "intelligent"; the Negroes "dominated" (this resulting, it is presumed, from a history course dealing with the American Civil War, and the confusion of African Negroes with Negro slaves in the American south); and a very few described Brazilians as "wealthy." The main content emphasis at all age levels, and in respect to all seven reference peoples, is on physical-racial characteristics, minor themes being political and material aspects, habits, language, clothing, and personality traits. The clothing and habits categories were particularly employed in respect to the Chinese, Indians, and Negroes. Clothing, in the case of the Chinese, referred for the most part to the traditional Chinese dress, not the Communist uniform; in respect to the Indians, the references were to "turbaned." References to Chinese habits were primarily to their classic manner of greeting; Indian habits meant "chasing animals through the jungle." Politics was mentioned by 14-year-olds in respect to all peoples except the Americans; for them the main descriptive categories, besides physical-racial, are material possessions, language, food, and personality traits. References to Indian politics, by a small group of 14-year-olds, primarily pertained to the pacifism of Nehru, who had visited Kyoto shortly before the children were questioned.

5.   In general the Japanese children were reluctant to express affection for the reference peoples or were indifferent. The number of children expressing indifference increases with age, until at the 14-year level indifference makes up a substantial proportion of the responses, and in the cases of the Brazilians, Chinese, and Indians the majority are indifferent. Thus, although the 14-year-olds are better informed about other peoples, they prefer to maintain an indifferent attitude toward them. This marked recurrence of the attitude of indifference among the older children may reflect a general Japanese characteristic. Middle-class 14-year-olds in particular show this indifference, while the lower-class children more often refuse to generalize. Response rates are very low among 6-year-olds except toward Americans and Negroes, in both cases the majority expressing dislike. The older children, if they were not indifferent or reluctant

to generalize, tended with age to like rather than dislike Americans, Brazilians, and Germans; to show a decrease in both liking and disliking Chinese; to change from dislike to indifference toward the Indians and Negroes; and to remain substantially the same in their attitudes toward Russians, the majority expressing dislike but a consistent minority expressing affection.

6. For conceptions and information regarding the reference peoples, the Japanese children, like the other national groups studied, relied mainly on parents at the 6-year level, and with advancing age cited television and movies particularly, along with school-related sources, books, and magazines, while the mention of parents declined markedly. The 6-year-olds mentioned parents as primary sources regarding the Americans, Chinese, and Russians, but cited television and movies as main sources for their conceptions of Germans, Indians, and Negroes. They did not have sufficient information about Brazilians to cite any sources, and response rates were low regarding the Germans. Television and movies were given as important sources at all age levels and in respect to all seven reference peoples, being even for 14-year-olds the principal source regarding Americans, Indians, and Negroes. American movies and some television productions are widely viewed in Japan. School courses assumed first place at the 14-year level in respect to the Brazilians, Chinese, Germans, and Russians. Direct contact was mentioned in connection with only two of the reference peoples, all age levels citing direct contact with Americans, and a few 10- and 14-year-olds mentioning direct contact with Negroes. The Japanese in Kyoto rarely see Chinese people in person, their conceptions of them being gained through books, movies, and television. Radio was mentioned as a source by a few 10- and 14-year-olds in connection with their knowledge of Russians.

THE LEBANESE STUDY

1. In response to the "What are you?" questions, many of the Lebanese children answered in terms of family or kinship. The self-definition "child" was not often used, the children apparently tending to view themselves as "the nephew of Ali" or some such relationship. Other frequent references by 6-year-olds were "boy" or "girl" (9%) or religious affiliation (9%). The 10- and 14-year-olds defined them-

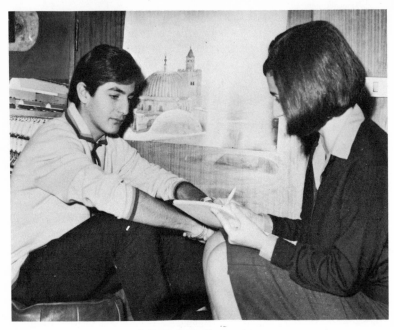

A Lebanese Interview.

selves in terms of assumed personal qualities (15%, 16%), as students (12%, 15%), as "boy" or "girl" (12%, 12%), or in terms of nationality, the latter response, which increases markedly with age (4%, 7%, 12%), specifying "Lebanese" or "Arab." The response "Arab" was given by four 10-year-old Moslems, two 14-year-old Christians, and fifteen 14-year-old Moslems, the frequency thus being related both to age and to sect. Religious identifications were frequently employed at all three age levels (9%, 12%, 6%); "person" was also used (2%, 7%, 7%); racial answers were entirely absent. Rates of no response at the three age levels 6, 10, and 14 were 49 percent, 19 percent, and 16 percent respectively.

In describing the Lebanese as a people, the children primarily used factual statements and assertions of similarities among themselves. A few made the evaluation that Lebanese are "good." Descriptive content dealt predominantly with physical characteristics for the 6-year-olds, followed by personality traits; for 10- and 14-year-olds personality traits are decidedly preponderant. Language and living habits are also important categories, as well as, for the 14-year-olds, political aspects.

2. The Lebanese children found it difficult to name peoples similar to themselves, as reflected in the number of no-responses (Table C.37). Some of this number is the result of children at all age levels giving responses, such as towns or regions in their own nation, that could not be classified as countries. In general, the people of nearby Arab nations (Syria, Egypt, Iraq) were most often mentioned as being similar, although the Americans, French, and British led a small list of non-Arab peoples also considered similar. Christian and Moslem children show marked differences in their conceptions of similar peoples, the former being much more likely than the latter to think of Americans, French, and British as similar, and the Moslems much more likely to cite Egyptians, Syrians, and Iraqis. Thus religious identification seems to influence not only the self-concept of the Lebanese child, but by extension his concept of those people seen as similar to himself.

As with most children in the other national studies, the Lebanese youngsters found it somewhat easier to name dissimilar than similar peoples (Table C.38). Americans, Africans, Chinese, and French were mentioned most frequently by 10- and 14-year-olds as being different from themselves, but the 14-year-olds also cited the Egyptians, Syrians, and British. Overall, the distribution of the responses is widespread, none of these dissimilar peoples being particularly emphasized.

3. In constructing tables to summarize the Lebanese children's choices of most and least perferred nationalities, a few arbitrary decisions were necessary. The "United Arab Republic" choices were combined with those of Syria, and choices of "Arab" were treated separately, even though some students may have meant "Arab Republic." Responses of "Hebrew" were treated together with those of "Israeli," inasmuch as most Lebanese children think of Israel as the Jewish or Hebrew state. The preference pattern is quite simliar at all age levels, the children finding American, Egyptian, or Syrian-UAR the most attractive nationalities (Table C.39). (If, however, Egyptian, Syrian-UAR, and Arab had been combined, such a choice would have the highest percentage ranking—34% for the 10-year-olds and 39%

for the 14-year-olds.) A number also stated they would not like to be anything else but Lebanese (*cf.* footnote to the French-Canadian study, item 3). Significant religious differences in the choices of desirable nationalities emerge: Christians chose the American and French significantly more often than did Moslems, while Moslems significantly more often chose the Egyptian. The question "Why?" was not asked of Lebanese children, since at the start of the investigation some parental opposition was aroused presumably as a result of recent political strife in Lebanon. Hence there are no evaluative or content category data in respect to the most and the least desirable nationalities in this instance.

Least desirable nationalities named by the Lebanese children were the African, followed by American, Israeli, Russian, Indian, and Chinese (Table C.40). Moslems mentioned the American and Israeli nationalities significantly more often than did Christians. Overall, two definite religion-based patterns emerged. If they were not Lebanese, the Moslem children would like to be Egyptian or Syrian-UAR and would not like to be American or Israeli. The Christian children, if not Lebanese, would like to be American or French and would not like to be African or Russian. There are deviations from the main patterns, of course. Some of the Moslems would like to be American and some Christians would like to be Syrian, but these are in a minority. In general, national preferences can be predicted from the religious affiliation of the children.

4.   The Lebanese children overwhelmingly perceived the seven reference peoples as different from themselves. In respect to Americans, the sectarian cleavage in the Lebanese population resulted in a cleavage in perceptions of similarity and dissimilarity; while almost all 6-year-olds who answered agreed Americans are dissimilar, the tendency to see them as similar increases sharply with age until at the 14-year level the proportions are split almost evenly. Most 6-year-olds saw all of the reference peoples as different. In the case of Brazilians, Germans, and Russians, 10-year-olds split equally in seeing similars and dissimilars, but at age 14 more saw these peoples as dissimilar than as similar. The Chinese, the Indians from India, and especially the Negroes from Africa were perceived as different from Lebanese at all three age levels; nevertheless, a few children said these peoples were similar to themselves. Except in respect to Americans, percep-

tions of dissimilarity increased with age, corresponding to a decrease in expressions of indecision.

At all three age levels, and in respect to all of the reference peoples, the most common categories of description were statements of facts, differences, and similarities. Evaluative adjectives were used only by a few of the older children: all of the peoples except Negroes were occasionally described as "good"; Americans, Indians, Negroes, and Russians as "bad"; Americans and Russians as "aggressive"; Americans, Germans, and Russians as "intelligent"; Americans as "cultured"; and Russians as "strong." The 6-year-olds mainly used the content categories of physical characteristics and language; the clothing of Americans, Chinese, and Indians interested some 6- and 10-year-olds; the two older age groups stressed personality traits, language, physical characteristics, living habits, and politics. Physical characteristics are predominant at all age levels in descriptions of Chinese, Indians, and Negroes. Politics are referred to in connection with Americans, Germans, Negroes, and particularly Russians. The religious habits of the Indian and Russian peoples also occasioned some mention.

5. The Lebanese children showed only a moderate tendency toward liking rather than disliking the standard reference peoples, with the older children more often expressing liking than the 6-year-olds. Differences between the number of expressions of liking and disliking were slight in respect to each of the reference peoples, minor shifts occurring from age level to age level but not in any meaningful patterns. The majority of 10- and 14-year-olds said they liked Americans, but sizable minorities said they did not. Brazilians drew almost equally split responses from those 6-year-olds who answered, but liking for them increased substantially at age 10 and 14, with a subgroup of 14-year-olds expressing indifference. The two older groups split almost evenly in expressions regarding Chinese, Indians, and Negroes; more said they liked Germans than disliked them; there was very little difference at all age levels between liking and disliking the Russians, although 10-year-olds showed a slight tendency to like and the 14-year-olds a slight tendency to dislike. Substantial subgroups of 14-year-olds expressed indifference toward Brazilians, Chinese, Indians, and Negroes, and a few toward Germans.

6. Parents were cited by the Lebanese children as a relatively

important source for their conceptions of the reference peoples, even to some extent by the older age groups. Direct contact, another important source at all age levels, also appears in connection with all of the reference peoples. While these two are essentially the only sources cited by 6-year-olds, the older children depend on them less, citing a wider variety of sources such as radio, movies, books, magazines, texts, courses, and friends. At all age levels direct contact was given as the chief information source about Americans. It is probable that the landing of American troops in Lebanon in 1958 and the frequent visits of the U.S. Sixth Fleet have provided Lebanese children with at least some brief contact with Americans. All age groups mentioned parents as the primary source of information about Brazil; possibly the children had heard parents speak frequently of Brazil, since many Lebanese emigrate there and have established a sizable colony. Direct contact was given by 6- and 10-year-olds as the major source of their conceptions of Negroes. At the 14-year level, however, there is a striking decrease in the mention of direct contact with Negroes as a source of information. For the older children magazines, followed by radio, supply most of the information about Russians, and radio is the major source with regard to Chinese, Indians, and Negroes.

THE TURKISH STUDY

1. In answer to "What are you?" questions, most of the Turkish 6-year-olds described themselves as "child," while others with lesser frequency said "person," "student," and "boy" or "girl." The older groups mainly defined themselves as "person" and "student," followed by references to sex, national background, and assumed personal qualities. Self-identification in terms of nationality is relatively infrequent, although it increases with age (5%, 9%, and 11%). Religion is another minor factor (2%, 8%, and 7%) while racial characteristics are not mentioned at all. Rates of no response for the three age levels 6, 10, and 14 are 38 percent, 17 percent, and 9 percent respectively.

In describing the Turkish people, most of the children at all three age levels stressed the "good" qualities of their own national group, with a number of 6-year-olds mentioning similarities among themselves, and facts. Many 10-year-olds saw their own people as "religious," "peaceful," "ambitious," and "patriotic," whereas a somewhat larger percentage of 14-year-olds saw them as "ambitious" and "patriotic," and a decreasing percentage as "peaceful" and "religious." The descriptive content deals preponderantly with personality traits, a theme increasing in frequency with age. The 6-year-olds also referred to physical characteristics and language. For 10- and 14-year-olds religion is a minor theme.

A Turkish Interview.

2.   Turkish 10- and 14-year-olds had practically no difficulty in naming peoples similar to themselves and showed a broad range of choice in total responses (Table C.41). Nominations are fairly evenly distributed among Americans, Germans, British, and French, with lesser mention of Persians (Iranians), Italians, Iraqis, and Greeks. The tendency to see Germans as similar increases with age, Germans ranking fourth in order for 6-year-olds, second in order at age 10, and first at 14. A substantial sex role differentiation in responding to questions about foreign peoples appears in the sample of Turkish

children. Girls at all age levels showed more difficulty in answering than did boys, giving significantly more responses of "don't know" or "can't decide." They also had more difficulty in expressing their feelings toward other peoples, and showed some differences from boys in the sources of their information about foreign peoples. Since girls presumably have the same schooling as boys, the differences may be a reflection of the tendency for Turkish women to maintain a social reserve.

Turkish 6-year-olds found it slightly more difficult to name peoples different from themselves, but both older age groups answered readily (Table C.42). The 6-year-olds most often saw Africans as dissimilar, while 10- and 14-year-olds named the Chinese. Next in order at the 10-year level were Africans and Japanese, followed by Russians and Arabs, then Hindus, British, and Greeks. The 14-year-olds named Africans and Russians for equal second ranking, followed closely by Japanese, with a few naming the British, Hindus, Greeks, and Arabs. Russians were more frequently named by the older children, Arabs less frequently.

3.   Many Turkish 6- and 10-year-olds, when asked what other nationalities they would most like to be, could not imagine being other than Turkish (Table C.43). (Cf. footnote to the French-Canadian study, item 3.) Of those who could, most 6-year-olds chose American, with a few naming German, British, and French. The 10-year-olds increasingly named American as the preferred nationality, with German as a distant second choice. American was still a slight choice for the 14-year-olds, but the number preferring German increased sharply. A few 14-year-olds said they would like to be Pakistani or British. Evaluative responses at age 6 stressed that the attractive nationalities were "good"; 10-year-olds said they were "good," and also described them as similar and "ambitious," while 14-year-olds saw them primarily as "ambitious" or "good." A few 14-year-olds also described them as "cultured," similar, "intelligent," "religious," and "wealthy." The content of most descriptions referred to personality traits, a tendency that became more frequent with age. A few 10- and 14-year-olds mentioned physical characteristics, religion, and material aspects. Hardly any references to political aspects were apparent when the children discussed their most desirable nationalities.

Least attractive nationalities in the eyes of the Turkish children are, for the 6-year-olds, African, Russian, Greek, and Giaour ("infidel" or non-Moslem), with a few naming American; for the 10-year-olds, decidedly the Russian, trailed by African, Chinese, and Greek (Table C.44). To 6-year-olds the unattractive nationalities were "bad," different, "aggressive," and "dirty"; at age 10, "bad" was even more often given, followed by different and, to a lesser degree, "aggressive" and "uncultured"; the 14-year-olds saw them as "aggressive," different, and "bad," and to a lesser degree, "uncultured." The content of most of the references deals with personality traits although minorities at all ages mentioned physical characteristics and at age 10 and 14 religious and political customs.

4.   In general, the Turkish children perceived two of the standard reference peoples—the Americans and Germans—as similar to themselves, and the rest as dissimilar. The 10-year-olds were most prone to perceive others as similar, the 6-year-olds the least. The response rate in respect to Brazilians is low at all age levels. In respect to most of the reference peoples (Germans and Negroes from Africa tending to be exceptions), girls showed more difficulty than boys in responding and in explaining their answers. The Chinese and the Negroes were practically unanimously perceived as different from Turks. Indians from India were also viewed as different to a marked degree, and Brazilians somewhat less so. Russians were more often perceived as dissimilar than similar. Americans and Germans were viewed by 6-year-olds almost equally as similar and dissimilar, but the 10- and 14-year-olds mainly saw them as similar.

Non-evaluative descriptions of similarities and differences, and factual statements, were most often used by children at all three age levels, although the older Turkish children tended with more frequency to use evaluative adjectives. A few 6-year-olds did describe Americans and Germans as "good," Chinese as "bad," and Negroes and Russians as "bad" and "aggressive." The 10- and 14-year-olds also gave these characterizations when referring to Americans, Germans, and Russians, but they described Negroes as "uncultured" rather than "bad." At age 10 the Chinese were still seen as "bad," and at age 14 as "bad," "aggressive," and "good." In addition, 10- and 14-year-olds saw Germans as "ambitious," 14-year-olds also attributing this quality to Americans. A few children described

Brazilians and Indians as "good." Content categories varied from people to people. The Chinese and Negroes particularly, but also Brazilians and Indians, were at all age levels preponderantly described in terms of their physical characteristics and the latter two peoples were increasingly referred to in terms of religious customs and personality traits. Religion was also frequently mentioned in respect to all the other peoples except the Negroes. Politics was a matter of interest to 10- and 14-year-olds in connection with Americans and Russians but not with Germans or any other of the peoples. While physical characteristics were of most concern to 6-year-olds in regard to six of the seven reference peoples, it was the presumed personality traits of Russians that were most referred to at all age levels. Reference to personality is the predominant category for 14-year-olds in descriptions of Americans and Germans, and for 10-year-olds in describing Americans.

5.   The Turkish children liked two of the reference peoples— the Germans and the Americans. Turkish girls when compared to boys more often failed to express their feelings, except in respect to Germans and Negroes, in which cases no noteworthy differences appear. Response rates with respect to Brazilians are low at all age levels, as they are for 6-year-olds with respect to the Indians. While 6- and 10-year-olds mostly disliked the Brazilians, 14-year-olds were almost equally split. The majority at all age levels expressed dislike of the Indians, 10-year-olds less so than the others. A substantial minority of 10-year-olds also expressed liking for Chinese, but this trend was reversed at age 14. Negroes and Russians were clearly disliked, unfriendly expressions toward the latter increasing with age. While 6-year-olds tended to dislike Americans and Germans, the tendency to like them increased markedly with age, so that a sizable majority of 14-year-olds expressed liking for Americans, and almost all said they liked Germans.

6.   Turkish 6-year-olds cited parents and friends as chief sources of their conceptions about the seven reference peoples. The girls tended more often to name friends and the boys more often to name parents. At the 10-year level, parents and friends were only rarely mentioned, the chief source of information in respect to all of the reference peoples being books, followed by school texts and courses, movies, and magazines. The 14-year-olds placed even more emphasis

on books, especially the boys, while girls were somewhat more likely than boys to cite movies. Movies were given as important sources of conceptions of the "highly visible" peoples—Chinese and Negroes (by all age levels) and Indians (by 10- and 14-year-olds)—and by 14-year-olds in respect to Americans; they were not cited as sources of conceptions about Brazilians, Germans, and Russians. In general, the boys were better able to name sources of information than were the girls, and were influenced by books more than by any other source. The girls relied relatively more on school courses and texts, and on movies, than the boys did. Direct contact was not given by the Turkish children as a source of conceptions regarding any of the reference peoples.

Part 2

Cross-National Comparisons

Each of the following chapters is organized around one of the general
questions we used as guides in planning the study. For example, in
Chapter 4 the orienting question is "What are you?" Since this question came first in the interview, before any discussion about nationalities or foreign peoples had taken place, the children's responses
reveal a good deal about their conceptions of themselves as individuals and as members of national groups. In the analysis, we give
particular attention to the actual descriptive themes stressed because
these very likely reflect the distinctive criteria children use in judging
people, foreign peoples as well as themselves. Chapter 5 is organized
around the question "What is your own group like?" The children's
spontaneous descriptions of their own national group are examined
in their own right and are also used for comparison with their views
of foreign peoples. Thus, the next two chapters deal with the children's views of themselves and their own national groups.

With Chapters 6 and 7 the focus of attention shifts to the comparisons children make between their own groups and foreign peoples.
In Chapter 6 we are concerned with the reactions of children to the
question "Which peoples from other places in the world are like you
and which are different from you?" From their responses we are

able to map out a rudimentary sociometry of nations; in the process we also discover how each group of children defines "similar" and "different."

Chapter 7 is developed around the question "What nationality would you *most* like to have and *least* like to have if you weren't what you are?" Through their responses the children produce interesting lists of popular and unpopular places to live. Moreover, as they explain their choices, they reveal the various criteria they use in categorizing nationalities as desirable or undesirable. They even, in certain cases, indicate how their own nations and ways of life might be made more desirable.

The question underlying Chapter 8 directs the children's thoughts to seven particular foreign groups: "What are your views of the Americans, the Brazilians, the Chinese, the Germans, the Indians from India, the Negroes from Africa, and the Russians?" This line of questioning permits us to look more deeply into the ways children develop images of foreign peoples, how these images change with age, and how they are shaped by various sources of influence.

In Chapter 9 we focus on the actual descriptions children give of foreign peoples. As we shall see, there are marked national and age group differences in descriptive diversity or richness, and these differences reflect the degree of friendliness of children's reactions to foreign peoples.

Chapter 10 deals with children's attitudes toward foreign peoples, that is, their tendencies to view others as similar or dissimilar, their readiness to express affection or antipathy toward them, and their ethnocentric feelings. As will become clear, there are important differences among national groups of children in the friendliness of their attitudes toward foreign peoples.

Finally, in Chapter 11 we bring together the major findings and discuss their significance in the light of current research and theory. On the basis of these findings we are able to outline a general theory of the origin and development of children's conceptions of homeland and foreign nations.

Before we get into Chapter 4, a statement of caution needs to be made about the interpretation of the findings. It will be recalled that nearly all who helped us gather the interview data in the various nations stated that they and the school authorities involved considered the children selected for the study to be representative of urban children with normal intelligence or better in that particular country. While we too believe that these children are representative in the nontechnical sense of the word, the fact remains that this is only a belief or a feeling. Our methods were not extensive or rigorous enough to assure representativeness, assuming one can ever be sure of this when working with national groups. Thus, the reader should remember we are dealing here, for example, with American children from the Boston area only, with Japanese youngsters from Kyoto, not Tokyo, with Brazilian children from Recife, not São Paulo, with English-speaking Canadians from Montreal, not Toronto. Had there been time, energy, and finances enough, we would have included at least two samples from each nation: from Chicago and Atlanta in the United States, for example, or from Paris and Marseilles in France. Even so, this extension would not have assured representativeness; at best it would only have increased our confidence in the generalizations we make about national groups. We do not wish—to quote ourselves—to make overgeneralizations about a whole national group from small and unrepresentative samples. Nevertheless, we will talk about national groups as such and make generalizations about them. Yet as we do so we shall have certain reservations about the matter of representativeness in mind, and we hope the reader will too.

We wanted to emphasize these reservations in the presentation and discussion of the findings by labelling the samples of national groups of children more precisely, but because the wording would be very complicated (e.g., Canadian French-speaking children from Montreal or South African Zulu and Sesotho children from Johannesburg) we have stayed with less exact designations.

Finally, when discussing national group differences we faced another interesting problem: the samples from one nation may be quite different from another with respect to the socio-economic background of the nation as a whole. Thus, the reactions of the Turkish children may differ from those of the Americans not because of national background but because of differences in socio-economic backgrounds that exist between these or any other countries brought into comparison. Here we encounter a methodological limitation: behavioral scientists have not yet developed a means of equating nations on this basis or of separating the effects of social class from national background, and we were not able to help in this matter with our approach. We feel, however, and this is another belief only, that social class differences between nations are not the only or the main reason for what differences or similarities we find among our national groups of children. We come to this conclusion because the differences of social class *within* national samples generally played a relatively minor role in the way children view foreign peoples or their own group.

4

Children's Self-Conceptions

Imagine asking large numbers of children of different ages from a variety of different nations to answer the question, "What are you?" On first thought, one might expect a multitude of different responses, too numerous to summarize or categorize neatly. Actually, the bulk of their self-descriptions are of seven general types. These are, in order of popularity, references to their *sex*, to the fact that they are *persons* or *human beings, students,* or *children,* and to their *national* or *regional, religious,* or *racial* backgrounds. Of course, the various national and age groups of children make their own characteristic uses of these standard descriptive categories, as we shall see.

The responses of the three age groups from all eleven nations are compared in Table 4.1. The table entries are percentages, based on the four answers each child gave to the questions, "What are you?" "What else are you?" "Anything else?" and "Can you think of anything else you are?" Percentages are used because, as we noted in Chapter 3, the younger children generally give fewer and less varied self-descriptions than the older ones do, and we would like here to focus attention on variations in the content of self-descriptions, disregarding richness and variety.

As one examines Table 4.1, it is evident that for most groups of children national references are only one feature of their self-conceptions, and generally not the most salient one. Although our original purpose in asking these questions was to see how prominent a role nationalistic feelings play in children's views of themselves, it now becomes evident that several other descriptive themes are equally

Table 4.1

Popular Categories of Response to the Four Questions Asking "What are you?"

(Table entries are percentages)

	Sex (Age)				Person (Age)				Student (Age)				Child (Age)				National or Regional (Age)				Religion (Age)				Race (Age)			
	Over-all	6	10	14	Over-all	6	10	14	Over-all	6	10	14	Over-all	6	10	14	Over-all	6	10	14	Over-all	6	10	14	Over-all	6	10	14
American	21	21	22	20	11	9	11	13	3	2	3	5	3	2	1	4	5	2	4	8	2	1	2	3	0	0	0	0
Bantu	12	7	12	17	10	4	13	14	2	0	2	5	10	12	8	10	0	0	1	0	0	0	0	0	14	9	22	13
Brazilian	17	16	20	14	6	8	6	5	12	4	12	20	1	1	3	0	2	2	2	3	4	2	4	5	0	0	0	0
English-Canadian	20	16	21	24	11	8	14	10	6	1	3	12	3	5	4	0	5	2	5	7	3	2	4	4	0	0	0	0
French	12	14	15	8	5	1	7	7	10	4	13	14	6	5	9	4	6	2	6	10	1	0	4	1	0	0	0	0
French-Canadian	19	23	17	17	4	3	6	4	12	2	14	18	5	6	7	2	4	2	6	4	2	0	3	2	0	0	0	0
German	18	21	21	13	11	9	13	10	13	7	15	16	10	8	13	9	8	4	8	11	2	2	3	3	0	0	0	0
Israeli*	0	0	0	0	11	8	12	11	8	7	8	10	23	21	22	26	6	4	8	7	4	3	2	6	0	0	0	0
Japanese	10	2	13	14	4	9	1	1	0	0	0	0	1	2	0	0	20	1	29	30	1	0	2	1	0	0	0	0
Lebanese	11	9	12	12	5	2	7	7	10	2	12	15	2	2	3	1	10	6	10	14	9	9	13	6	0	0	0	0
Turkish	11	9	8	15	16	12	15	22	15	10	15	19	12	17	13	7	9	6	9	12	6	2	8	7	0	0	0	0

*In Hebrew there is no way to separate references made to sex and child. That is, if an Israeli boy says he's a "child," he also indicates that he's a male child. Because of this inevitable linkage, all such responses have been arbitrarily placed in the child category but are not interpreted as such.

90

interesting. For example, if children from certain nations stress religious, racial, or national background in describing themselves, we would expect them to be more likely to use these same criteria in judging foreign peoples than other groups that do not emphasize these themes in describing themselves. We shall, therefore, examine every aspect of the children's self-conceptions since they all shed light on the criteria different groups typically use in judging themselves and, we presume, foreign peoples as well.

NATIONAL COMPARISONS OF SELF-DESCRIPTIONS

The American and English-Canadian children at all three age levels refer mainly to their sex, to the fact that they are persons, and, in the case of the 14-year-old English Canadians, to their role as students. The predominant tendency, however, is to describe themselves as boys or girls, all other descriptive themes, in comparison, appearing infrequently. The picture is slightly different for French-Canadian children since at the 10- and 14-year levels they refer to themselves as students nearly as often as they do to the fact that they are boys or girls, and they refer to themselves as persons only infrequently. Hardly any of the American, English-Canadian, or French-Canadian children describe themselves in nationalistic, religious, or racial terms.

This marked emphasis on sex in self-descriptions is not characteristic of all national and age groups, however. In Brazil, France, and Germany, sex is the most popularly used category of self-description at the 6- and 10-year levels, but not at the 14; these 14-year-olds place more emphasis on their role as students. For the Bantu children sex is the most frequently used descriptive theme at the 14-year level, but it is closely followed by references to one's self as a person of a particular racial background. The 6- and 10-year-old Bantu children describe themselves mainly as children of a particular race, referring to person and sex much less frequently.

In Israel the category used with the highest frequency, even at the 14-year level, is "child." However, because the word for child in Hebrew also includes a reference to the sex of the speaker, we cannot directly compare Israel with the other national samples with regard to use of either the sex or child categories. Nevertheless, the

Table 4.2

Popular Categories of Response to "What are you?" Questions*

Percentage of Responses	Sex	Person	Student
21-25	American		
16-20	Brazilian English-Canadian French-Canadian German	Turkish	
11-15	Bantu French Lebanese Turkish	American English-Canadian German Israeli	Brazilian French-Canadian German Turkish
6-10	Japanese	Bantu Brazilian	English-Canadian French Israeli Lebanese
0-5	Israeli**	French French-Canadian Japanese Lebanese	American Bantu Japanese

Child	National or Regional	Religion	Race
Israeli**			
	Japanese		
Turkish			Bantu
Bantu German French	French German Israeli Lebanese Turkish	Lebanese Turkish	
American Brazilian English-Canadian French-Canadian Japanese Lebanese	American Bantu Brazilian English-Canadian French-Canadian	American Bantu Brazilian English-Canadian French French-Canadian German Israeli Japanese	All others are zero

* Data for all three age groups per nation combined.
** In Hebrew one cannot determine whether a child has referred to himself as a "male *child*" or as a "*male* child."

Israeli children in general emphasize the fact that they are persons and students, and, as they get older, they also frequently refer to their national and religious backgrounds.

The Turkish 6-year-olds describe themselves primarily as children, and, as one would expect, the use of this category steadily decreases through the age groups, while references to person and student increase. The Turkish children rarely describe themselves as boys or girls at any age level, whereas national references are comparatively frequent. Moreover, in contrast to the other groups, the Turkish children have varied self-descriptions, that is, all categories except race are used with a certain frequency at all age levels, including the youngest group.

For the Lebanese 6-year-olds, sex and religious references are the only themes occurring with a fairly high frequency. The 10- and 14-year-old Lebanese children refer mainly to their role as students, to their sex, and to their national or regional and religious backgrounds.

The pattern for the Japanese children is essentially unique. They give the fewest responses to the "What are you?" questions and their self-conceptions at all age levels are very restricted. That is, the 6-year-olds describe themselves mainly as persons, whereas the 10- and 14-year-olds typically refer to themselves as Japanese boys or girls. No more than 1 percent or 2 percent of the responses for any age group of the Japanese children fall in other than the national-regional and sex categories. It would almost seem as if the 10- and 14-year-old Japanese children could conceive of no other way of describing themselves.

THE COMPARATIVE IMPORTANCE OF VARIOUS SELF-DESCRIPTIONS

Reference to Sex

One can isolate two clusters of national groups that place quite different emphasis on sex in self-descriptions. One group, comprising American, English-Canadian, French-Canadian, German, and Brazilian children, makes more frequent references to their sex than do the Japanese, Turkish, Lebanese, Bantu, and French children. Furthermore, for certain groups (the Japanese, Turkish, Bantu, Lebanese, and English-Canadian children) there is an increase with age in the frequency of sex references, while for others (the French-Canadian, Brazilian, German, and French children) there is a decrease. Thus, for certain national groups (the French-Canadian, German, and Brazilian children) sex is a salient feature of self-description at the early ages but gradually decreases in prominence by the teens; for others (the Japanese, Turkish, Bantu, and Lebanese) it is not a dominant theme at 6 years but gradually increases in salience; for others (the American and English-Canadian) it is a prominent aspect of self-description at all three age levels; and for the French, interestingly enough, it is not especially prominent at age 6 and its use as a descriptive theme diminishes even further by the teen ages.[1] These contrasts are of interest since they demonstrate that for certain national groups of children no theme is as dominant as sex in their conceptions of themselves whereas other groups of children find various other themes of equal or more importance.

Reference to Person or Human Being

One can also distinguish two clusters of national groups that give different stress to being a person or human being. The Turkish children make frequent use of this category as do the American, English-Canadian, German, Israeli, and Bantu. The children of five other nations—the Japanese, French-Canadian, French, Lebanese, and Brazilian— make relatively few references to the fact that they are persons.

Although it is difficult to be certain what significance this category had for the children, the differences in its use could reflect cultural variations in the privileges and rights granted children. That is, in certain cultures children may be taught to look at themselves as persons or human beings with rights of their own, while other children, for example, may be taught that they are primarily children, or colored, or Jewish. Thus, we might expect some relation to be found between the frequency of use of this theme and reactions to foreign peoples who may, for certain groups of children in particu-

---

[1] Although it is incidental to our main purposes, these comparisons may be of major interest to behavioral scientists studying cultural variations in sex-role differentiation.

lar, also be thought of first as human beings. We shall examine this possibility and several similar ones in the final chapter.

References to Student

There is a great deal of variability in the use of student as a descriptive theme. The Turkish youngsters describe themselves in this way frequently while, at the other extreme, the Japanese children never refer to themselves as students. Older children in general use this category more frequently than the younger ones do.[2]

References to Child

There are few noteworthy differences among groups in their use of the child category except that the Turkish, Bantu, and German children refer to themselves as children more often than other groups do, suggesting that more attention may be given to age-group differentiations in these cultures than in others.

National or Regional References

In general, it appears that national or regional references are a comparatively small feature of children's self-conceptions, at least as these were estimated by our procedures. The exception to this general rule is the marked tendency of Japanese children to make frequent references to their national and regional affiliations, a tendency that increases sharply after age 6. Compared to other groups, the Lebanese, Turkish, and German children also make relatively frequent refer-

[2] One might argue that the differences among nations in their use of the student reference reflect underlying differences in earnestness to get ahead in life through education. We tested this possibility by comparing the eleven nations on both their use of the student category and their "need for achievement" as established by McClelland in a cross-national study. (D. C. McClelland. *The achieving society.* Princeton: Van Nostrand, 1961; see especially pages 461-462). McClelland's indices of achievement need were determined by analyzing the content of stories in children's readers for achievement themes. Fortunately nine of our eleven nations were included in McClelland's study, and the correlation between achievement scores and student self-references is statistically significant ($rho = .62$, $n = 9$, $p < .05$), lending strong support to the notion that self-references reflect cultural values that in turn influence behavior. National variations in achievement needs are examined further in Appendix E.

ences to national or regional background, whereas the Bantu, Brazilian, and French-Canadian children only infrequently refer to themselves in these terms, and there is no increase in their use with age. What variations there are in the use of national references may well reflect basic differences in the salience or importance of nationality that could affect children's reactions to foreign peoples. For example, we might expect the Japanese youngsters to make sharper distinctions between their own and foreign groups because they place so much importance on national or regional background in thinking about themselves.

References to Religion

The Lebanese children in particular and the Turkish somewhat less so, commonly describe themselves in religious terms. The variations among national groups in this regard suggest that religious differentiations are of personal importance only in certain nations, such as Lebanon and Turkey, but are much less important in others, even in Quebec where one might have thought that children would identify themselves as Catholic or Protestant. On the basis of these results, we would expect the Lebanese and Turkish children to make distinctions among foreign peoples along religious lines, just as we would expect the Bantu children to use race as a criterion for evaluating peoples, since they were the only children who frequently described themselves in racial terms.

In summary, it was found that the various national and age groups of children made use of a very similar set of descriptive categories in describing themselves, although they still revealed their own distinctive self-conceptions. The noteworthy ones are: the American and English-Canadian children's marked tendency to identify their sex to the relative exclusion of other self-descriptions; the stress given to race by the Bantu children, the dominant theme for them, and their infrequent use of student and national references; the Japanese children's very common references to national or regional background and their infrequent use of the student category; the Turkish children's relatively frequent references to themselves as persons, and their infrequent references to their sex; and the Lebanese children's relatively common references to religion and their infrequent use of the person category. These findings reveal the common and unique features of the children's self-conceptions, and at the same time indicate the relative importance of nationality, race, and religion in their self-descriptions, which are ways of thinking about themselves that could affect their views of foreign peoples.

5

Children's Conceptions of Their Own National Group

Near the end of the interview, each child was asked to describe his own national group. The question was placed late in the interview so that the children would be more likely to describe their own group in comparison with the many other countries and people they had just been asked to think about and discuss in some detail. The comparisons to follow are based on each child's response to one question put to him in a standard form; for example, the Lebanese children were asked "What are the Lebanese like?"

Certain descriptive terms are characteristically used by children of various national backgrounds while others turn up in the responses of one or two groups of children only. For instance, although all of the children make frequent use of *factual statements* in describing their own groups, those from certain nations make more use than others of such descriptions. Compared to most of the national groups, the Bantu, Brazilian, and Israeli children frequently give factual descriptions, whereas the Turkish children, especially the 14-year-olds, rarely use factual statements at all, emphasizing instead subjective descriptions of personality traits when talking about their own group.

The second most frequent general characteristic of the children's descriptions of their own groups is the common reference to *good qualities.* Even so, not all groups of children emphasize the goodness of their own group, nor do they all make such references with the

99

same degree of regularity. Those with a tendency to stress their own group's good qualities are the American, English-Canadian, French-Canadian, French, German, Turkish, and Brazilian children, and in all cases, except the Brazilian, "goodness" is popularly used by children of all three ages, although particularly so by the older ones. In the case of Brazil, the 6-year-olds hardly ever refer to the goodness of their own group, although the older Brazilian children do so frequently. Compared to these seven national groups, the Lebanese and Israeli children make comparatively few such references, and the Bantu and Japanese children are distinctive because they hardly ever refer to the good qualities of their own people. We shall speculate about the meaning of these differences later in the chapter.

Several national groups, interestingly enough, make frequent use of *similarity statements* in describing their own people. This means that the Lebanese child, for example, when asked to explain what the Lebanese are like, answers that "they are like us," "they dress as we do," or that they have similar habits, customs, or personality characteristics. Apparently subgroups of children in certain countries do not consider themselves full-fledged members of the nation in which they live. In other words, children in certain national settings seem to make a differentiation between themselves, or their family, religious, or ethnic group, and everyone else, even though they recognize a bond between themselves and their countrymen. We might expect that 6-year-olds would sometimes respond this way because they are not clear about their nationality,[1] but the use of similarity statements is fairly common for various 10-year age groups and for 14-year-olds in certain cases. For instance, the Lebanese and Bantu children at all age levels frequently make similarity references of this sort as do the 6- and 10-year-old, but not the 14-year-old, Brazilian and German children. The Israeli children also use this descriptive category to a certain degree at all ages, but less so than the Lebanese or Bantu. These findings may reflect important social divisions within those nations where ethnic, religious, linguistic, or other distinctive

[1] See J. Piaget and A. M. Weil. The development in children of the idea of the homeland and of relations with other countries. *Int. soc. sci. Bull.*, 1951, *3*, 561–578.

See also, G. Jahoda. The development of children's ideas about country and nationality. *Brit. J. educ. Psychol.*, 1963, *33*, 47–60 and 143–153.

subgroups draw off or divide children's allegiances, making it difficult either to identify with or form a clear concept of the superordinate national group. One might expect American children to have this difficulty too, but apparently "American" is a clear concept for them despite their various ethnic and national backgrounds. We would also expect Canadian children to face the same difficulty but in fact hardly any similarity references were given by either English- or French-Canadian children. This is very likely due to the cultural and educational isolation of these two groups. Furthermore, the wording of the questions helped to delimit the superordinate group referred to, since *"les Canadiens"* in the question *"Comment sont les Canadiens?"* would very likely mean *French* Canadians to French-Canadian children just as "the Canadians" in the English version would likely be taken as *English* Canadians by the English-Canadian children.

Five groups frequently refer to the people of their own country as "intelligent." These are the older children from France, Brazil, Germany, Israel, and the 10-year-olds from Japan. The description "wealthy" is used frequently by the 10-year-olds from English and French Canada, Germany, and by the 10- and 14-year-old American children. In contrast, many 14-year-old Japanese children refer to themselves as "poor." "Ambitious" is used often by 10- and 14-year-old German and Turkish children and by the 14-year-old Israeli children. The 14-year-old Brazilians, on the other hand, frequently describe their own group as "unambitious." "Peaceful" is a popular description of the 6- and 10-year-old Turkish children, the 10- and 14-year-old Israeli, and the 14-year-old French-Canadian children. Finally, the term "cultured" is used by the older children from France, Brazil, and English Canada.

Some descriptive terms are used by only one or two national groups. For example, in discussing their own group, the older Brazilian and French children frequently describe themselves as "happy." The older American and English-Canadian children stress the term "free." The older Turkish and French-Canadian children commonly use the term "patriotic." The Israeli children at all ages and the older Turkish children refer to themselves as "religious." The 6-year-old Turkish children quite frequently describe themselves as "clean." One of the more interesting findings is the use made by the older

Japanese children and, to a less marked extent the French, of the self-descriptive term "bad."

The distinctive descriptive patterns of each national group of children, listing the terms in approximate order of their frequency, can be summarized as follows:

American: good, wealthy, free
Bantu: mainly factual statements and similarity references
Brazilian: good, intelligent, cultured, happy, unambitious
English-Canadian: good, wealthy, free, cultured
French-Canadian: good, wealthy, peaceful, patriotic
French: good, intelligent, cultured, happy, bad
German: good, ambitious, wealthy, intelligent
Israeli: good, religious, peaceful, intelligent
Japanese: poor, intelligent, bad
Lebanese: similarity references and good
Turkish: good, peaceful, ambitious, religious, patriotic, clean

COMPARATIVE FEATURES OF OWN NATIONALITY AND DESIRABLE NATIONALITY

If we compare the children's descriptions of their own groups with their characterizations of those foreign nationalities they think of as desirable,[2] the correspondences and incongruities that appear provide us with information for inferring how satisfied each group of children is with its own way of life, and how it might be improved, from a child's point of view. Take as an example the French children who are attracted to foreign countries made up of good, cultured, and interesting people, and who find their own people to be mainly good, cultured, intelligent, and happy, if somewhat bad. There is substantial agreement between actual and ideal in this case as there is for American children, who are attracted to good and peaceful people, and who find their own people mainly good. We might conclude, therefore, that the French and American children are happy with their lot, that is, their people have the qualities they consider desirable. The incongruities between descriptions of one's own group and those of attractive nationalities are perhaps more significant. For

[2] In Chapter 7 we shall examine in detail how the children define desirable and undesirable nationalities.

example, the German children are attracted to good, wealthy, and peaceful nations, whereas they consider their own group as good, wealthy, intelligent, and ambitious, with no reference made to peaceful. The failure to see themselves as peaceful could signify a potential source of dissatisfaction with one's own national group since peacefulness is apparently a valued characteristic. A similar contrast is apparent in the case of Brazilian and Israeli children. We may infer that both these groups of children value wealth since they stress this feature in describing their choices of desirable nationalities, but they fail to mention wealth in the descriptions they give of their own national group.

The inconsistencies are very clear for the Japanese children. They admire other peoples who are good, wealthy, peaceful, cultured, and clean, whereas they think of their own people as poor and bad, albeit intelligent. One can interpret these inconsistencies as signs of unrest or dissatisfaction, especially for the older children of Japan. It would be interesting to examine this matter more carefully, to determine if inconsistencies of this sort actually signify real dissatisfactions or envy of foreign countries. With the limited information available here, one should consider these speculations as interesting hypotheses only.

Finally, when we compare the children's descriptions of their own groups with their manner of describing foreign peoples (see Chapters 3 and 7), certain age changes in the structural content of their statements are of interest. When describing both their own groups and foreign peoples, references to physical features generally decrease in importance as the children grow older while personality traits, political issues, and habits become more dominant descriptive themes. There are, however, instructive exceptions to this general tendency: the Bantu and Japanese children, the two non-white groups included in the study, make comparatively frequent references to the physical traits of their own group, even at the 14-year level. These groups also emphasize the physical characteristics of foreign groups somewhat more than other groups of children do, indicating that this topic is particularly salient in their thinking.

Of somewhat greater significance for the present discussion, however, is the fact that the 6-year-olds, who generally make fewer non-evaluative references to personality characteristics than the older children do, still clearly give more subjective evaluations of personality characteristics when describing their own national groups than they do when describing foreign peoples. They typically make only statements of well known or obvious facts about foreign peoples whereas older children give the more evaluative descriptions of the personality characteristics of a whole national group of people. This contrast suggests that stereotyped thinking about *foreign* people may become part of children's repertoires after they have developed stereotyped modes of thought about their *own* people. That is, young children may first learn to make stereotyped classifications about their own people in comparison with certain other peoples, and only later, in the early teen years, generalize this mode of thinking to foreign peoples.

In summary, we have looked into the ways children describe their own national groups and were able to survey, albeit superficially, the culturally distinctive criteria children use to explain what their people are like. When these conceptions are compared with their views of foreign peoples they say they admire, we are given hints that certain groups may be proud and others ashamed of particular aspects of their own ways of life.

6

Foreign Peoples Seen as Similar and as Different

Early in the interview, before their attention had been directed to specific examples, the children were asked to mention several foreign peoples they considered to be similar to their own group and several others they thought of as being different. The words actually used were "like you" and "not like you." In this chapter we shall examine the children's spontaneous responses to these questions.

One can think of the analysis to follow as a type of sociometry of nations in the sense that certain people will receive many nominations, either as similar or dissimilar, while others will be infrequently or never mentioned, just as certain individuals become sociometric "stars" and others "isolates" when members of a school class are asked to name classmates they particularly like and others they dislike. It should be kept in mind, however, that there are clear limitations to how far the outcome of this sociometry of similars and dissimilars can be generalized since it is based on the choices of eleven national groups of children only, none of which are from within the Communist world. But, as we shall see, we at least have a start here.

PEOPLES CONSIDERED SIMILAR

The figures presented at the end of this chapter (Figures 6.1-6.11) summarize, for each national group of children, the most popular choices of similars and dissimilars. The general trends to be discussed are apparent in the choices of all three age groups of

105

children although they are more pronounced in the case of the older children. The people most frequently mentioned as "like us" are the *Americans*, chosen as similar by all except the Bantu children. The Americans are the first choice of the English-Canadian, German, and Israeli children, the second choice of the Brazilian and Turkish children, and the third choice of the French, Lebanese, Japanese, and French-Canadian children.

The next group also popularly considered as "like us" is the *British*, nominated by all national groups of children except the Bantu, Lebanese, and Brazilian. The British are the first choice of the American and French children, the second choice of the German, Israeli, and French- and English-Canadian children, the third choice of the Turkish, and the fourth choice of the Japanese children.

The *French*, the third most popularly mentioned, are frequently considered as similar by six national groups; the exceptions are the Lebanese, Japanese, English-Canadian, and Bantu children. They are the first choice of the French Canadians, the third choice of the American, Brazilian, German, and Israeli children, and the fourth choice of the Turkish children.

The *Germans*, the *Italians*, and the *Russians* are each mentioned by two countries as being similar, and no other nation receives as many as two nominations.

PEOPLES CONSIDERED DIFFERENT

The *Chinese* and *African Negroes* are most frequently nominated as dissimilar. All national groups of children except the Japanese and Bantu nominate the Chinese, and they are the first nomination of four groups of children (*i.e.*, the Brazilian, English- and French-Canadian, and Turkish), the second nomination of four other groups (the American, French, Israeli, and German children), and the third nomination of the Lebanese children.

All national groups of children except the Brazilian and Japanese nominate the *African Negroes* as dissimilar. They are the first nomination of three groups (the French, German, and Israeli children), the second nomination of the Lebanese, English-Canadian, and Turkish children, and the third nomination of the American and French-Canadian children.

The *Japanese* are the third most frequent choice for dissimilar. All except the Lebanese, Bantu, and Israeli children refer to them as different. Although they are not the first choice of any of the groups, they are the second choice of the Brazilian and French-Canadian children, the third choice of the French, German, and Turkish children, and the fourth choice of the American and English-Canadian children.

The *Americans* and *Russians* are also frequently mentioned as being "not like us." Five national groups include the Americans among those commonly considered as different; they are the first choice of the Lebanese and Japanese children and the fourth choice of the Brazilian, French, and German children. It is of interest that five national groups appear to have ambivalent conceptions of Americans: a certain subgroup of Brazilian children considers Americans as "like us" while others view them as "not like us"; a subgroup of French children also regards Americans as similar, while another subgroup sees them as different; and the same trend is noted in the samples of German, Japanese, and Lebanese children.

Five groups also nominate *Russians* as dissimilar. They are the first choice of the American children, the third choice of the Brazilian and English-Canadian children, and the fourth of the Turkish and French-Canadian children. The tendency to view the Russians as different is primarily found among the 14-year-old children of these five nations.

The specific pattern of choices for each group of children can also be seen in the accompanying figures. Many American children, for example, consider the British, in particular, and, less frequently, the Canadians, the French, and the Italians as similar. On the other hand, the Russians, Chinese, Africans, and Japanese are commonly seen as different by American children. The pattern suggests that American children choose others as similar either on the basis of historical and cultural origins as reflected in the choices of British, French, and Italian, or on the basis of geographical proximity, if this nearness brings to light a historical and ethnic similarity with another national group, as is the case with Canada. They apparently consider foreign people as dissimilar or "not like us" on the basis of ideological differences (the Russians) or on the basis of ethnicity and distance, as is reflected in the choices of the Chinese, the African

Negroes, and the Japanese. When consideration is given to the choices of all groups of children, it seems that foreign peoples may be categorized as similar or different on the basis of such factors as historical ties or animosities, ethnic similarities or contrasts, geographical proximity, and similarities and contrasts in customs, language, values, and beliefs. These trends should be looked at as suggestions for further investigations designed specifically to examine in detail the way children perceive foreign groups in relation to their own. Such research would be of great value in helping us understand not only how children define similarity and dissimilarity when thinking about foreign peoples, but also how the comparisons that they make between their own national group and foreign peoples contribute to their own national identity.

PEOPLES POPULARLY MENTIONED AS SIMILAR AND DISSIMILAR TO ONE'S OWN NATIONAL GROUP

Figure 6.1
American Children's Responses.

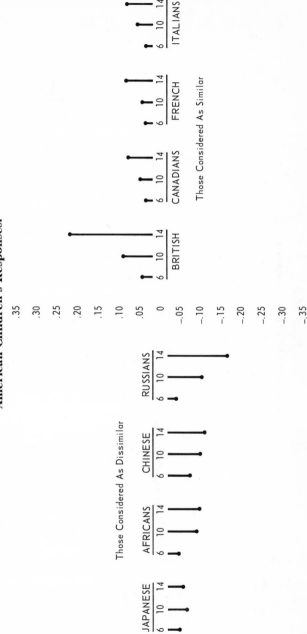

Figure 6.2
Bantu Children's Responses.

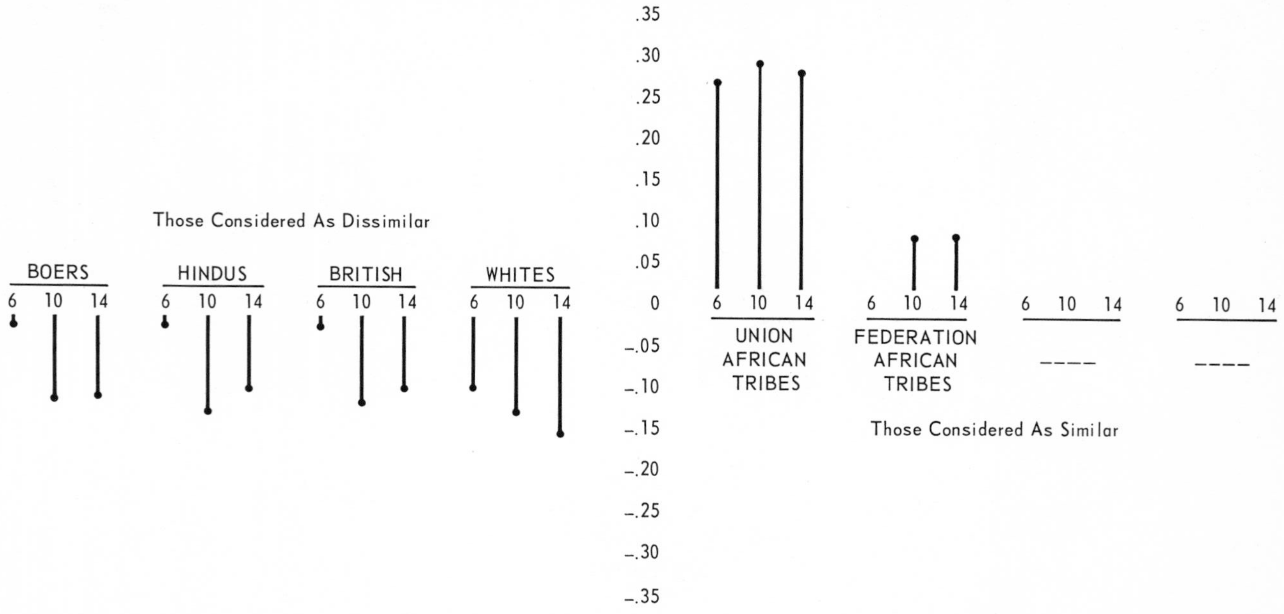

Figure 6.3
Brazilian Children's Responses.

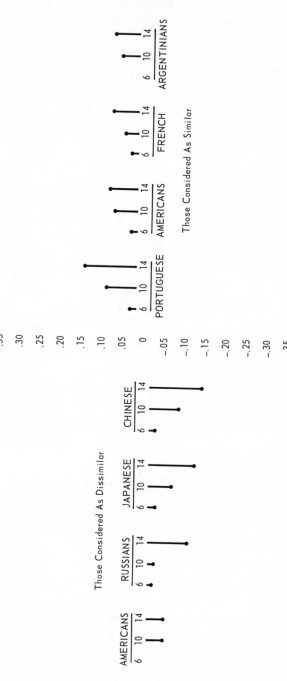

Figure 6.4
English-Canadian Children's Responses.

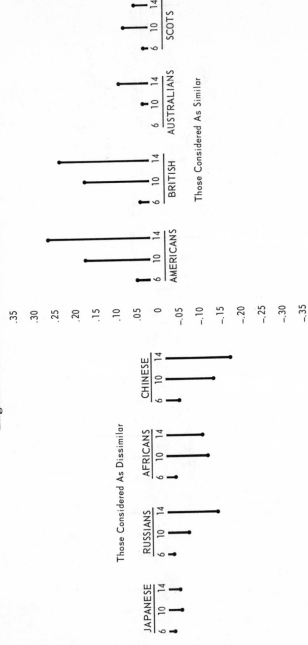

Figure 6.5
French-Canadian Children's Responses.

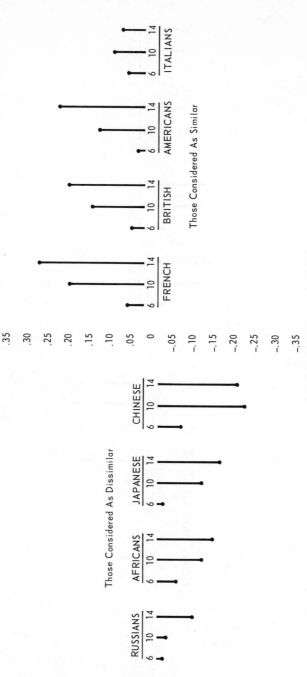

Figure 6.6
French Children's Responses.

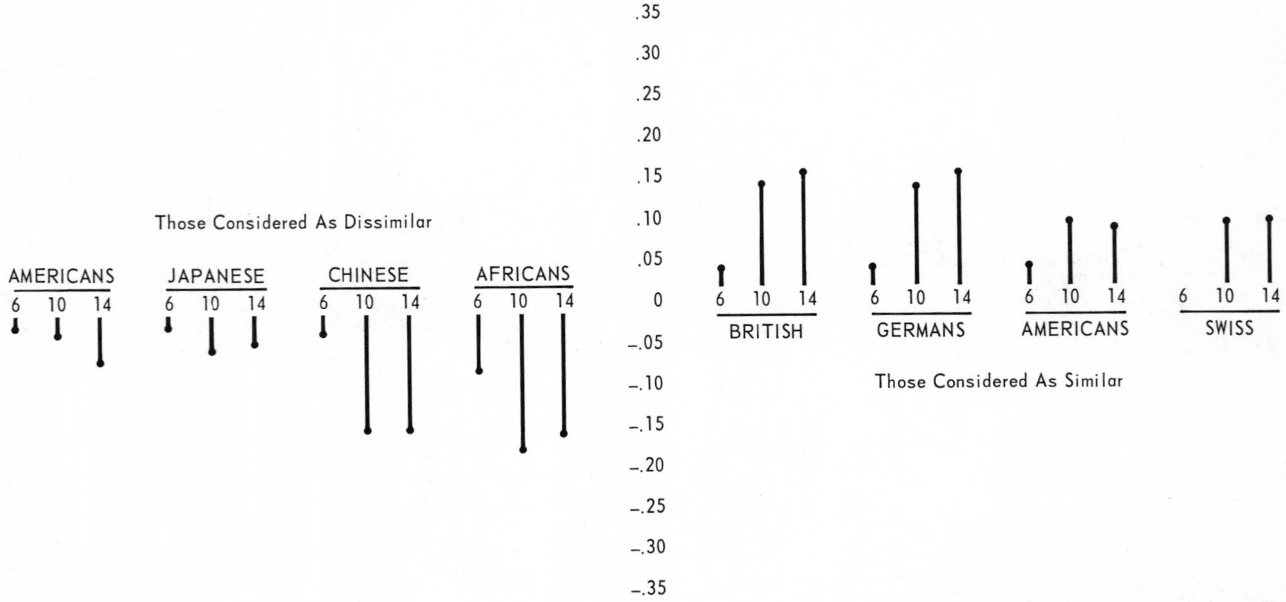

Those Considered As Similar

Those Considered As Dissimilar

Figure 6.7
German Children's Responses.

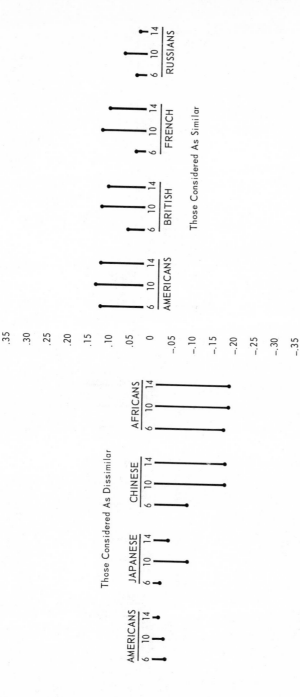

115

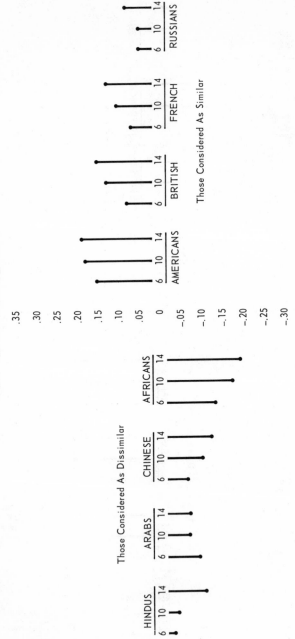

Figure 6.8
Israeli Children's Responses.

Figure 6.9
Japanese Children's Responses.

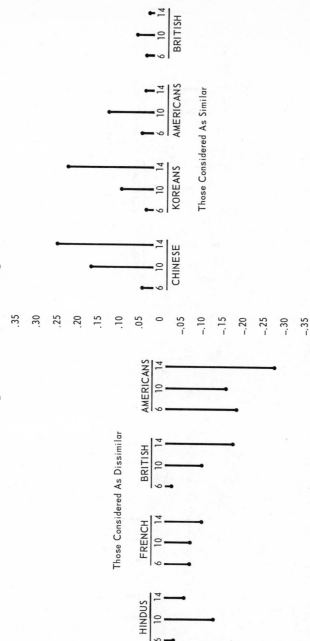

117

Figure 6.10
Lebanese Children's Responses.

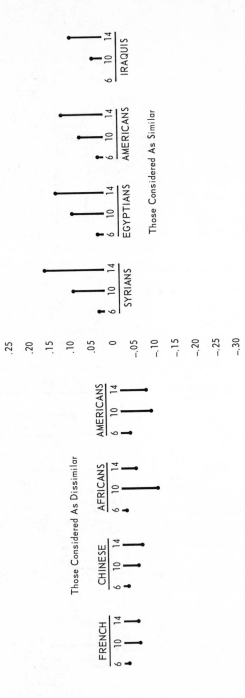

118

Figure 6.11
Turkish Children's Responses.

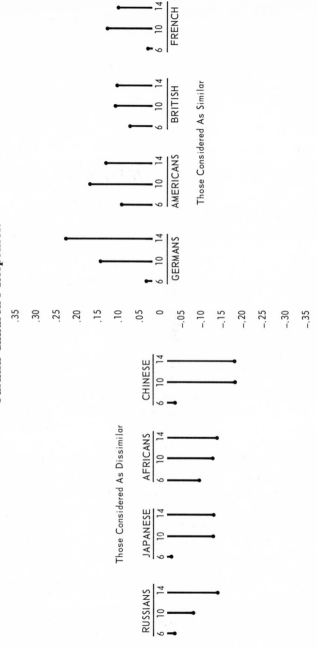

7

Desirable and Undesirable Nationalities

When the eleven groups of children were asked what nationality they would most like to have and least like to have, excluding their own nationality from consideration, most had favorite choices, as we shall see.[1]

"MOST LIKE TO BE"

Which nationalities are especially attractive and desirable for children from various parts of the world? As is apparent in Figures 7.1-7.11, the American nationality is a very popular choice. In fact, all but two of the eleven groups make the American their predominant first choice, the two exceptions being the Bantu children who frequently mention "Whites" without specifying a national group, and the French Canadians who divide their first choices between French and American.

The popularity of the American nationality generally increases in the 6- to 10-year age range, and in four cases (with Brazilian, French, French-Canadian, and German children) increases further

[1] As noted in Chapter 3, some would not let their imaginations play on these questions; for example, the younger children from Turkey, French Canada, and Lebanon frequently stated they would rather be what they are. Since there may have been subtle differences in the attitude of interviewers that account for these tendencies, we shall not attribute special importance to them.

in the 10- to 14-year age range. Its popularity drops off, however, for the 14-year-old Japanese children, who are particularly attracted to Switzerland, and for the Turkish 14-year-olds, who find German nationality especially desirable.

The second most popular nationality is British. It is mentioned relatively frequently by seven of the national groups of children (the American, Bantu, English-Canadian, French-Canadian, German, French, and Israeli). Its popularity increases with age for the American, English-Canadian, and Israeli children, but falls off for the 14-year-old French-Canadian and German children.

The third most popular choice is French nationality, mentioned frequently by the French-Canadian, Brazilian, Israeli, and Japanese children. Its popularity increases regularly with age for French-Canadian and Brazilian children, but decreases slightly for the 14-year-old Japanese children.

Although American, British, and French are generally popular choices, still each national group of children has its own distinctive set of nominations. The American children, for example, show no one favorite nationality; instead, they distribute their choices among British, Italian, and Canadian. If they were not Bantu, the Bantu children would like to be either "White" or British. The Brazilian children in general consider American, particularly, and Portuguese or French nationalities desirable. The English-Canadian children choose American as their favorite, and only infrequently mention British and Scottish nationalities. In contrast, the French-Canadian children find French or American, and to a lesser extent British, nationalities desirable. The continental French children have no special favorite. They distribute their nominations among American, British, Spanish, and Swiss. The German children choose American nationality as their clear favorite, but also mention British, African (a nomination of the younger children), and Italian. Similarly, the Israeli children select American as their clear favorite, with British and French as second choices. American is also the distinctive favorite of the Japanese children who, in comparison, only infrequently mention French, Swiss, and Russian. The Lebanese children, depending upon their religious or ethnic background, choose American or Egyptian nationalities as their favorites, with Syrian and United Arab Republican clearly less popular choices. Finally, the Turkish children divide their choices mainly between American and, for the older children, German nationalities, with British mentioned only infrequently.

Reasons for Choices of Desirable Nationalities

The children were asked to tell why they had chosen a particular nationality as a desirable one.[2] Their responses shed considerable light on how children think about or define a comfortable and desirable way of life because they emphasized quite different themes in the explanation of their choices. The themes themselves are valuable examples of contrasts in cultural values. Let us examine some of the more prominent ones.

There is, first, a widespread tendency for children to describe their favorites as nations where people with *good personal qualities* live. Only the English-Canadian children failed to stress good qualities in explaining their choices. In addition, the descriptions of desirable nationalities typically make reference to facts known about the geography, habits, and language of the countries involved.

Many children also stressed the similarity between their own national groups and their favorite choices. This is so for the American, English-Canadian, and Turkish children and the 6-year-old German, Israeli, and French Canadian children. Perhaps of more interest are the national groups that failed to mention similarity as one aspect of their definitions of desirability. This latter tendency is noted among the Bantu, Brazilian, and Japanese children and the older German, Israeli, and French-Canadian groups. Thus some groups of children appear to choose their favorite nations on the basis of similarity while other choose on the basis of contrasts with their own nationalities. It is interesting in this regard that the Bantu, the Japanese, and, to a lesser extent, the Brazilian children form a distinctive cluster of groups that stress "wealth" and "material possessions" as a theme in their descriptions of favorites. Furthermore, the older German, French-Canadian, and Israeli children also made

[2] In Lebanon certain parents were so annoyed by this question that it was only asked in a few cases at the start of the study. These parents wanted to know why their children were asked, "Why?" when they mentioned, for example, that they would like to live in the United Arab Republic if they were not Lebanese.

frequent references to wealth. This trend suggests that certain national groups may envy the wealth and material possessions of other national groups and find these nations especially desirable ones.

Other groups of children, notably the older German, Japanese, and French, stress the "peacefulness" of their favorite choices. This finding suggests that children from nations that were particularly involved in recent wars make peacefulness an important criterion in their choices of favorite places to live.

Several national groups appreciated those nations they consider to be "cultured." This theme appears among Japanese, French, Turkish, and French-Canadian, as well as the older Bantu children.

Two other distinctive themes are apparent. The French children stressed the "interesting" features of the nationalities they chose, and the Turkish children emphasized the "ambition" of their favorites.

"LEAST LIKE TO BE"

Several nations were popularly mentioned as undesirable in the sense that they were not attractive places to live from the children's perspectives. The Russian nationality is a prominent choice for six national groups: the American, English- and French-Canadian, Brazilian, German, and Turkish children. The nomination of Russia as undesirable increases with the age of the children in all cases except Germany where it decreases for the 14-year-old group.

The African nationality is more frequently chosen as undesirable than the Russian inasmuch as all eleven national groups mentioned it, but it did not receive the number of nominations among the various national groups that Russia did. There is an increase from 6 to 14 years in the tendency for the American, Japanese, Lebanese, and Turkish children to specify African as unattractive. In contrast, the French, French-Canadian, Israeli, Brazilian, and English-Canadian children show either little change or a reduction in the references made to Africa.

Seven groups nominated the Chinese nationality as undesirable, but in general it was not as frequently mentioned as were Russian and African. Those reacting in this fashion to Chinese are the American, Brazilian, French, French-Canadian, German, Japanese, and Turkish children. In general, references to China as an undesirable nation decrease in frequency with age except for the German children who, as they grow older, increase their nominations of Chinese as unattractive.

Four national groups nominated Germany as an undesirable place to live. These are the English-Canadian, French, Israeli, and American children. In general, there are not large numbers of children contributing to this trend except for the 14-year-old Israeli children, a sizable number of whom concur that German nationality is undesirable.

Thus, the four nationalities commonly mentioned as undesirable by nearly all national groups were Russian, African, Chinese, and German. Few other nominations that are distinctive for any particular group of children appeared. The national groups of children do differ, however, with respect to their manner of ordering the undesirability of nationalities. For the American children, particularly the 10- and 14-year-olds, Russian nationality is clearly the most commonly considered as undesirable; the African, German, and Chinese nationalities were mentioned much less frequently. The neighboring Union African tribes are the common choice for the Bantu children of all three ages, the Boers and Indians being mentioned much less frequently. A substantial number of the older Brazilian children consider Russia as an undesirable country, whereas generally small proportions nominated Africa, China, and Japan. The younger English-Canadian children consider German, African, Russian, and Indian nationalities as undesirable, whereas an increased proportion of the 14-year-olds concur that Russian is undesirable. The continental French children have no one particular choice, distributing their nominations among African, German, Chinese, and Russian nationalities. The younger French-Canadian children find the African, Chinese, Russian, and Indian nationalities unattractive, whereas a larger proportion of the 14-year-old group nominated Russian as their main choice, as did the English-Canadian teen-agers. For the German children at all three age levels, Russian is the first choice with relatively fewer nominations going to Chinese, African, and Indian. For all age groups of Israeli children Arab nationality is the major choice, although African, Egyptian, and German nationalities were also nominated. For the Japanese 6-year-olds, American is particularly unattractive, whereas the main choice of the older children is

African nationality. The Lebanese children have no one major choice. Instead they distribute their nominations among African, American, Russian, and Hebrew-Israeli nationalities. Finally, the 6-year-old Turkish children distribute their choices among African, Russian, Greek, and Chinese, but a larger proportion of the 10- and 14-year age groups make Russia their first choice as a nation they would rather not live in.

Reasons for Choices of Undesirable Nationalities

The various themes used by the children in explaining their nominations of undesirable nationalities are instructive. The most general theme is that the nations categorized as undesirable are made up of "aggressive" and "bad" people. This conception comes through with regularity for all eleven national groups of children.

The second most prevalent theme is that the undesirable nations are "uncultured." A sizable number of the older children from six nations concurred on this theme, namely the older American, Bantu, Brazilian, Japanese, Israeli, and Turkish children. Incidentally, the children did not stress "culture" to this extent when discussing the nations they found to be attractive.

The third most generalized theme is that undesirable nations are "under domination." This description of the political atmosphere of nations is prevalent in the thinking of many of the 14-year-old American, English-Canadian, French-Canadian, German, and Japanese children.

The older Bantu, French, and Israeli children stressed the idea that their choices of undesirable nations were populated by "unintelligent" people. The converse of this theme, it will be recalled, was unique to the Israeli children when explaining their choices of desirable nationalities. Apparently the older Israeli children value intelligence because they both choose and reject other nations on this basis. It is of interest that the Bantu and French children share this value only with regard to their nominations of unattractive places to live.

Two other themes are of some importance. First, the older French and German children stressed the "poverty" found in the nations they chose as undesirable, and they are the only two groups to mention this feature to any extent. On the other hand, "wealth" was a generalized theme for many different groups of children in describing the nations they found attractive. Apparently other considerations, such as lack of culture and being dominated, were of more importance in describing unattractive nations. Second, the Japanese children of all age levels and the 10-year-old Bantu children stressed the "dirtiness" of unattractive nations. The Japanese youngsters also used this theme ("clean") in describing attractive nations, but its use is much more pronounced in the case of unattractive ones. These are the only two national groups that referred to cleanliness to any noticeable extent.

There is one additional trend of interest here. Only four national groups, the American, Brazilian, English-Canadian, and French-Canadian, made much use of *facts* known about peoples they considered to be unattractive, whereas the use of facts was a very general mode of describing attractive peoples, indicating that children are apparently better informed about those countries they find attractive than about those they find unattractive.

In summary, this analysis highlights the ways children of different ages from various parts of the world think about foreign nations they consider to be attractive or unattractive. The comparisons bring to light the different themes children use to define what to them are desirable and undesirable places to live. Some themes are common to the thinking of children from many national backgrounds, others were touched on only by children from certain nations, suggesting that such themes may reflect both common and specific cultural values. More comprehensive research along these lines would help us understand more thoroughly how children's values affect their views of foreign peoples.

Figure 7.1

Figure 7.1
American Children's Responses.

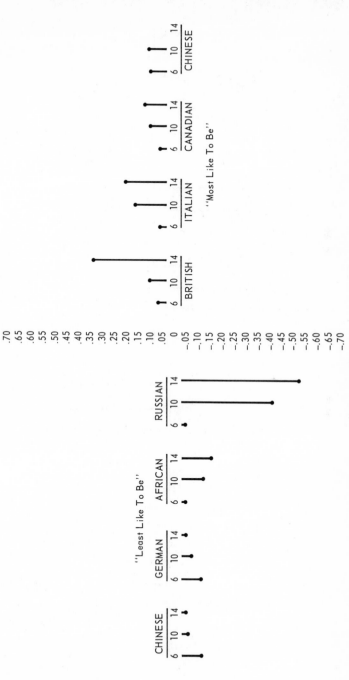

Figure 7.2
Bantu Children's Responses.

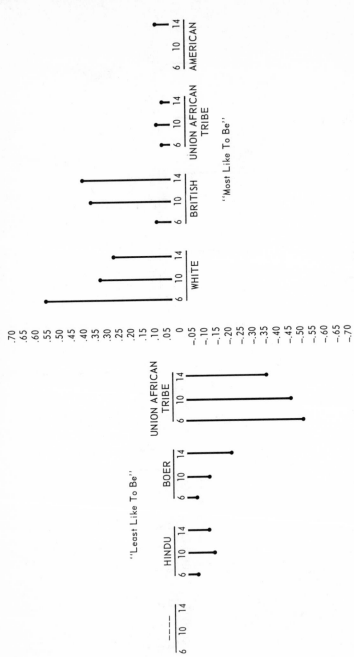

Figure 7.3
Brazilian Children's Responses.

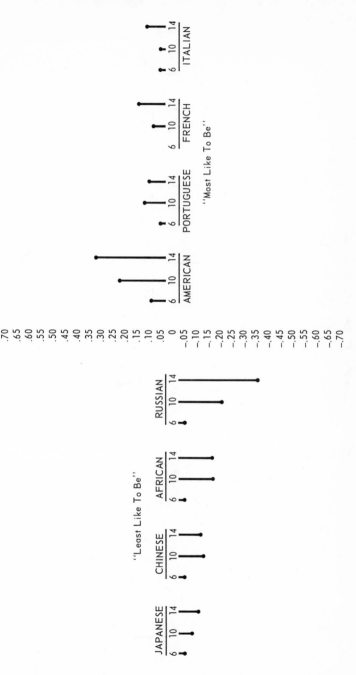

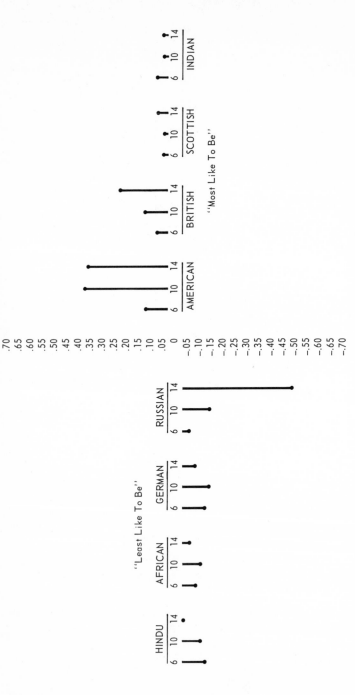

Figure 7.4
English-Canadian Children's Responses.

130

Figure 7.5
French-Canadian Children's Responses.

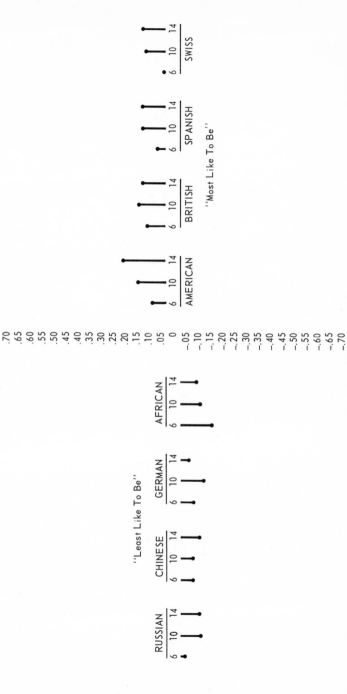

Figure 7.6
French Children's Responses.

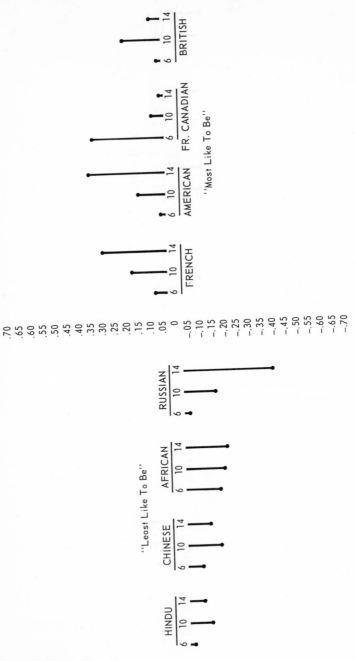

Figure 7.7
German Children's Responses.

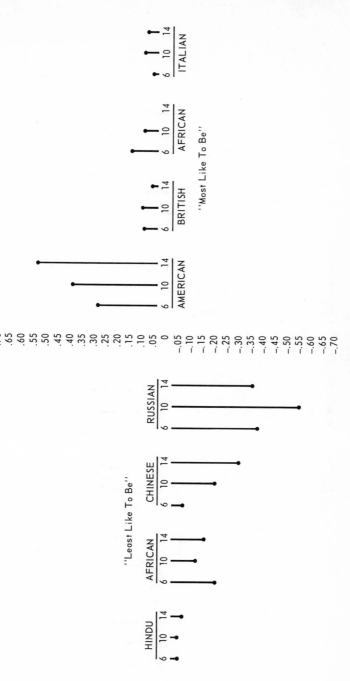

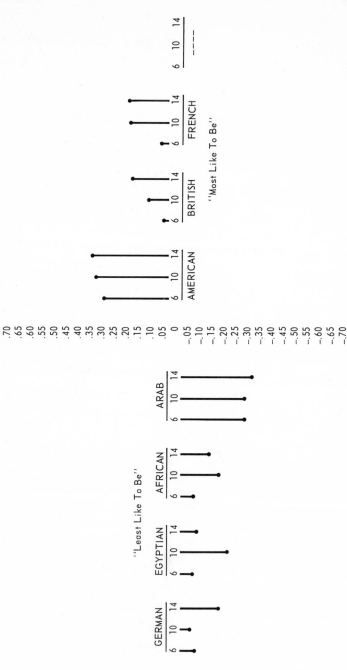

Figure 7.8
Israeli Children's Responses.

134

Figure 7.9
Japanese Children's Responses.

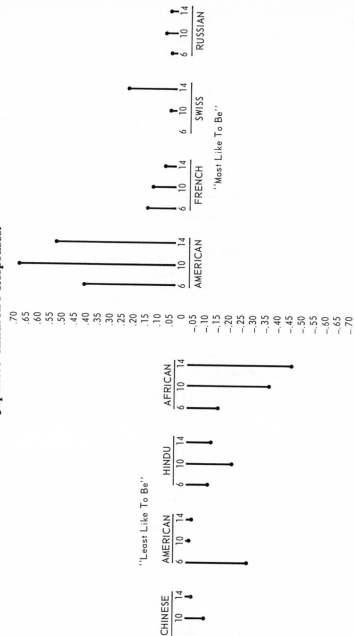

Figure 7.10
Lebanese Children's Responses.

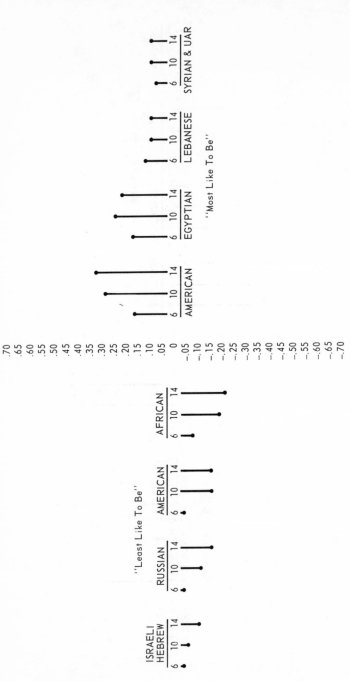

136

Figure 7.11
Turkish Children's Responses.

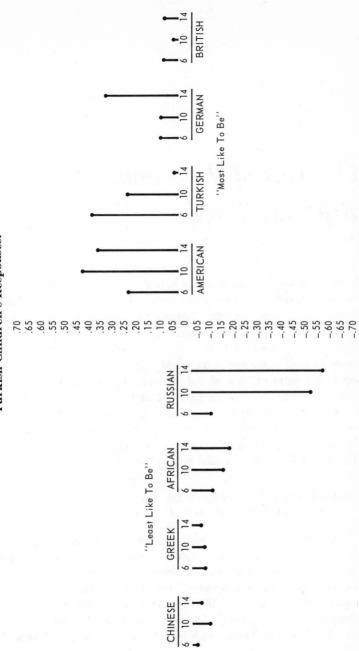

137

8

Concepts of the Standard Reference Peoples

In this chapter we shall examine how the eleven national groups of children viewed each of the seven reference peoples—the Americans, Brazilians, Chinese, Germans, Indians from India, African Negroes, and Russians. The discussion will be organized around the following question: Does each of these reference peoples project a consistent image of itself to the rest of the world or does the image vary according to the point of view of the onlooker, considering not only his cultural background but his age, sex, and social class as well? We shall start by searching for the conceptions, both common and unique, that the children have of the reference peoples. Then we shall examine the variations in children's conceptions according to differences in their age, sex, social class, and cultural background.

CHILDREN'S CONCEPTIONS OF THE STANDARD REFERENCE PEOPLES

For the most part, the *Americans* were considered as similar by the children in most of the countries studied. Even so, the youngest children frequently saw them as dissimilar or had difficulty in conceptualizing them. Furthermore, two national groups, the older Japanese and the Bantu children, emphasized the physical and racial dissimilarity of Americans, and sizable minorities of Lebanese, Brazilian, Turkish, and French children also saw them as different. In general, the descriptions of Americans involved references to differences or similarities in their physical appearance and personality characteristics, and, to a lesser degree, their habits and language. References to the good qualities of Americans occurred frequently while descriptions of material wealth and political activities in America were only occasionally mentioned. Although the Americans were generally liked, sizable numbers of the youngest Turkish, Japanese, Bantu, Lebanese, and French children expressed dislike, but this tendency generally decreased with the older groups. In fact, in all countries more 10- than 6-year-olds expressed affection for Americans. There is no general pattern, however, from 10 to 14 years; in five cases more 14- than 10-year-olds said they like Americans, while in six cases there is essentially no change from the 10- to the 14-year age groups. Mass media, including movies, television, and magazines, were the most important universal sources of information about Americans, although direct social contact was also frequently cited. The 14-year-olds also learned about them in school, and the youngest from their parents.

Children in all countries were relatively uninformed about the *Brazilians* and had difficulty describing them. They were apparently not even easily categorized as similar or different since sizable subgroups in most countries viewed them as similar while others saw them as dissimilar. No unique descriptive categories appeared in the descriptions given of Brazilians. Good evaluations, facts, and differences and similarities in terms of physical and personality traits, habits, and language were generally given. Much ambivalence appeared in the feelings expressed toward the Brazilians, especially among the older children who commonly said they were indifferent to them. However, a favorable impression of Brazilians tended to emerge in the descriptions given by American, French, German, and Lebanese children. The mass media for all children, and school for the older groups, were the sources of what little information the children had about Brazilians.

The *Chinese* were clearly conceptualized as dissimilar by all groups of children, with the exception of those from Japan. Most descriptions stressed differences and facts about their physical characteristics and, to a lesser degree, their personality traits, habits, clothing, and language. Good evaluations also were given by a few national groups, as were descriptions of material poverty, religion, and political issues. In most groups, feelings were divided between liking and disliking the Chinese, and although there were generally more favorable than unfavorable reactions, the Turkish children in particular expressed dislike of the Chinese. The typical information sources were drawn upon, that is, mass media for most children, supplemented by parents for the youngest, and school for the oldest.

Opinion about the similarity of the *Germans* was divided in most cases, except that the older Turkish, French, and American children considered them mainly as similar and the older Japanese and Bantu children saw them as different. Accordingly, strong emphasis was given to both similarities and dissimilarities in the descriptions of Germans. They were described as good by most of the national groups, yet they were also seen as aggressive and bad, although to a lesser extent. Physical and personality characteristics were the usual descriptive themes, followed by references to language and politics. Despite the disparity of descriptive evaluations, affective reactions were surprisingly consistent; most national groups tend to like the Germans, the tendency increasing from the youngest to oldest age groups. The noteworthy exception was the Israeli group, which showed an increasing dislike of Germans. Sizable subgroups of 6-year-old Lebanese, French, Bantu, French-Canadian, and Turkish children also expressed dislike of Germans. The typical sources of information were relied upon—mass media, parents, and friends at the younger ages and school at the older ages. Direct contact with Germans was also cited by a number of groups.

Large majorities of most groups of children considered the *Indians from India* as dissimilar. Although many of the younger children were unable to answer, the conception of Indians as dissimilar increased markedly from 6 to 14 years. Most of the descriptions of Indians involved statements of differences and facts, although they were also evaluated as good and, less frequently, as poor. Attention was mainly given to the physical traits of Indians, and to their habits and clothing, although the older children also referred to their personality characteristics and their religion. The Indians were liked by most national groups except for the Japanese, Lebanese, and Turkish children who, in general, showed more dislike or indifference than affection. Most information about the Indians came from the mass media, especially movies and television, and for the older children, from school-work and reading. Parents were important information sources for some groups of youngest children.

As a group, the *Negroes from Africa* were almost unanimously considered dissimilar, except for the Bantu children whose opinions were divided. The Negroes were described mainly as being different, although they were also seen as bad, dirty, unintelligent, uncultured, and good. The descriptions tended to emphasize their physical traits and, to a lesser degree, their habits. References to their personality characteristics were common in the descriptions of the older children; linguistic differences and references to their material possessions, especially their lack of wealth, were minor descriptive themes. Most of the national groups displayed a tendency that increased with age to like the Negroes. However, Turkish and Japanese children definitely disliked Negroes and the Lebanese and Israeli children, as groups, had divided feelings, some liking, others disliking them. Information about Negroes came from the mass media in most cases, from parents in the case of the youngest children, from schoolwork with the older children, and in some instances, particularly in Lebanon, from direct contact.

The *Russians* were considered to be dissimilar by six national groups, while five (the German, French, Israeli, Lebanese, and French-Canadian children) were, as groups, divided in their opinion. Most descriptions of Russians involved factual statements or general references to their differences and similarities. Still a certain number of children gave evaluative descriptions, referring to them as good, aggressive, intelligent, and politically dominated. Personality and physical characteristics were the most common descriptive themes, followed in importance by language and habits, and for the oldest children, political issues. Affective reactions toward Russians were ambivalent; some national groups (the American, Bantu, and French) displayed a positive feeling, and some (the Turkish and German) a negative, while the others (Brazilian, French-Canadian, Israeli, Lebanese, and Japanese) were either ambivalent in their feelings or indifferent toward Russians. The children's sources of information about the Russians were mainly the mass media, but in this case, in particular, radio was a very commonly mentioned source.

The youngest children relied on the views of their parents, while the older groups in certain countries emphasized schoolwork.

Those Viewed as Similar and Dissimilar

Certain summary statements can be made about the findings presented above. First, only the Americans are commonly viewed as being "like us" by the various national groups of children studied, whereas the Chinese, Indians from India, and Negroes from Africa are generally considered as "not like us." Three other peoples (the Brazilians, Germans, and Russians) are not so definitely conceptualized inasmuch as sizeable numbers of children from each nation considered them as similar while large subgroups saw them as dissimilar.

The conception of peoples as similar or dissimilar is also apparent in the actual descriptions the children gave. That is, in describing foreign peoples, children frequently referred to either the similarities or dissimilarities of the people in question. This tendency is due in large part, we presume, to the fact that the children were explicitly asked at the start of the interview to think of peoples who were different or similar. However, in respect to most reference peoples, *both* similarities and differences entered into the descriptions, while the Chinese, Indians, and Negroes were almost exclusively described, and presumably conceptualized, in terms of their dissimilarities. One would therefore surmise that most of the information and indoctrination the children received about Chinese, Indians, and Negroes stressed their differences. It is also possible that these groups, because of their distinctiveness for white children, have been used in many parts of the world as examples for contrast with more familiar peoples and more familiar ways of life.

Common Evaluative Descriptions

Second, if we consider the children's purely evaluative statements, we note that there is a great deal of agreement among many national groups in the ways they describe the standard reference peoples; in certain instances, nearly all groups of children ascribe the same characteristics to particular peoples. To summarize, Americans are thought of as good (mentioned by 10 groups out of 10 since in this case the American children were not asked to describe Americans), wealthy (5 out of 10), intelligent (5), and aggressive (2); although little is known about Brazilians, still 8 out of 10 groups of children made some reference to their good qualities; Chinese are seen as good (9 out of 11), poor (3), aggressive (3), and bad (2); Germans are good (9 out of 10), aggressive (7), intelligent (4), and bad (2); Indians from India are good (10 out of 11) and poor (4); African Negroes are good (7 out of 11), uncultured (7), unintelligent (4), dominated (3), poor (2), bad (2), and aggressive (2); and Russians are seen as aggressive (10 out of 11), good (6), intelligent (6), bad (6), and dominated (3). Although these common descriptions of foreign peoples are usually minor themes, appearing in context with many non-evaluative factual statements or references to general similarities or differences, still, as spontaneous reactions, they are prominent enough to suggest that the older children we studied are starting to give overgeneralized, stereotyped descriptions. It is possible that the stereotyping process is stimulated by the apparent *universality* of a conception of a foreign group. That is, an otherwise purely personal or local and usually unexpressed view of a particular foreign group may become a full-blown stereotype if, through information coming from parents, school, or the mass media, children come to believe that "everyone," "everywhere" knows that "they are like that."

Affective Tendencies

Third, there are general trends in the way children from the eleven nations feel about the standard reference peoples. The bar graphs that follow (Figures 8.1-8.7) help summarize the relation between conceptions of similarity or dissimilarity of each reference people and the affection or lack of affection expressed for that group. It will be noted that some groups of children consistently expressed affection for foreign peoples, even those clearly viewed as dissimilar from their own groups. Yet certain other groups of children did not demonstrate this generalized affection, showing instead a consistent tendency to align their conceptions of similarity and the degree of affection expressed by liking those viewed as similar and disliking those viewed as different.

THE SIMILARITY OR DISSIMILARITY AND THE AFFECTION OR LACK OF AFFECTION EXPRESSED FOR THE STANDARD REFERENCE PEOPLES.

Figure 8.1
Conceptions of Americans.

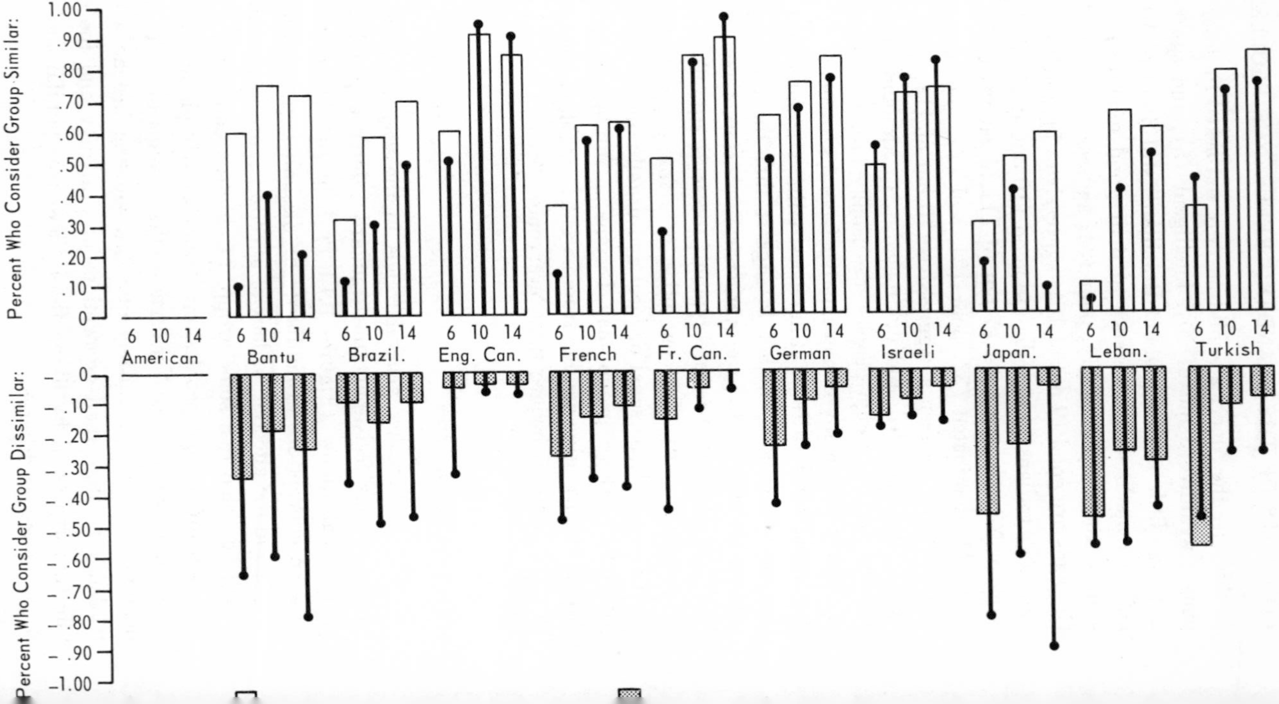

144

Conceptions of Brazilians.

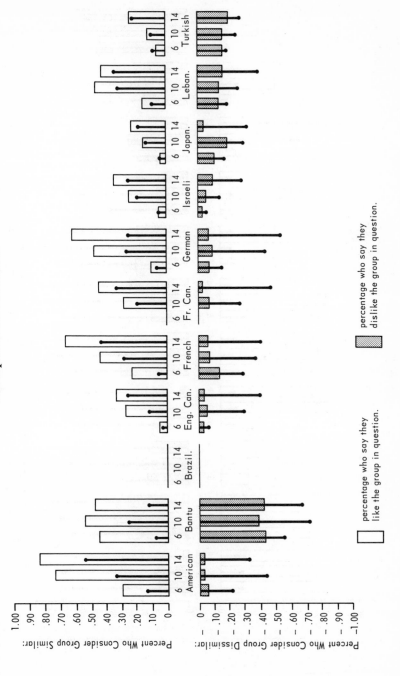

percentage who say they like the group in question.

percentage who say they dislike the group in question.

145

Figure 8.3
Conceptions of Chinese.

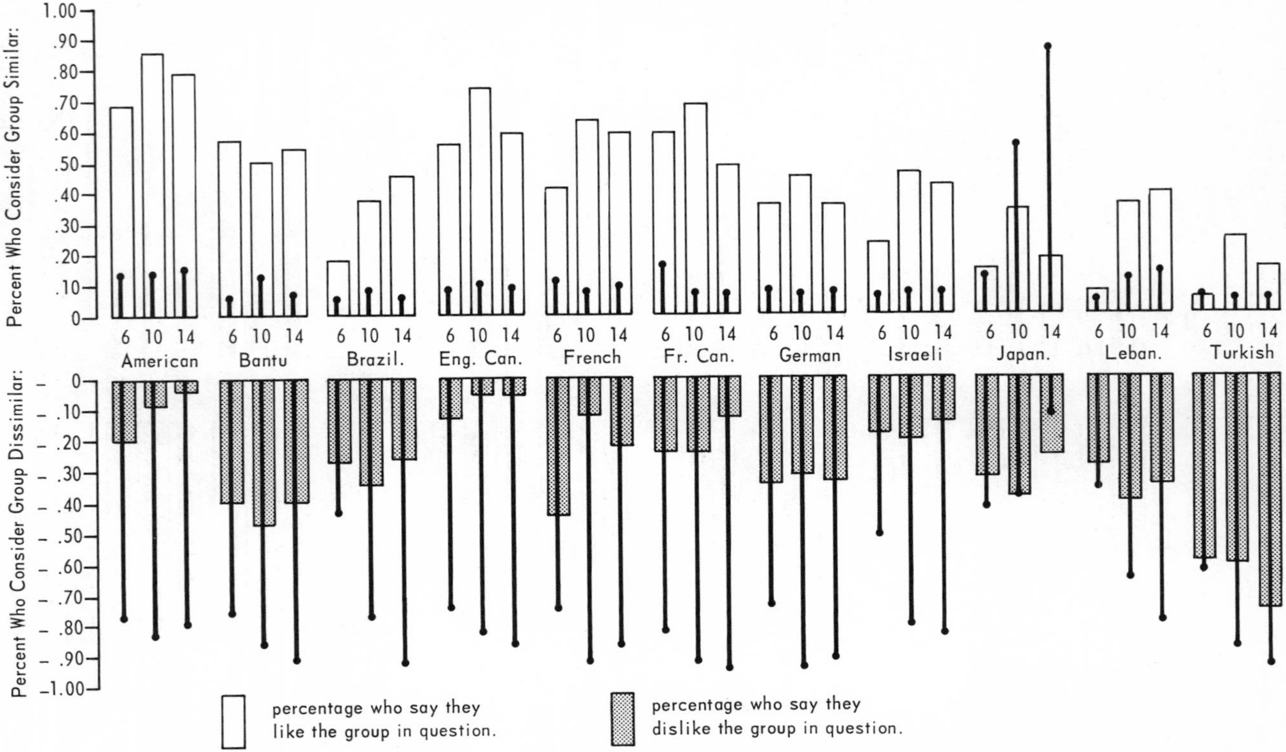

percentage who say they
dislike the group in question.

percentage who say they
like the group in question.

Conceptions of Germans.

Percent Who Consider Group Similar:

Percent Who Consider Group Dissimilar:

percentage who say they like the group in question.

percentage who say they dislike the group in question.

147

Figure 8.5
Conceptions of Indians.

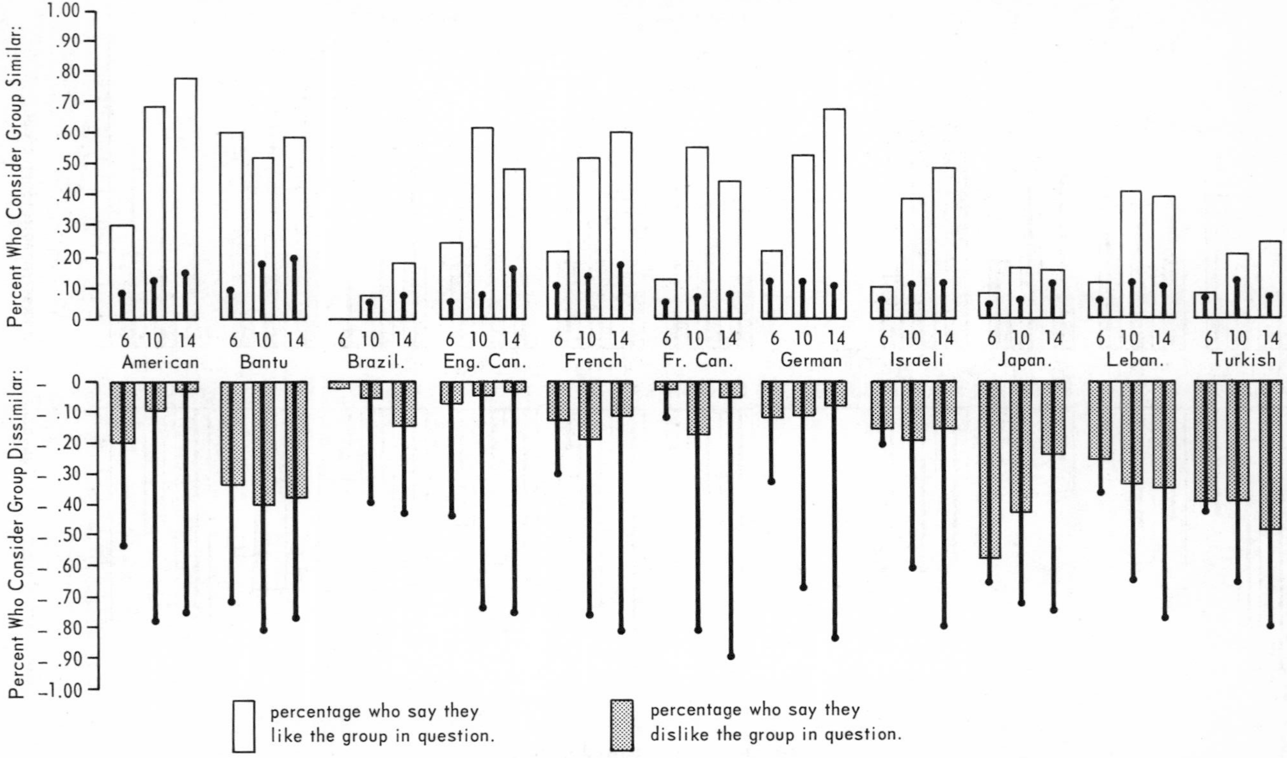

Percent Who Consider Group Similar:

1.00 .90 .80 .70 .60 .50 .40 .30 .20 .10 0

Percent Who Consider Group Dissimilar:

0 -.10 -.20 -.30 -.40 -.50 -.60 -.70 -.80 -.90 -1.00

American   Bantu   Brazil.   Eng. Can.   French   Fr. Can.   German   Israeli   Japan.   Leban.   Turkish

6 10 14

□ percentage who say they like the group in question.

▨ percentage who say they dislike the group in question.

148

Conceptions of African Negroes.

percentage who say they like the group in question.

percentage who say they dislike the group in question.

149

Figure 8.7
Conceptions of Russians.

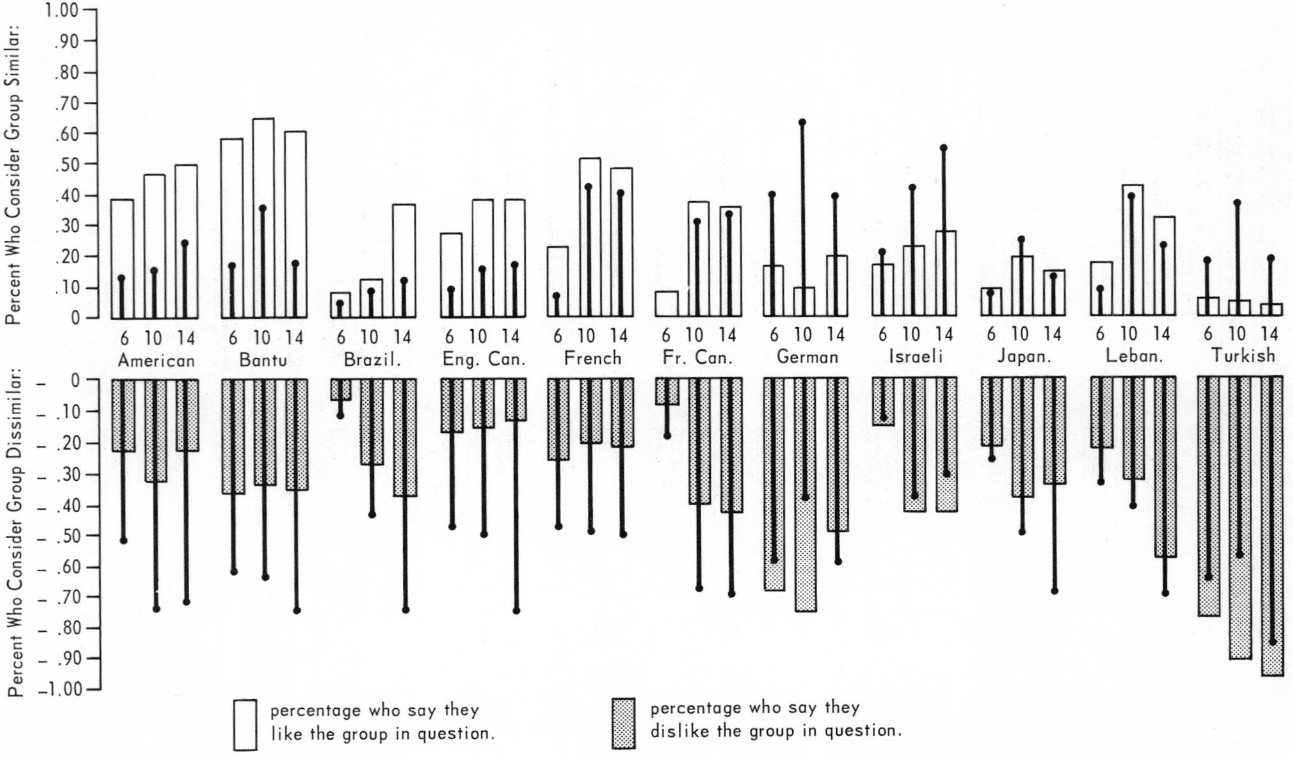

Percent Who Consider Group Similar:

Percent Who Consider Group Dissimilar:

American   Bantu   Brazil.   Eng. Can.   French   Fr. Can.   German   Israeli   Japan.   Leban.   Turkish

□ percentage who say they like the group in question.

▨ percentage who say they dislike the group in question.

150

It was the American children of all age levels who most consistently expressed a liking for foreign peoples. This fact is represented in the graphs by the surplus of affection over conceptions of similarity and by a very small amount of disaffection expressed toward any groups. When the American children discussed the Russians, there was a slight tendency to express dislike but even in this case it is much less pronounced than the tendency to like. However, when the peoples in question are clearly seen as dissimilar—the Chinese, the African Negroes, and the Indians (Figures 8.3, 8.5 and 8.6)—then there were other groups of children in addition to the American, notably the English- and French-Canadian, the French, and the German children, who also expressed a great deal of affection.

In contrast to the children who were prone to express affection, three groups (the Turkish, Japanese, and Lebanese) tended to align their conceptions of similar with affection and their conceptions of dissimilar with dislike.

One might expect children to express affection for those peoples they view as similar. However, certain instructive exceptions to such a rule become apparent in this analysis. When the Germans were being discussed (Figure 8.4), the older French and the Israeli children at all age levels indicated they were more similar than they were liked. Also, the older Japanese children considered the Chinese as similar to a marked extent (Figure 8.3), but they did not express an equivalent degree of affection for them. When the discussion turned to the Russians, they were seen as similar to a greater extent than they were liked by German, Israeli, and Turkish children (Figure 8.7).

The Bantu children did not fit any pattern in this regard. Generally, a large proportion of them consistently expressed affection for others, whereas a sizable minority expressed dislike.[1]

AGE VARIATIONS IN CONCEPTIONS OF FOREIGN PEOPLES

The generalizations just made about the children's reactions to the standard reference peoples did not take into account the potentially important considerations of age, sex, or social class variations. Sev-

[1] We shall examine the interrelations of affective tendencies and conceptions of similarities more fully in Chapter 10.

eral striking age trends in children's ways of viewing foreign peoples become apparent when descriptions of the reference peoples are examined.

First, the 6-year-olds respond less frequently than the older children to the questions asked them.[2] When one considers the responses they do give, it is apparent that they are mainly non-evaluative descriptions or statements of well known facts about the reference peoples in question. Compared with the older children, the 6-year-olds make few evaluative descriptions with the exception of "good" and "bad." As between the two older age groups, there is a progressive increase in the number of evaluative categories used, the popular ones being: good, bad, intelligent, aggressive, poor, wealthy, peaceful, dominated, ambitious.

Second, there is a strikingly clear and progressive change with age in the content of the descriptive statements made about other peoples. Younger children's descriptions typically refer to physical features, clothing, language, and habits, whereas the older children concentrate more on personality characteristics, habits, political and religious aspects of the group in question, and statements about material possessions. This change in the structure of descriptions of foreign peoples is general, except for one national group: the older American children do not make references to personality characteristics of foreign peoples as often as those from the ten other nations do. Instead the American children emphasize habits. This finding may reflect the relatively strong influence of social scientific findings and theories, especially those bearing on prejudice and discrimination in American education.

The difference between the non-evaluative, nonpersonal descriptive patterns of the younger children and the highly evaluative, personality-oriented patterns of the older children may be of importance. It suggests that our research has, as we planned, fairly well bracketed the age prior to the active use of stereotyping (that is, 6 years) and the upper age where the stereotyping process has begun to mark children's thinking of foreign peoples. This developmental change is probably due in part to the older children's greater command of the linguistic means of giving sophisticated descriptions of other peoples

[2] The whole matter of responsiveness to questioning is examined in Appendix C.

and to a change in interest toward the more complex aspects of one's social and personal environment. However, this linguistic development and change in interests rest in large part on what is learned from others about what should be said and what should be of interest. That is, children between 6 and 14 may well learn how to communicate about foreign peoples in an increasingly more stereotyped manner from members of their own social environment. Of course, the modifications in the manner of describing others may also be due to changes in the information sources typically available to the older children. We shall examine this possibility in a later section.

Third, a remarkable degree of cross-national agreement emerges in the evaluative and content nature of the descriptive statements. The common use made of the good-bad descriptive dimension by the children of all ages, especially the younger ones, from all nations suggests that this dimension may be a particularly simple and convenient category for expressing one's feelings and reactions. The good-bad category may be learned early in life because it is frequently used by those who train children. But why it is so notably popular is a matter of current interest to behavioral scientists, especially C. E. Osgood and his colleagues,[3] who have found it to be a common descriptive category in a variety of different cultures.

Even the sophisticated evaluations of the older children have a surprising similarity across the eleven national groups. Most of these common categories of thought about foreign peoples also correspond to those found to be popular in the seventeen cultures Osgood and his associates studied. Future research will perhaps determine whether these cross-national similarities of descriptive categories appear spontaneously in each of the cultures or are mainly determined by the transmission of descriptive information from culture to culture.

BOY-GIRL DIFFERENCES IN CONCEPTIONS
OF FOREIGN PEOPLES

To determine whether boys and girls generally have the same or different views of foreign peoples, the basic tables of the national reports were examined for statistically reliable boy-girl differences

[3] C. E. Osgood. Studies on the generality of affective meaning systems. *Amer. Psychol.*, 1962, *17*, 10-28.

in manner of responding. The most important contrast uncovered by this analysis concerns the relative degree of affection expressed for the standard reference people. For five national groups, the boys are more affectionate than girls. This is the case for the 10-year-old boys in America, France, Germany, Japan, and Lebanon. The 6-year-old American boys and the 14-year-old German and Japanese boys are also more affectionate than girls of the same ages. In fact, in only two cases do girls show more affection than boys—the English-Canadian samples at all age levels and the two older Brazilian samples. There are no sex differences of this sort for the Bantu, French-Canadian, Israeli, and Turkish samples at any age level.

These findings supplement several conclusions reported earlier. For example, we noted that the Japanese children tend to align their conceptions of similarity and the degree of affection they express. Since we now know that Japanese boys are more affectionate, it is apparently the Japanese girls who, by being selective in expressing affection, actually determine the overall pattern attributed to the Japanese children. The similar instance of alignment noted with the Lebanese children is more complex, for although 10-year-old girls are less affectionate than boys, they nevertheless view others as similar more often than boys do at both the 6- and 10-year levels. Thus both boys and girls contribute to the alignment in the case of Lebanon.

The only other recurrent difference between the responses of boys and girls concerns the sources of information used. Boys from four nations—those of all age levels from America, the 10-year-old French-Canadian and German, and the 10- and 14-year-old French boys—mention television and movies as sources of information more often than girls do. The 14-year-old boys from Turkey, on the other hand, mention movies as an information source less often than do girls. These findings may be a reflection of cultural differences in the freedom given boys and girls to attend movies or watch television. In any case, television and movies apparently have not been negative sources of information for the 10-year-olds of America, France, and Germany, for in these three instances boys used these two sources of information more often than girls and yet boys were the more affectionate. It could be that movies and television, very visual and personal media, enhance a sense of familiarity with foreign peoples and that affection is generated by the familiarity. With only this information available, however, we cannot conclude that television and movies contributed in any essential way to the greater degree of affection expressed.

In summary, there were no universal boy-girl differences in modes of responding to questions about foreign peoples. Only in certain national settings do sex differences contribute to the manner of reacting to foreign groups. In general, sex differences had relatively little effect on the manner of viewing foreign peoples for the Bantu, French-Canadian, Israeli, and Japanese children, whereas they played a relatively greater role in determining the modes of responding of the Turkish, American, Brazilian, English-Canadian, French, and German children. Sex differences were an important determiner of the amount of affection expressed toward foreign peoples, and boys, especially at the 10-year level, were found to be more affectionate than girls in a number of national samples. There were also sex differences in regard to the types of information sources popularly mentioned: boys, especially 10-year-olds, cited television and movies more frequently than did girls.

SOCIAL CLASS VARIATIONS IN CONCEPTIONS OF FOREIGN PEOPLES

For this analysis the basic tables of the national reports were examined for statistically reliable differences between lower- and middle-class children in their manner of responding to questions asked them about the seven reference peoples, and, as was the case with the boy-girl comparisons, there were more reliable differences attributable to variations in social class for some national groups of children than for others. In general, social class differences had a greater influence on modes of responding for American, English-Canadian, Israeli, Japanese, and Lebanese children than for the Bantu, Turkish, French, and German children. Furthermore, social class differences are also most apparent when one examines the amount of affection expressed toward foreign peoples. In general, the middle-class children were more affectionate than the lower-class, a trend that held for seven national groups: the younger English-Canadian, French-Canadian, and French groups, and the older groups from America, Brazil, Israel, and Lebanon. However, in three cases—the 6-year-old German, the 14-year-old French-Canadian, and the 14-year-old Japanese—the middle-class children were less affectionate, or more indifferent, toward foreign peoples than were lower-class children.

The second general pattern involves social class differences in conceptions of the similarity or difference of foreign peoples. In four instances the middle-class children considered fewer foreign groups as similar. This was so for the older American and Lebanese children, and the younger English-Canadian and French children. It is noteworthy that the same age groups from these four nations also contributed to the first pattern, described above—a relation that seems to be more than accidental. The middle-class children of these four nations were more affectionate toward foreign peoples but were, at the same time, less prone to consider them similar. Stated otherwise, the lower-class children in these nations tended to view foreign peoples as similar to themselves but, at the same time, were particularly prone to dislike foreign groups. It is possible that the lower-class children express dissatisfaction with their own lower-class status by disliking foreign peoples in the same social position as their own. In contrast, the middle-class children in these four nations may be intrigued by the exotic differences of foreign peoples and therefore express affection for them. Although these are speculations only, they deserve further study because they point to a possible feeling of unrest among the lower-class children from certain nations that may manifest itself in a dislike of foreign peoples.

Two other patterns are relatively minor in that few groups contribute to them. First, the older middle-class children in Japan, Israel, and Brazil referred more frequently to personality characteristics when describing foreign peoples than did the corresponding lower-class children. This trend is of significance for these three nations inasmuch as generalizing about personality traits of whole groups of people appears to be one of the bases of the stereotyping process.

Second, the older middle-class English- and French-Canadian children mentioned more sources of information for their knowledge about foreign peoples. Since we have already noted that the middle-class English-Canadian children are relatively *more* affectionate whereas in the middle-class French-Canadian children are relatively *less* affectionate, it may well be that the content of the information about foreign peoples, directed from many sources toward the middle class in these two ethnic groups in Canada, is quite different yet powerful enough to determine how affectionate or unfriendly the groups of children are toward foreigners.

In summary, it appears that in certain nations social class membership plays a more important role in determining how children will respond than it does in others. Social class differences mainly affect the degree of affection children express toward foreign peoples and their conceptions of the similarity of foreign groups.

SOURCES OF INFORMATION ABOUT FOREIGN PEOPLES: AGE AND NATIONAL VARIATIONS

Table 8.1 summarizes the various sources of information about foreign peoples commonly mentioned by the different groups of children. Our interest here is in the general types of information most easily accessible to children of different ages and cultural backgrounds.

The most outstanding trend is a contrast in the types of information most often received by 6-year-olds in comparison to 10- and 14-year-olds. The typical information sources for the 6-year-olds are parents, television and movies, and direct contact. In all groups except the English-Canadian and French-Canadian, parents are a popular source of information about foreign peoples. Thus, the young child generally learns about others through parents, mainly, or through television and movies. However, there is a very clear change from 10 years on; judging from the sources they recall when questioned, the older children in general receive little or no information about foreign nations from people in their environment, not even from their parents. In no instances are parents a popular source for the 14-year-old children and in only two cases (the Bantu and French) are parents frequently mentioned as information sources for the 10-year-olds. Furthermore, school teachers are not often mentioned in this regard. In fact, in only two cases (the Bantu and Japanese) are teachers popularly referred to. Finally, friends are not important sources of information about foreign peoples; friends are only mentioned to any notable degree by the Israeli and Lebanese children.

Table 8.1

Comparisons of Popularly Used Sources of Information*

Nationality of Children

	American	*Bantu*	*Brazilian*	*English-Canadian*	*French*
6-year-olds	T.V.—movies (parents)	parents	parents (contact)	T.V.,** contact	parents
10- and 14-year-olds	T.V.—movies, books, courses, texts, magazines	parents, (10 years only), contact, teachers	movies, magazines, contact	T.V., courses, texts, books	parents (10 years only), texts, books, magazines (14 years only)
Specific instances: (10- and 14-year-olds only)	*contact* for Germans and Chinese; *radio* for Russians	*movies* and *books* for Americans and Negroes; *friends* for Russians	*school* for Negroes; *radio* for Russians	*radio* for Russians	*contact* for Americans; *radio* for Russians

158

French-Canadian	German	Israeli	Japanese	Lebanese	Turkish
T.V.**	parents, T.V.— movies (contact)	parents, friends	parents, T.V.— movies	contact, parents	parents, friends
T.V., texts, books, magazines (14 years only)	T.V.— movies, books, maga- zines, courses, contact, radio	books, friends, courses, movies, maga- zines	T.V.— movies, courses, texts, teachers, maga- zines	books, magazines, radio, movies, texts, friends, contact	books, texts, courses, movies, maga- zines
	parents for Russians	radio for Russians			

* Listed in approximate order of frequency. Those in parentheses are not as frequently mentioned as the others.

** Since children in Montreal are not allowed to attend movie theatres until they are 16 years of age, it was presumed that television was the major source coded in the T.V.—movies category.

Thus, for older children the major sources of information about foreign peoples are impersonal ones—television and movies, books, school course work, textbooks, magazines, and, to a lesser extent, direct contact. Apparently, parents, schoolteachers, and friends do not often communicate about foreign nations to children over 10 years of age, or if they do their comments are not well remembered. What the older children know about foreign peoples they learn through the mass media, through reading, or through direct contact with small samples of people from the country in question (which often means they have merely seen an occasional Chinese person or an American tourist).

Information about Russians is apparently hard to come by. The older children in many nations rely on the radio, in particular, and on parents or friends for their knowledge of Russians. The Americans, in contrast, are easier to learn about because television and movies often deal with American themes, and Americans are frequently encountered through direct contact.

The eleven nations differ with regard to the variety of their information sources. The older children in certain countries, in particular the older Lebanese, German, Israeli, and American children, have varied sources of information about foreign peoples. On the other hand, the Bantu children apparently have relatively few available sources, most of them of a personal nature. The Brazilian children also have a comparatively restricted range of sources of information about foreign peoples.

It is difficult to draw conclusions concerning the ways in which information sources affect children's thinking about foreign peoples. One might argue that the distinctive modes of thinking about foreigners noted among the 6-year-olds, their tendency to refer to the more concrete differences and similarities of foreign peoples, for example, are traceable to the types of information sources they commonly use, in particular their parents. Perhaps parents do give children selected examples of how foreign groups look, dress, or behave, keeping their descriptions concrete because it is assumed that 6-year-old children can only comprehend concrete examples. Children's television and movie offerings might also be planned with similar conceptions of the young child's interest in mind. On the other hand, it may be that parents actually communicate very generalized and stereotyped versions of what foreign peoples are like, including references to habits and personality traits, but that these descriptions are not understood by young children who select out the more concrete aspects of such descriptions. Without a more complete study of what is actually communicated from the source, whether it be a personal or an impersonal one, we are unable to explain what effect different sources of information have on the child. The findings uncovered here, however, indicate that further research on this topic would be of great usefulness.

The results of the present analysis are valuable in their own right because they indicate which sources are likely to be used by children of different ages in different national settings. This information can be of value in developing plans to change conceptions or introduce new ideas about foreign peoples. It also highlights the responsibility parents, educators, and those who control the mass media have when they discuss foreign nations and their inhabitants with children. The mass media are particularly important for children of certain groups, notably the English and French Canadians, who hardly consult parents, teachers, and friends at all, and for the older children in most nations studied, because these more impersonal sources turn out to be the major sources of information about foreign peoples. There is no indication in these findings, however, that television and movies damage the children's conceptions of foreign peoples. For example, the American children at all ages rely heavily on television and movies for their information and yet, of all the national groups studied, they have the most friendly outlook toward foreign peoples, making the least use of widely-generalized statements about personality characteristics. In contrast, the Turkish children do not use television as a source of information, nor movies to a great extent, and yet they have a particularly unfriendly attitude toward foreign peoples.

9

Descriptive Diversity in Children's References to Foreign Peoples

When asked to describe people from a foreign nation, some children mention only one or two characteristics while others touch on a large number of distinguishing features of the people in question. If one examines the descriptions of a particular people given by whole groups of children—for example, the one hundred 10-year-olds from each national setting—it is also apparent that certain groups make references to only a few traits or features whereas others produce a great variety of descriptive references. In this chapter we shall say that the descriptions of a group of children are *diversified* if a large variety of different characteristics of a foreign people are referred to when other comparable groups of children, given the same opportunities to respond, refer to only a few different characteristics.

A statistical measure of descriptive diversity was developed for our purposes by Professor George A. Ferguson of McGill University. This index reflects variations in the distribution of descriptive statements given by groups of any size, producing a high score when comparatively few different descriptive references are made and a low score when references are made to a number of characteristics of the people in question. Thus, the higher a group's score, the more consensus there is on the elements introduced into the description. The formula[1] for what we shall call the consensus index is:

$$C.I. = \Sigma p^2 = \frac{\Sigma f^2 + f_o}{(\Sigma f)^2}$$

where $f =$ the frequency of descriptions falling in any one descriptive category, and where $f_o =$ the frequency of descriptions falling in the "other" category provided for relatively idiosyncratic descriptions. Each idiosyncratic reference is given special weight in the formula. To illustrate, suppose that the descriptions given by a group of 23 respondents limited to one description each were categorized into five standard code categories and an "other" category. If the descriptions distributed themselves as follows, the consensus index would be .16.

	f	f^2
Category 1	4	16
Category 2	3	9
Category 3	5	25
Category 4	6	36
Category 5	2	4
Other	3	(3)
	23	93

$$C.I. = \Sigma p^2 = \frac{93}{(23)^2} = \frac{93}{529} = .16.$$

In other words, when the descriptions cluster in only a few categories, the consensus index is high. For example, if the 23 responses had been distributed in only two categories, say 11 in one and 12 in the other, the index would be .50. Furthermore, the magnitude of the coefficient does not depend on the number of descriptions being considered but only on their distribution. Thus, if 46 descriptions were distributed in the same manner as the 23 illustrated above, the index would still be .16. This makes the index very appropriate for our purposes since, in the analyses to follow, we shall disregard children's failures to respond so that the actual number of descriptions given by different groups will not be equivalent.

Using this index, we shall compare the statements of various national and age groups of children for descriptive diversity. The children's descriptions, it will be recalled, were coded into two distinctive types of categories (see Appendix B). The *evaluative* cate-

[1] The index is mathematically similar to one proposed by B. Freund. The degree of stereotypy. *J. Amer. Statist. Ass.*, 1950, 45, 265-269.

gories were used to classify the nature of the child's evaluations of foreign peoples, that is, to classify such responses as (*a*) "they are kind," (*b*) "they are dominated," or (*c*) "it is too cold where they live." The *content* categories were used to classify the general content of the references made in the same descriptive statements. Following the examples just given, the same statements would be classified in the content categories as references to: (*a*) personality characteristics, (*b*) political system, and (*c*) geography or climate. As will become evident, the diversity noted in the evaluative features of the children's descriptions often has a quite different meaning from that noted in the content features.

NATIONAL AND AGE VARIATIONS IN DESCRIPTIVE DIVERSITY

Evaluative Diversity

Tables 9.1-9.3 present the national and age variations in the diversity of *evaluative* statements. Certain trends are apparent when the three tables are compared. First, there is a general increase in the diversity of evaluative statements from 6- to 10- to 14-year age groups. There are, however, exceptions to this overall age trend: the Japanese children show essentially no age change, the descriptions of Israeli children are least diversified at age 10, and the Lebanese children show little change from 10 to 14 years of age.

Considering next the peoples being described, least evaluative diversity is noted at all three ages in the descriptions given of Chinese and Indian peoples. There is a noteworthy tendency toward consensus in the evaluative statements made about Negroes by 6-year-olds in contrast to 10- or 14-year-old children. Similarly, the evaluative statements made about Russians are relatively constricted for the 10-year in contrast to the 14-year age groups.

Considering next the groups of children giving the descriptions, the Bantu children at all three age levels give the least diversified evaluative descriptions of foreign peoples. The American and English-Canadian children, relative to other national samples, also lack evaluative diversity at all three age levels in contrast to the Israeli and the younger Japanese children whose evaluative descriptions are especially diversified.

Table 9.1

Indices of Descriptive Consensus Among 6-Year-Olds: Evaluative Categories

Standard Reference Peoples

Respondents	Americans	Brazilians	Chinese	Germans	Indians	Negroes	Russians	Averages
American	–	.28	.42	.23	.39	.41	.23	.33
Bantu	.41	.50	.45	.49	.47	.41	.40	.45
Brazilian	.23	.23*	.28	.22	.50	.08	.24	.25
English-Canadian	.30	.26	.46	.22	.43	.44	.25	.34
French	.20	.35	.31	.21	.27	.29	.20	.26
French-Canadian	.22	—**	.32	.21	.28	.39	.23	.28
German	.19	.17	.31	–	.21	.32	.20	.23
Israeli	.20	.16	.18	.16	.12	.13	.13	.15
Japanese	.18	.20	.16	.19	.20	.23	.17	.19
Lebanese	.30	.28	.31	.23	.24	.29	.27	.27
Turkish	.16	.28	.28	.17	.27	.30	.20	.24
Averages	.24	.27	.32	.23	.31	.30	.23	

* Argentinians.
** In this case no index was calculated because too few responses were available.

Table 9.2

Indices of Descriptive Consensus Among 10-Year-Olds: Evaluative Categories

Standard Reference Peoples

Respondents	Americans	Brazilians	Chinese	Germans	Indians	Negroes	Russians	Averages
American	—	.27	.39	.23	.40	.20	.39	.32
Bantu	.32	.42	.39	.36	.35	.39	.37	.37
Brazilian	.20	.20*	.30	.24	.10	.16	.17	.20
English-Canadian	.42	.30	.36	.20	.40	.17	.41	.32
French	.15	.18	.28	.19	.20	.15	.23	.20
French-Canadian	.26	.24	.28	.16	.29	.17	.31	.24
German	.16	.16	.25	—	.22	.18	.20	.20
Israeli	.17	.16	.22	.18	.17	.10	.16	.17
Japanese	.16	.19	.16	.19	.18	.16	.22	.18
Lebanese	.17	.20	.29	.17	.31	.17	.23	.22
Turkish	.20	.23	.23	.16	.24	.22	.21	.21
Averages	.22	.23	.29	.21	.26	.19	.26	

* Argentinians.

166

Table 9.3

Indices of Descriptive Consensus Among 14-Year-Olds: Evaluative Categories

Standard Reference Peoples

Respondents	Americans	Brazilians	Chinese	Germans	Indians	Negroes	Russians	Averages
American	—	.24	.36	.18	.39	.30	.22	.28
Bantu	.26	.41	.36	.34	.32	.27	.26	.32
Brazilian	.13	.21*	.28	.15	.24	.16	.15	.19
English-Canadian	.34	.25	.28	.12	.29	.27	.13	.24
French	.10	.11	.16	.15	.19	.16	.10	.14
French-Canadian	.23	.20	.22	.17	.28	.23	.16	.21
German	.14	.12	.20	—	.18	.16	.08	.15
Israeli	.12	.08	.17	.16	.12	.12	.08	.12
Japanese	.18	.21	.23	.19	.24	.20	.17	.20
Lebanese	.14	.24	.26	.18	.28	.28	.24	.23
Turkish	.20	.14	.19	.19	.17	.25	.20	.19
Averages	.18	.20	.25	.18	.25	.22	.16	

* Argentinians.

167

Certain national groups of children are particularly constricted in their evaluative descriptions of certain peoples. For example, the American children at all ages lack diversity in the evaluative descriptions they give of Chinese and Indian people. Similarly, the Brazilian 6-year-olds are restricted in their evaluative descriptions of Indians, whereas the 10-year-old Brazilians show much more diversity in regard to the same group. One might expect, judging from the Brazilian case, that once children develop descriptive diversity at a certain age level, they will maintain it, but this is not a general rule. For instance, both the English- and French- Canadian children are restricted in their evaluations of Negroes at age 6, while the 10-year-olds are much more diversified; however, by 14 years, the diversity has decreased.

In summary, we can conclude that there is an overall increase in evaluative diversity from 6 to 10 to 14 years although several national groups form interesting exceptions to this rule. In general, children of all ages are particularly limited in the evaluative descriptions they give of the Chinese and Indians. The 6-year-olds also lack diversity in their evaluations of Negroes as the 10-year-olds do when describing Russians. Compared to other national groups, the Bantu, American, and English-Canadian children generally lack evaluative diversity, whereas the Israeli and the younger Japanese children are comparatively diversified in their evaluations of foreign peoples.

Content Diversity

The indices presented in Tables 9.4-9.6 permit us to make national and age group comparisons of the *content* diversity of children's descriptions of foreign peoples. There is a universal tendency for content diversity to increase from 6- to 10-year age levels, but there is no consistent trend between the 10- to 14-year levels. Three national groups show an increase in content diversity from 10- to 14-year levels (the Bantu, Brazilian, and Japanese children), four a decrease (the American, French, French-Canadian, and Turkish children), and four show no essential change (the English-Canadian, German, Israeli, and Lebanese children). These inconsistencies from 10- to 14-year age groups may be due in part to the unreliability of the measure when indices become smaller than .20; that is, there

Table 9.4

Indices of Descriptive Diversity Among 6-Year-Olds: Content Categories

Standard Reference Peoples

Respondents	Americans	Brazilians	Chinese	Germans	Indians	Negroes	Russians	Averages
American	—	.19	.23	.16	.20	.19	.13	.18
Bantu	.63	.70	.67	.66	.70	.73	.70	.68
Brazilian	.22	.18*	.42	.27	1.00	.46	.18	.39
English-Canadian	.19	.18	.23	.19	.19	.18	.14	.19
French	.17	.23	.26	.18	.18	.33	.18	.22
French-Canadian	.25	—**	.32	.27	.25	.44	.23	.29
German	.22	.23	.31	—	.16	.35	.17	.24
Israeli	.21	.22	.36	.22	.22	.41	.17	.26
Japanese	.49	.46	.35	.44	.33	.55	.50	.45
Lebanese	.36	.30	.25	.18	.23	.25	.25	.26
Turkish	.27	.31	.31	.30	.24	.48	.28	.31
Averages	.30	.30	.34	.29	.34	.40	.27	.31

* Argentinians.
**There were too few responses available for this group to apply the formula.

169

Table 9.5

Indices of Descriptive Diversity Among 10-Year-Olds: Content Categories

Standard Reference Peoples

Respondents	Americans	Brazilians	Chinese	Germans	Indians	Negroes	Russians	Averages
American	–	.16	.16	.17	.17	.14	.19	.17
Bantu	.54	.59	.43	.46	.50	.50	.45	.50
Brazilian	.22	.23*	.42	.32	.32	.20	.22	.28
English-Canadian	.15	.15	.14	.17	.15	.15	.14	.15
French	.12	.13	.17	.12	.18	.12	.15	.14
French-Canadian	.16	.13	.16	.20	.24	.19	.15	.17
German	.18	.25	.26	–	.28	.16	.20	.22
Israeli	.17	.18	.27	.24	.27	.15	.19	.21
Japanese	.34	.23	.22	.31	.41	.23	.35	.30
Lebanese	.22	.18	.20	.21	.26	.19	.20	.21
Turkish	.25	.19	.23	.20	.27	.19	.16	.21
Averages	.23	.22	.24	.24	.28	.20	.22	

* Argentinians.

Table 9.6

Indices of Descriptive Diversity Among 14-Year-Olds: Content Categories

Standard Reference Peoples

Respondents	Americans	Brazilians	Chinese	Germans	Indians	Negroes	Russians	Averages
American	—	.13	.18	.17	.18	.30	.22	.20
Bantu	.44	.43	.50	.40	.37	.46	.38	.42
Brazilian	.16	.15*	.29	.16	.20	.34	.15	.21
English-Canadian	.15	.11	.13	.21	.14	.15	.25	.16
French	.19	.18	.16	.18	.16	.20	.14	.17
French-Canadian	.26	.18	.21	.29	.15	.24	.24	.22
German	.19	.18	.21	—	.16	.25	.18	.20
Israeli	.19	.16	.18	.26	.16	.21	.16	.19
Japanese	.36	.17	.28	.23	.23	.32	.22	.26
Lebanese	.27	.16	.18	.23	.14	.23	.19	.20
Turkish	.38	.17	.25	.37	.18	.31	.32	.28
Averages	.26	.18	.24	.25	.19	.27	.22	

* Argentinians.

may be a minimum number of categories that are likely to be used by any group, thus limiting the sensitivity of the index as this point is approached. Because of this possibility, we shall not attempt to interpret the changes from 10 to 14 years. The general increase in content diversity from 6- to 10- year age levels, however, appears to be a genuine phenomenon.

The average amounts of diversity do not vary much from one reference group to another, except for the case of the 6-year-olds, whose descriptions of African Negroes are especially restricted. However, there are more marked differences among the national groups of children. Again, the Bantu children at all ages have the least diversified descriptive content when describing foreign peoples. Although not as marked as the Bantu case, the Japanese children at all ages also are restricted in the content of their descriptions as are the younger Brazilian children. In contrast, the American, English-Canadian, and French children are more diversified in their descriptive content at all three age levels. Note that the American and English-Canadian children use a relatively restricted range of evaluative categories but a relatively broad range of content categories when describing foreign peoples, whereas the reverse holds for the Japanese children, that is, their descriptions of foreign peoples are diversified in evaluative features but restricted in content. We shall return to this point later.

Several national groups have interesting descriptive habits. For example, the French, French-Canadian, German, and Israeli 6-year-olds are restricted in their descriptive content when discussing Negroes but are more diversified at the 14-year level. In contrast, the American 6- and 10-year-olds use diverse descriptive content when referring to Negroes whereas the 14-year-olds are much more restricted, suggesting that the older American children are not receiving, or are not utilizing, as many different types of information about African Negroes as are children from many other nations. It is also noteworthy that the Japanese and Turkish 14-year-olds are restricted in their descriptive content when discussing Americans, just as the Israeli and Turkish 14-year-olds lack content diversity when describing Germans.

CORRELATES OF DESCRIPTIVE DIVERSITY

From a theoretical point of view, we might expect descriptive diversity to be correlated with favorable or friendly reactions. In other words, we might expect the more unfriendly groups of children to be less diversified in their thinking about foreign peoples. On the other hand, other factors would influence the relationship since a group of children could be restricted in its views of those foreign peoples they particularly admire in which case they would not, of course, be unfriendly. To examine these possibilities, we ranked the eleven national groups, one age group at a time, with regard to their average consensus scores (based on their descriptions of all seven reference peoples) and then correlated group variations in descriptive diversity with the degree of affection each group expressed for foreign groups, both those viewed as similar and those seen as dissimilar. (This measure of expressed affection is described in detail in the next chapter, see Table 10.1.) These correlations are presented in Table 9.7.

There are several important trends in this table. First, note that the correlations are all positive for the rows dealing with evaluative categories and all negative for those concerned with content categories. This means that in the case of descriptive content, as we expected, the less diversified the content features of a group's descriptions are, the less friendly that group is likely to be both toward foreign peoples they see as similar and foreign peoples they see as dissimilar. However, quite contrary to expectations, the less diversified the *evaluative* features of a group's descriptions are, the *more* friendly that group is likely to be toward foreign peoples. Stated otherwise, these correlations indicate that the degree of affection national groups of children express for foreign peoples is reflected in the diversity of their descriptions of these peoples. In general, the descriptions given by the more friendly groups of children are composed of restricted evaluative statements with diversified descriptive content, whereas the descriptions of foreign peoples given by less friendly groups of children have a diversity of evaluative statements but a restricted range of descriptive content.

Perhaps this important point will be clearer if we reconstruct the general form of the descriptions given by the more and less

Table 9.7

Correlates of Descriptive Diversity

Descriptive Consensus and Affection

	6-year-olds	10-year-olds	14-year-olds
Evaluative Categories	.66*	.61*	.22 n.s.
Content Categories	-.33 n.s.	-.67*	-.41 n.s.

Descriptive Consensus and Affection for Similars

	6-year-olds	10-year-olds	14-year-olds
Evaluative Categories	.40 n.s.	.69*	.58*
Content Categories	-.31 n.s.	-.56*	-.12 n.s.

Descriptive Consensus and Affection for Dissimilars

	6-year-olds	10-year-olds	14-year-olds
Evaluative Categories	.69*	.61*	.23 n.s.
Content Categories	-.34 n.s.	-.60*	-.38 n.s.

*Indicates that the correlation is significant at better than the .05 level of confidence, based on rank-order correlations; n = 11 in each case.

affectionate groups. The more friendly groups apparently think of foreign peoples as, for example, "good" (a restricted evaluative description if it were the only one given) in terms of their "personalities," "customs," "political systems," and "physical features" (a diversification of the descriptive content). The unfriendly national groups apparently have a different way of thinking about foreign peoples. They display a diversity of evaluative statements (for example, Russians are "different," "bad," "dominated," "intelligent," and "untrustworthy") but are restricted in their descriptive content (Russians are different, bad, untrustworthy *people*—all classified as references to one feature, "personality characteristics").

Of course, we cannot tell from correlations alone what the sequence of events is that leads to such differences in describing foreign peoples. We do not know whether, through educational and socialization experiences, children learn about the diversified aspects of other peoples and on the basis of this knowledge develop a liking for others, or whether they first develop a generally favorable attitude toward certain peoples and then, as a consequence of liking them, increase and diversify the information they have about them. The solution of this problem calls for long-range studies of actual changes that take place in children's views of people from other lands.

The important generalization suggested by these findings is that national groups of children with a friendly orientation toward foreign peoples are well informed about various aspects of the ways of life, habits, and personalities of these peoples and yet describe them with a minimum of evaluative references. An illustrative example of how this process might appear in the thinking of one person is the tourist who was really impressed with her trip to England and who exclaims, "Everything was wonderful, just wonderful," while revealing her detailed knowledge of the country, its institutions, politics, and so forth. In contrast, national groups of children who have a relatively unfriendly orientation either do not have diversified information about foreign peoples (or fail to use it if they do) while at the same time they tend to proliferate evaluative references, suggesting that when little objective information is available, children elaborate vague evaluative descriptions, analogous in one sense to the elaborate network of rumors that get established in poorly informed groups working under stress. The best we can do is describe this prominent trend and point out its potential importance in children's thoughts about foreign peoples. We cannot explain it. It could mean that those who are favorably disposed to foreign groups come to justify their feelings with information, or that those who are well informed are more likely to become friendly whereas those who are unfriendly are not motivated to become informed, justifying their feelings with vague evaluative references. We shall comment on these and other possible explanations in Chapter 11.

It should be noted that this trend comes from the contrast between negative and positive correlations in Table 9.7, but since only some of the correlations are statistically reliable, we should limit our generalizations to the 10-year-old age groups of children. Why the pattern is particularly strong at that age level is not clear from this investigation.

In summary, we have uncovered striking differences between the evaluative and content features of children's descriptions of foreign peoples when these were analyzed for their diversity. We also found marked national and age group variations in degree of descriptive diversity in regard to particular foreign peoples. Further research using the consensus index would be extremely valuable in extending our understanding of the structure of children's thoughts about foreign peoples.

10

Children's Attitudes Toward Foreign Peoples

Our purpose in this chapter is to compare the eleven national groups of children with regard to three aspects of their reactions toward foreign peoples: their tendency to regard foreigners as similar or different, their readiness to express affection or disaffection, and their general ethnocentrism. After examining each separately, we shall focus attention on how interrelations of these component reactions provide somewhat novel descriptions of children's attitudes toward foreign peoples.

To help the reader follow whatever inferences we may draw, it seems appropriate to outline briefly the details involved in measuring each reaction component. First, the *index of similarity outlook* is a simple ratio score, determined for each child, of the number of foreign peoples categorized as similar over the total number of peoples thought of as either similar or different, including those mentioned spontaneously and those asked about specifically. In cases where it was clear from his subsequent descriptions that a child knew little or nothing about one of the standard reference groups, that group was not included in the ratio. It is noteworthy that the ratio scores were based on each child's reactions to peoples from various parts of the world (Americans, Brazilians, Chinese, Germans, Indians, Negroes, and Russians) as well as six (or fewer) other peoples the child spontaneously mentioned as being similar or different. With this procedure, all groups of children probably had generally equivalent samples, from their respective points of view, of similar and dissimilar peoples to think about and describe. The ratio would, of course, reflect a child's inability to supply three nominations of similar and three of dissimilar peoples; for example, if he could nominate dissimilar foreign peoples easily but had difficulty recalling similars, his ratio would be lowered accordingly.

Second, the children were asked whether they liked or disliked each of the standard reference peoples and the other peoples they mentioned spontaneously. The measure of the tendency to like foreign groups is also a simple ratio, determined for each child, of peoples liked over the total number he was well enough informed about to describe in some detail. In addition to this overall index of affection, separate indices of the affection or lack of it shown for similar and dissimilar peoples were also calculated.

Third, it will be recalled that the 14-year-olds in each country were asked to respond to the questions of Else Frenkel-Brunswik's Ethnocentrism scale. Dr. Frenkel-Brunswik developed and validated these items by carefully analyzing the responses of two comparison groups of children; one whose observable behavior and reactions in clinical interviews indicated they were prejudiced and distrustful of people who were not members of their own group but of some alien national, regional, or religious group. The contrasting validation group gave every indication of being tolerant and without prejudice toward foreign people and ideas; in their thinking the ingroup-outgroup dimension played a relatively insignificant role.

Average scores for each of these variables were determined for all eleven national groups (see Table 10.1), and the differences between national samples were tested by a multiple-group comparison statistic, the Duncan Range Test.[1] The rank of placements of national groups and the statistical reliability of the separation of ranks are diagrammed in the graphs that follow.

[1] See D. B. Duncan. Multiple range and multiple F tests. *Biometrics*, 1955, *11*, 1-42.

In Figures 10.1-10.5, a solid line linking one country to another (or others) indicates that the national samples involved do not differ significantly from each other. A dotted line indicates a significant difference at the .05 level of confidence. If there is no connecting line, the countries differ significantly at the .01 level. For example, in Figure 10.1, the Israeli 6-year-olds differ significantly (.05 level) from the German children with regard to similarity outlooks and from all others at the .01 level of significance. The Turkish children do not differ from the Germans, and the English Canadians are not different from the Turkish although they are significantly different from the German children.

Figure 10.1
Similarity Outlooks.

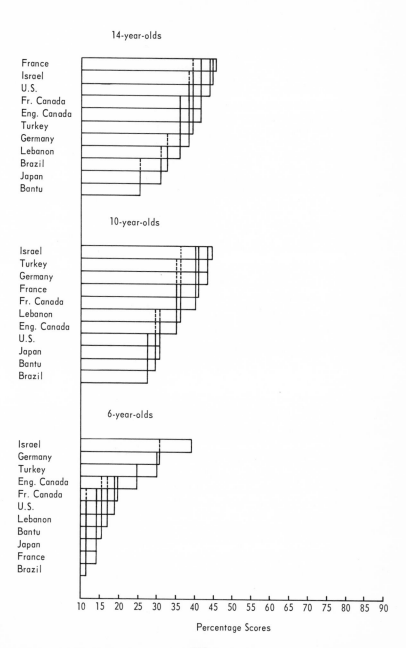

179

Figure 10.2
Affection Index.

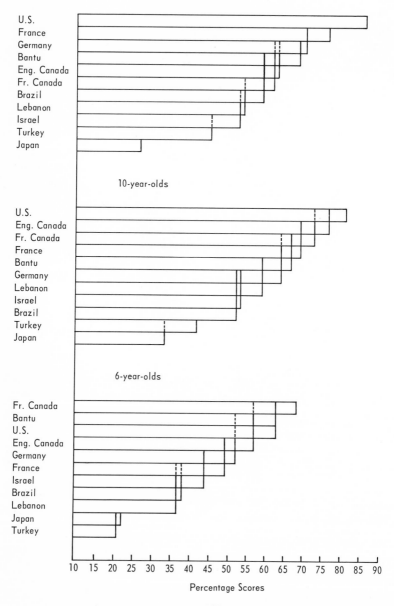

14-year-olds

10-year-olds

6-year-olds

Percentage Scores

Figure 10.3
Affection for Similars.

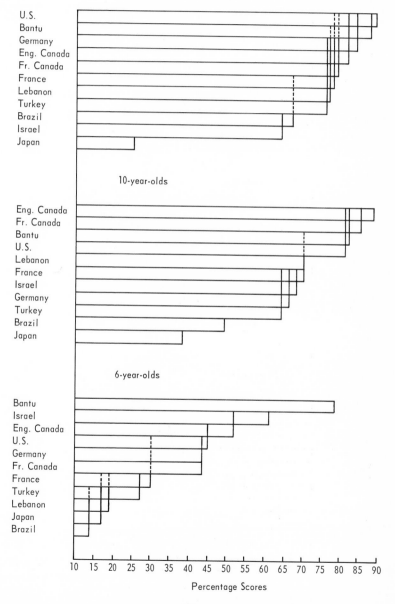

Percentage Scores

181

Figure 10.4
Affection for Dissimilars.

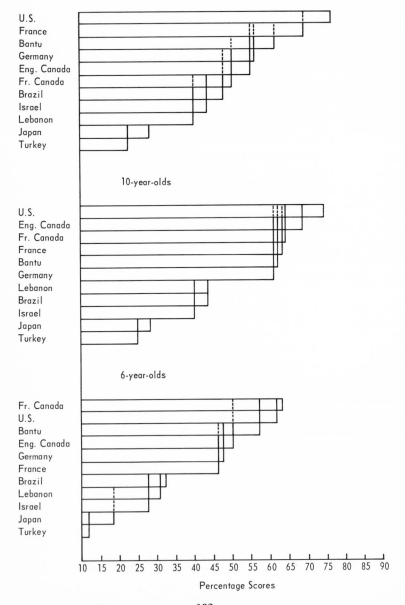

14-year-olds

10-year-olds

6-year-olds

Percentage Scores

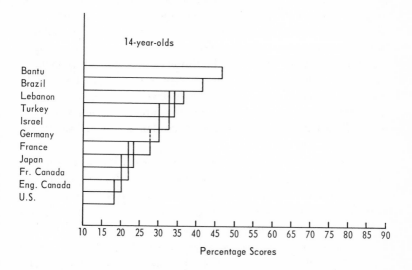

Figure 10.5
Ethnocentrism Scores.

SIMILARITY OUTLOOKS

Figure 10.1 presents the cross-national comparisons of similarity outlooks, one age group at a time. It is apparent that three national groups—the Brazilian, Japanese, and Bantu children—have comparatively narrow similarity outlooks in the sense that they consider most of the samples of foreign peoples as dissimilar to themselves, and this is consistent for all three age groups. Apparently these three national groups of children, compared to the others included in our study, think of themselves as unique or isolated national or cultural groups. In contrast to these three, the Israeli children at all age levels consider a wide range of foreign peoples as "like us." In fact, as a group they have the broadest similarity outlooks at 6- and 10-year levels and the next to largest at age 14. At 14, it is the French children who show the widest similarity outlooks, followed by a cluster of national groups comprising the Israeli, American, French-

Canadian, English-Canadian, and Turkish children, ranking in that order.

These comparisons may be in part a reflection of differences among the national groups of children in experience with foreign peoples, since countries like Israel, France, the U.S., and Canada have long been, or are now becoming, popular reception centers for immigrants from all over the world, and it is possible that children in such settings may learn more easily the similarities among peoples who differ in ethnic backgrounds. However, it is also likely that the differences noted here reflect more than variations in the heterogeneity of population in the countries involved—they may reflect differences in basic orientations toward foreign peoples that have been inculcated through particular education and socialization experiences.

There are several noteworthy changes from one age group of children to another in the relative breadth of similarity outlooks. First, the French children at age 6 have a very narrow view of who is "like us," but at ages 10 and particularly 14 this outlook is distinctively broader. Second, the American children at 6 and 10 years have a comparatively narrow view of similarity, but a striking change takes places by age 14 when the American sample moves into the group of nations with the broadest outlooks. Third, the Turkish and German children's similarity outlooks become both absolutely and comparatively narrower after the age of 10, changing from relatively broad ones at 6 and 10 years of age to intermediate ones at age 14.

There is a nearly universal tendency for 6-year-olds to think of the social world about them as populated more by people who are different from than similar to their own group. In fact, for ten of the eleven cultures examined, the 6-year-olds view foreign peoples as different from their own group reliably more frequently than do 10- or 14-year-olds.

This general age trend corresponds to one aspect of the normal intellectual development of children. The results of intelligence testing indicate that children learn to make differentiations among events in their environments before comprehending similarities. Thus, a child can comprehend and explain the differences between a bicycle and an automobile, for example, or an orange and an apple before he can comprehend broader, superordinate categories such as "means of transportation" and "fruit." In Vygotsky's[2] terms, "awareness of similarity requires a more advanced structure of generalization and conceptualization than awareness of dissimilarity. . . . consciousness of likeness presupposes the formation of a generalization, or of a concept, embracing the objects that are alike; consciousness of difference requires no such generalization." It may therefore be that similarities are basically more difficult for young children to grasp than differences, in the sense that contrasting or coordinate categories of thought are more easily used than are superordinate ones. Furthermore, it also may be that differences are stressed more often than similarities by those who socialize young children; that parents and teachers in their discussions with young children emphasize contrasts and differences of foreign peoples. The residue of this type of training seems to appear in the young children's descriptions, as we shall point out in the next chapter.

By 10 years of age, the tendency to regard foreign peoples as "like us" reaches its maximum and, in general, does not change much between 10 and 14 years. There are, however, exceptions to this leveling off tendency: for the American and English-Canadian children similarity outlooks increase in scope from 6 to 10 to 14 years. For Israeli children, on the other hand, there is no reliable change in this tendency from 6 to 14 years of age. Clearly, it would be extremely worthwhile to investigate the factors that contribute to or determine these cultural differences and age variations in children's views of foreign peoples and to examine how this orientation toward foreigners affects other features of children's behavior.

AFFECTION EXPRESSED FOR FOREIGN PEOPLES

Even though a child regards most foreign peoples as different from his own group, he may still show affection for them. We have noted this tendency to like foreign groups, regardless of their similarity, in the national profiles, and the same pattern can be seen on

---

[2] L. S. Vygotsky. *Thought and language.* M.I.T. Press and Wiley, 1962, p. 88 f.

a larger scale by comparing Figure 10.2 with Figure 10.1. It is clear that in general the children express an affection for others more readily than they regard them as being similar.

Nevertheless, important differences emerge among the national groups with regard to the tendency to like foreign peoples. The Japanese, Turkish, and Israeli children at all three age levels show least affection toward foreigners. At the other extreme, the American children at all ages have the most marked tendency to express affection for foreign peoples. Between these extremes, the Lebanese and Brazilian children at all three age levels fall near the center of the distribution of national groups in this regard.

Again, there are several distinctive changes from one age level to another. The 6-year-olds show least affection in seven of the eleven cultures examined, and yet also for seven of the eleven nations there are no reliable changes between the 10- and 14-year levels. In general, affection expressed toward foreign peoples increases from 6 to 10 years and then levels off. For three groups, however—the French-Canadian, English-Canadian, and Japanese—it is the 10-year-olds who show most affection toward others while the 14-year-olds are only about as affectionate as are the 6-year-olds. The American children and, to a less marked degree, the French, show a regular increase in affection from 6 to 10 to 14 years. In comparison, the Bantu children show no reliable changes from 6 to 14 years.

The striking differences and changes noted here prompt one to try to explain them, to speculate why, for example, the 14-year-old Canadians are less affectionate than the 10-year-olds toward foreigners, or why the Canadians fall out of the most affectionate cluster of nations at 14 years. Rather than offering almost pure speculations, however, it seems more appropriate to leave the findings as puzzles so that others may be interested in undertaking systematic research, both cross-national and intranational studies, that will throw light on the factors that determine cultural variations and age changes in these affective tendencies. That is, we could suggest that we are viewing here expressions of different national value systems, that, for example, American values press children to seek affection from others and to be nice to others, whereas Turkish values stress restraint of affection. Although we hope that ideas of this sort will come to mind, still we feel that readers may appreciate more a clear statement of the findings so that they can see new ways of determining what value systems, for example, actually are and why they vary from one national or age group to another.

AFFECTION FOR SIMILARS

On first thought, one would expect to find a direct relationship between children's similarity outlooks and their affection for foreign peoples; that is, that they would like people they consider as similar to themselves. It is clear from Figure 10.3 that there is not a perfect agreement and that there are large national differences in this regard. First, only the Bantu children at all age levels show a consistently high tendency to express affection for peoples considered as similar. On the other hand, Brazilian, Japanese, and Turkish children at all age levels expressed relatively little affection for those people they regarded as similar. Note especially the Japanese case, where the children at the three age levels said they like only 18, 37, and 24 percent of those peoples they considered similar.

For all national groups of children, there is an increase in the affection expressed for similars from the 6- to 10-year age levels. That is, the 6-year-olds, again, are least affectionate in all eleven countries, significantly so in eight of the eleven instances. No difference appears, however, between the 10- and 14-year-olds for the majority of national groups, there being no statistically reliable change from 10 to 14 years in seven of the eleven cases. The exceptions to this trend, however, are of interest. In Japan, the 10-year-olds express the most affection toward people viewed as similar, whereas the 14-year-old Japanese children are no different from the 6-year-olds. For the American, Brazilian, German, and Turkish children the tendency to express affection progressively increases from 6 to 14 years. In Israel and among the Bantu, there are no reliable differences in this regard from 6 to 14 years.

AFFECTION FOR DISSIMILARS

Figure 10.4 depicts the children's tendency to express affection for those people they considered as "not like us." Using adult logic we might in this case, too, expect a relationship between dissimilarity and disliking, but, as is apparent, there is little correspondence of this sort noted for the children sampled here. In fact, the figure makes it clear that children of these ages typically separate their conceptions of similarities and differences from the affection they express. In other words, they are quite ready to express affection for those they consider to be "not like us." If we compare this figure with Figure 10.3, it is clear that at age 6 there is, in general, as much affection shown for dissimilars as for similars. However, by the tenth and especially the fourteenth year, a discrepancy appears, and, generally, less affection is shown for dissimilars. This trend suggests that a correspondence does set in during the mid-teen years; in other words, children commence to dislike and like foreign peoples on the basis of their dissimilarities or similarities. As noted earlier, this may be due in part to a shift in the criteria used for judging similarity, that is, a shift away from judgments based on physical characteristics, common for the 6-year-olds, to judgments based on personality features which are particularly common for the 14-year-olds.

The 6-year-olds are clearly the least friendly toward dissimilars, and in no case is the 14-year age group more friendly than the 10-year-olds. In French Canada, the 14-year-olds are the least friendly of the three age groups toward dissimilars. Among English Canadians, the 10-year-olds are the most friendly to dissimilars but, as was the case with the French Canadians there is a statistically reliable decrease in affection expressed from the 10- to 14-year age groups. For the Bantu children, no reliable age variation occurs from 6 to 14 years.

Several generalizations can be made about the findings discussed so far. It is clear that 6-year-old children, at least those included in our small sample of societies, regard a restricted number of foreign peoples as similar to their own group. They are less prone to express affection toward foreign peoples, whether the peoples in question are considered similar or dissimilar to their own cultural group. The 10-year age period seems to be the critical one, for at this age children are most ready to consider other peoples as similar and are particularly friendly. By age 10 the readiness to like people who are dissimilar also reaches its maximum, for in none of the national groups studied is there a reliable increase in affection for dissimilars from 10 to 14 years. In fact, this tendency typically decreases after age 10.

From the other information we have about the children, we feel that these age changes in affection for foreign peoples are due in part to parallel changes in the way children define "like us" and "not like us." The 6- and 10-year-olds generally think of foreigners as different if they have clearly visible physical differences, whereas the 14-year-olds consider foreign peoples as different if their personality characteristics and habits are not similar to their own. Thus, when the older children categorize foreign peoples as different, they actually imply a negative evaluation of the latters' personalities and customs. We would expect, therefore, that 14-year-olds would be less likely to express affection for peoples they categorize as different.

This is not the complete explanation, however, since other factors, presumably cultural ones, clearly play a role, too. The older children from certain nations show a decrease while others show an increase in friendly attitudes toward foreigners. For example, the French Canadians and Japanese show significant decreases in their affection indices between the ages of 10 and 14. Further investigation is needed to determine what the factors are that disturb or change the favorable orientations toward foreigners noted among the 10-year-olds in these cultures. Moreover, the American children's overall similarity outlooks and their expressions of affection for foreign peoples increase significantly from the 10- to 14-year period. The English Canadians are also of special interest because in their case the similarity outlooks increase in scope from 10- to 14-years, while the expression of affection decreases, mainly because the 14-year-olds, in comparison to the 10-year-olds, say they do not like people they consider dissimilar. For the Brazilian, German, and Turkish children there are reliable increases from the 10- to 14-year age levels only in affection expressed for similars. That is, no general increase in friendliness is noted for these cultural groups, but only a greater tendency to like foreigners who are viewed as similar. For other national groups there are no age group changes; no changes in affection for similars occurs for the Israeli or Bantu children from 6 to 14 years. Each of these special cases, of course, deserves further investigation.

ETHNOCENTRISM

The distribution of ethnocentrism scores for the various groups of 14-year-old children is presented in Figure 10.5 where three clusters of national groups emerge. At one extreme, the Bantu and Brazilian 14-year-olds are the most ethnocentric while the American, English-Canadian, French-Canadian, Japanese, and French are the least. The other national groups (Lebanese, Turkish, Israeli, and German) form a cluster having an average degree of ethnocentrism. Within each cluster there are reliable differences among national groups, as can be seen in the figure. Some of these national differences in ethnocentric thinking are particularly interesting. For example, a great number of investigations using American high school and college students have formed the empirical bases of many prominent theories of prejudice and ethnocentrism, and the present results suggest that these theories have drawn on data taken from a country in which the children (though possibly not the adults) constitute one of the least prejudiced groups in the world.

Several important questions are raised by these findings. Why, for example, should the children from Brazil, a country noted for its lack of prejudice in race relations within its borders, rank as high as it does on the ethnocentrism measure, concerned as it is with attitudes toward foreign ideas and peoples? Why does the Bantu group rank so very high? Is it characteristic of those who have been coerced into segregation to be suspicious of foreign peoples? Why do the Japanese children, who showed so little affection for foreign peoples at age 14 and who thought of so few as being similar, rank so low on ethnocentrism? Even though the present study does not provide final answers to these questions, it does nevertheless suggest a new way of thinking about attitudes that may help in the search for answers.

PATTERNS OF ATTITUDE COMPONENTS

It may be profitable, before we turn to the configurations formed by all these indices, to consider similarity outlooks and expressions of affection as two important components of children's attitudes that determine how friendly or unfriendly they will be toward foreign peoples. Our findings make it clear that national groups of children vary greatly in both respects; some have extremely narrow similarity outlooks, as though they made rigorous use of various criteria for judging others, whereas others are much less restrictive, giving the impression that differences of skin color, language, and cultural habits are superficial ones for them. Similarly, national groups of children vary also in their readiness to express affection for foreign peoples, some making it clear they like a broad variety of peoples, whether judged as similar or different, while others are extremely selective, often misanthropic, suggesting that they have, as groups, developed a capacity to dislike foreigners, even many of those they think of as similar. Furthermore, there are certain indications that these two attitude components are independent. For instance, when we rank the eleven national samples of 14-year-olds for each component and calculate the rank-order correlation, it is not statistically significant ($rho = .36, df = 10$). This statistical independence implies that some groups of children may be very restrictive in their similarity outlooks but yet freely express affection toward foreign peoples, whereas others may have a broad similarity outlook and still be unlikely to express affection.

It follows that a more adequate description of a prejudiced or stereotyped attitude can be given if information is available about both the tendency to differentiate others from one's own group—a cognitive aspect of the attitude—and the readiness to express affection—an emotional aspect of the attitude.[3] In the present study we have information of these two sorts about children from various nations, and for the 14-year-olds we also have an indication of their ethnocentrism. When one examines the configurations formed by all three indices in the case of the 14-year-old groups, or by the two components in the case of the younger children, it becomes apparent that descriptions of attitudinal orientations and tendencies to react toward foreign peoples are incomplete and insufficient if based on only one index, such as a standard measure of prejudice, especially when it is used in cultures other than the one for which it was standardized. For example, three national groups of children who would

[3] For a fuller discussion of attitude components, see Chapter 4 of W. W. Lambert and W. E. Lambert. *Social Psychology.* Englewood Cliffs, N.J.: Prentice-Hall, 1964.

be considered ethnocentric, judging from their average scores, differ markedly in their reactions to foreign peoples: one group presents a consistent pattern of narrow similarity outlooks and a weak tendency to express affection; another shows a broad similarity outlook but a weak tendency to express affection; and the third has a very narrow similarity outlook but a very strong tendency to express affection. Obviously, the attitudes represented in each of these cases are basically different. Consider also a fourth example where the group has a very low ethnocentrism score at the same time as it has the strongest tendency to dislike foreign peoples and a very narrow similarity outlook. In this case (the Japanese 14-year-olds) the ethnocentrism score alone would be an inadequate description of the actual attitudes involved.

Let us now examine the configurations formed by all three indices for each of the eleven national groups.

1. Compared with the other national samples, the *American* children show the least amount of ethnocentrism at the 14-year level, a relatively restricted similarity outlook at the 6- and 10-year levels which broadens by age 14, and an extremely large affective tendency at all age levels, both for those peoples considered similar and those seen as different from their own group. Although there is the tendency for the younger children to be exclusive about who and how many foreign peoples are conceptualized as similar, the American pattern, compared to the others, is an encouraging one in the sense that these children appear friendly and receptive toward foreign peoples.

2. The 14-year-old *Bantu* children have the highest ethnocentrism score of all the national groups of children examined. Furthermore, at all age levels they consider very few foreign peoples as similar although they show an above-average affective tendency for similars as well as dissimilars. The inconsistencies of this pattern are of interest. Since the Bantu is the only group studied whose rights in their own country are seriously limited by legalized discrimination and segregation, it is possible that members of such a minority group may interpret the items of the ethnocentrism scale in some fashion that artifically increases their scores. A few of the 13 items (see Appendix A) may well be biased for the Bantu children: they could, for instance, justifiably reject item 2 (our country is

better off because of the foreign races that live here), and endorse item 4 and (there will always be war, it is part of human nature) because of suspicions and tensions existing for them in their own country, and thereby inappropriately increase their ethnocentrism scores. However, other items such as 7 and 1 may be biased in the opposite way. Thus, if we assume that the scale is appropriate and not badly biased for the Bantu children, then their scores likely reflect an above-average degree of ethnocentric thinking, at least as ethnocentrism is conceptualized by those who developed the measure.[4] The pattern then suggests that Bantu children have learned to consider themselves as a different and unique group, but they have apparently also learned to express affection for other peoples, even those considered dissimilar. Thus, the Bantu children's potential suspiciousness of foreign groups, inferred from their high ethnocentrism score and their narrow similarity outlook, may be offset by an unexpectedly strong affective tendency. Incidentally, it is possible, too, that the inconsistencies noted here may reflect discordant thoughts and feelings of the Bantu children that are sources of personal conflict for them.

3. The *Brazilian* children present a generally unfriendly pattern. The 14-year-olds rank very high in ethnocentrism. Furthermore, at all ages the Brazilian children consider very few foreign peoples as similar, and they are generally not affectionate toward foreigners, disliking both similars and dissimilars. All aspects of this pattern are negative, making the Brazilian children, in comparison with the other national samples, appear generally hostile toward foreign peoples.

4. The 4-year-old *French-* and *English-Canadian* children show comparatively little ethnocentrism. For similarity outlooks, their rank changes from slightly below to slightly above average from ages 6 to 14. The French-Canadian children show a regular decrease from 6 to 14 years in the degree of affection shown toward other peoples,

---

[4] The Bantu case makes it very evident that much more work is called for on this measure (and other measures) of ethnocentrism to determine if suspiciousness of foreigners expresses itself in a cross-culturally stable manner. Until more information is available, we can only assume that we have used an appropriate measure for all of the national groups involved, but in making this assumption, we run the risk of reifying a concept (ethnocentrism) that may actually have no real psychological basis, at least for children from certain cultures.

Table 10.1

Cross-National Comparisons of Similarity Outlooks, Affective Tendencies, and Ethnocentrism by Age Groups*

National Groups	Similarity Outlooks 6	10	14	Affection Indices 6	10	14	Affection for Similars 6	10	14	Affection for Dissimilars 6	10	14	Ethnocentrism 14
American	.19	.31	.44	.63	.81	.86	.45	.81	.88	.61	.73	.77	.18
Bantu	.16	.30	.27	.63	.66	.65	.78	.82	.87	.57	.62	.61	.46
Brazilian	.12	.28	.33	.38	.52	.59	.14	.48	.66	.32	.44	.48	.41
English-Canadian	.24	.36	.42	.57	.76	.62	.52	.87	.80	.50	.68	.51	.21
French	.14	.41	.46	.49	.69	.74	.30	.70	.77	.46	.63	.68	.26

Significance levels between adjacent age groups (6–10, 10–14):

- American — Similarity Outlooks: .01, .01; Affection Indices: .01, .05; Affection for Similars: .01, n.s.; Affection for Dissimilars: .05, n.s.
- Bantu — Similarity Outlooks: .01, n.s.; Affection Indices: n.s., n.s.; Affection for Similars: n.s., n.s.; Affection for Dissimilars: n.s., n.s.
- Brazilian — Similarity Outlooks: .01, n.s.; Affection Indices: .01, n.s.; Affection for Similars: .01, .01; Affection for Dissimilars: .05, n.s.
- English-Canadian — Similarity Outlooks: .01, .05; Affection Indices: .01, .01; Affection for Similars: .01, .01; Affection for Dissimilars: .01, .01
- French — Similarity Outlooks: .01, n.s.; Affection Indices: .01, n.s.; Affection for Similars: .01, n.s.; Affection for Dissimilars: .01, n.s.

194

Note: This table is printed rotated 90° on the page. Entries are mean scores; brackets between adjacent values indicate significance levels (.01, .05, or n.s.).

Group													Final
French-Canadian	.20	.40	.42	.68	.73	.61	.44	.84	.78	.63	.64	.50	.23
	.01	n.s.		n.s.	.01		.01	n.s.		n.s.	.05 / .05		
German	.31	.43	.39	.52	.64	.69	.44	.66	.83	.47	.61	.58	.30
	.01	.05 / n.s.		.01 / n.s.			.01	.01 / n.s.		.01	.01 / n.s.		
Israeli	.39	.44	.45	.44	.53	.52	.61	.67	.63	.28	.40	.44	.32
	n.s.			.05 / n.s.	n.s.		n.s.			.05	.01 / n.s.		
Japanese	.14	.31	.31	.22	.32	.27	.17	.37	.24	.18	.28	.28	.24
	.01 / n.s.			.01 / n.s.	n.s.		.01 / n.s.	.01		.05	.01 / n.s.		
Lebanese	.17	.37	.37	.37	.59	.53	.18	.70	.76	.31	.44	.40	.35
	.01 / n.s.			.01 / n.s.	.01		.01	.01		.05	.01 / n.s.		
Turkish	.30	.43	.40	.21	.41	.44	.27	.64	.75	.12	.25	.22	.33
	.01 / n.s.			.01 / n.s.			.01	.01		.01	.01 / n.s.		

*Entries are mean scores for each age group.
N's are 100 for each age group; t-value must be 1.98 for the 5% confidence level or 2.63 for the 1% level, using two-tailed tests of significance. When variances were not homogeneous, t-values are computed according to formula given on page 273 of A. Edwards, *Statistical methods for the behavioral sciences*. New York: Rinehart, 1954.

moving from the highest amount of affection at age 6 to an average degree at age 14. The English-Canadian children also become relatively less affectionate toward foreign peoples, if we compare the 10- and 14-year age groups. The pattern for both Canadian groups, therefore, is not a consistent or stable one: although they show relatively little ethnocentrism, they are exclusive about whom they classify as similar, and they show a relative decline in affection for foreign groups by the teen ages.

5. The *French* children present a generally favorable and friendly pattern. The 14-year-olds have a relatively low ethnocentrism score, and there is a marked change in similarity outlooks, from a particularly restricted view at age 6 to the broadest of all at age 14. Similarly, the affection index moves regularly from an average position at age 6 to a high position by age 14, due mainly to an increase in affection shown toward dissimilars.

6. The pattern for the *German* children is neither particularly friendly nor hostile. The 14-year-olds are at about the median of all national groups in terms of ethnocentrism. The samples of younger children show a relatively strong tendency to consider foreign peoples as similar, but the trend reverses to an average position by age 14. At all age levels, the German children are slightly above average in their expression of affection toward foreign groups and this trend increases slightly by age 14.

7. The *Israeli* pattern is inconsistent and, overall, it is an unfriendly one. At all ages the Israeli children have a relatively strong tendency to consider other peoples as similar. However, they have a generally weak tendency, especially noticeable with the 14-year-olds, to express affection for foreign peoples, either for similars or dissimilars. Furthermore, the 14-year-olds rank about at the median on ethnocentrism.

8. The *Japanese* children present an intriguing pattern of components. They rank extremely low on the tendency to regard foreign peoples as similar, and they express little affection for other peoples. In fact they have the lowest affection indices of all, even in the case of foreign peoples considered as similar to themselves. However, they have a very low ethnocentrism score. The Japanese pattern, like the Brazilian, is essentially an unfriendly one, characterized by a narrow similarity outlook and a tendency to dislike foreign peoples.

But whereas the Brazilian children ranked very high in ethnocentrism, thereby showing a consistent pattern, the Japanese children rank very low. There may be many possible interpretations of this inconsistent pattern. The one we have arrived at requires a preliminary comment about the nature of standard measures of prejudice. Most items of a prejudice scale require the examinee to make comparisons between his own reference group and others. If he feels that others are untrustworthy or inferior when compared with his own group, he will score high on prejudice. On the other hand, he could obtain a low score on a measure of prejudice if he had a generalized suspicion or hatred *which included his own group,* for in this case he would not make invidious comparisons and credit his own group with more favorable traits than other groups. Since we have evidence that the Japanese children expressed a marked degree of dislike of foreign peoples, it is possible that they direct disaffection toward their own group as well as foreign ones. There is some independent evidence that supports this interpretation. It will be recalled that the Japanese children, when asked to describe themselves, were particularly critical of their own group. In fact, the Japanese children were unique in the degree of negative evaluations made about their own national group. Even with this indirect support, however, our interpretation of the Japanese pattern should only be looked on as an hypothesis for further and closer examination.

9. The *Lebanese* 14-year-olds are above average in their degree of ethnocentrism, and at all age levels the Lebanese children are slightly below average in their similarity outlooks. Their affective tendency also falls somewhat below the average, especially at age 14, for foreign peoples viewed either as similar or dissimilar. In general the Lebanese pattern, although not a pronounced one, is more unfriendly than friendly.

10. The *Turkish* children have an inconsistent pattern that is generally unfriendly toward foreign peoples. At all ages the Turkish children have a relatively broad similarity outlook, but, relative to the other children, they do not show affection toward others, either in the case of foreign groups seen as dissimilar, where their tendency to dislike is extremely strong, or in the case of foreign peoples considered as similar. The 14-year-olds rank about average on ethno-

centrism. Thus their relatively broad conceptions of similarity do not offset their generally negative affective tendency toward other peoples.

In summary, the American, French, English-Canadian, and French-Canadian children emerge as comparatively friendly toward foreign peoples. In contrast, the Japanese, Brazilian, Turkish, and Israeli children appear relatively unfriendly. The German, Lebanese, and Bantu patterns are not easily categorized. What factors determine friendliness or unfriendliness of this sort? What accounts for the age and national variations in the breadth of similarity outlooks, in affective tendencies, and in degrees of ethnocentrism? These questions are as interesting and important as were the original ones that prompted us to begin the fact-finding aspect of this study. The next steps in research, that is, to examine these matters in detail, will depend on the efforts of social scientists from each national region, as well as those interested in cross-national comparisons.

11

Children's Views of Foreign Peoples: In Perspective

In this final chapter we shall first collect and summarize the large number of findings already presented in the earlier chapters. Reviewing the results in this fashion will give the reader a clearer overall view at the same time as it will permit us to relate the findings, where possible, to those of other investigators, and place them in proper perspective by pointing out the need for further study of many of the issues raised. In the final section, we shall integrate the major findings with those of other researchers who have been concerned with the development of prejudiced and stereotyped thinking of children and thereby sketch out the beginnings of a theory of how children's views of foreign peoples develop.

CHILDREN'S SELF-CONCEPTIONS

Our purpose in asking the "What are you?" questions at the very start of the formal interview was to capture the terms spontaneously used by various national groups of children when describing themselves. Considering the diversity of their ages and backgrounds, the children used a surprisingly small number of different self-descriptive themes. In order of their popularity of use these were: references to their sex, to the fact they were persons or human beings, students, or children, and to their national, regional, religious, or racial backgrounds. We assumed that the categories of

thought evident in self-descriptions would give some indication of
how the children thought about and judged other people, compatriots
as well as foreigners. Thus, if certain groups of children stress religion, race, or national background when describing themselves, they
might well categorize and evaluate foreign peoples in terms of the
same criteria. As it turned out, national or regional background,
religion, and race were not important descriptive categories for most
groups of children studied, although they were very apparent in the
thinking of certain groups.[1] For instance, national or regional background was prominent in the thinking of even the youngest Japanese
children and became increasingly noticeable with the older age
groups. Although relatively minor issues when compared to the Japanese case, national and regional references were of some importance
also for the Lebanese, Turkish, and German children; in contrast,
this matter was apparently unimportant for the Bantu, Brazilian,
and French-Canadian children, even at the 10- and 14-year age levels.
We were not able to determine why certain groups stressed national
or regional background, but the differences in usage merit further
study because they apparently reflect basic variations in the importance of nationality that could affect children's reactions to foreign
peoples. At this point, however, many questions are left open as to
why nationality is more salient for some groups than for others. Does
the spontaneous occurrence of these references reflect national pride
in certain cases, or does it in other cases indicate only an admission
of an unpleasant fact? Are national references more prominent for

---

[1] Other researchers have used a similar approach with children. For example, Hartley, Rosenbaum, and Schwartz (Children's use of ethnic frames
of reference. *J. Psychol.*, 1948, *26*, 367-386) asked young American children
"What are you?" and, in contrast to our findings, they received a large number
of national, ethnic, and religious responses (*e.g.*, Jewish, colored, Catholic,
English, Italian) and only a few references to sex. The use of ethnic-religious
references was particularly marked with Jewish children in contrast to non-
Jewish white children. The difference in the results of the two studies is very
likely due to two factors: the context in which the question was asked, and the
characteristics of the samples of children interviewed. For Hartley *et. al.*, the
question followed a discussion of "What kind of people live around your house?"
and since the children came from a region of New York City where families
of various ethnic and religious backgrounds lived, it is quite certain that they
would have been talking and thinking about the religious and ethnic affiliations
of their neighbors just before answering the "What are you?" question, thereby
highlighting the salience of these characteristics.

those living in nations composed of many ethnic and immigrant groups where distinctions of this sort may become socially relevant? Does the ethnic composition of the child's environment affect his use of such references, as the study of Hartley *et al.* suggests?

Ethnic references played a prominent role in the thinking of only one group, the Bantu children, the only Negro group included in our study. Clearly race is of major social significance in South Africa and it is not surprising that it manifested itself in the thinking of those South Africans who are discriminated against because of their skin color.

Religion was the dominant self-descriptive reference of the Lebanese children, and a popular category of thought for the Turkish children, too, suggesting that in these nations socially important distinctions are made along religious lines. Using the same argument, one would expect the Canadian children to make frequent references to their religious or ethnic affiliations since the Province of Quebec is noted for its English-Protestant and French-Catholic tensions. Although a small subgroup of 6-year-old French Canadians did refer to themselves as *"enfant de Dieu,"* religion did not otherwise enter into the self-descriptions of either group of Canadian children. This interesting finding calls for further study of the conditions that promote religious differentiation in the thinking of children from various nations.

Thus the children from certain nations when describing themselves highlighted particular characteristics that may also be stressed in judging foreign peoples. We might, for example, expect the Japanese children to judge others according to their national background, the Bantu to evaluate others in terms of race, and the Turkish and Lebanese youngsters to react to both the national and religious backgrounds of foreign peoples (the Lebanese in particular since they rarely referred to themselves as persons, which is a common self-reference for most of the other groups of children). In contrast, we would not expect the American or English-Canadian children to make distinctions along these lines since their dominant self-reference was to the fact that they were boys or girls and persons. Although our procedures were not precise enough to trace through the effect of these types of thinking on the children's reactions to foreign peoples, still certain results are consistent with the notion that such an effect is operative. As we noted in Chapter 10, the Japanese, Lebanese, and Turkish children have comparatively suspicious and unfriendly attitudes toward foreign peoples in contrast, especially, to the American and English-Canadian youngsters, who are generally inquisitive about and friendly toward foreign groups. Furthermore, the Bantu children make it clear that race is important to them when they say they would like to be "White" if they were not Bantu and when they frequently use the term "White" to identify dissimilar foreign groups. As noted in Chapter 10, though, this dominant category of thought does not apparently influence the Bantu children's readiness to express affection for others.

Although we are suggesting here that children's self-conceptions reveal the salient modes of thought used to judge and evaluate not only themselves but foreign peoples as well, it should be clearly understood that much more research, specifically designed to examine this important question, is called for before we can give a comprehensive account of how the process actually works.

CHILDREN'S CONCEPTIONS OF THEIR OWN NATIONAL GROUP

Even though nationality was apparently not foremost in the thoughts of most groups of children when they described themselves, still they generally did have definite views of their own national group when directly asked about it. Yet, even this generalization has interesting limitations. When certain groups of children were asked to describe members of their national group, they explained that these people were "similar to us" or "like us" in various ways. The cases in point are the Lebanese, Bantu, and, to a less marked degree, Brazilian, German, and Israeli children, many of whom either did not consider themselves as full-fledged members of superordinate national groups, or were unclear about the definition of such groups.

However, these interesting similarity references did not obscure the images children had of members of their own national group, as these are inferred from the evaluative descriptions they gave of their own people's personality traits. The American children saw Americans as good, wealthy, and free; the Bantu children when asked to describe the Zulu or Sesotho peoples, whichever was appropriate, gave few evaluative descriptions, instead typically making references to similarities or referring to physical characteristics; the Brazilian children thought of Brazilians as good, intelligent, cultured, happy, and unambitious; the English-Canadian children saw the Canadians as good, wealthy, free, and cultured; the French-Canadian children saw *les Canadiens* as good, wealthy, peaceful, and patriotic; the French children saw the French as good, intelligent, cultured, happy, and bad; the German children saw the Germans as good, ambitious, wealthy, and intelligent; the Israeli children saw Israelis as good, peaceful, religious, intelligent and ambitious; the Japanese children saw the Japanese as poor, intelligent, and bad; the Lebanese gave mainly similarity references or described the Lebanese as good; and the Turkish children saw their own national group as good, peaceful, ambitious, religious, patriotic, and clean.

For certain groups of children, we can compare their views of their own group with the views other peoples hold of them. In a recent study conducted in Switzerland, Fischer and Trier[2] found that "autostereotypes" (group A's stereotyped views of their own peoples) were less exaggerated but very similar in content to "heterostereotypes" (group B's views of people A). That is, the German-Swiss thought of themselves as being angular, dry, and conservative (rating scales with these adjectives, among others, were provided), and the French-Swiss while agreeing on the particular traits saw the German-Swiss as even more angular, dry, and conservative. By way of comparison, we noted in our study that the American children's views of their own people generally agreed with other groups' views of Americans—that Americans are good, wealthy, and politically democratic —but in this case the autostereotype was clearer than the heterosterotypes in that it was not accompanied by the addition of negative traits mentioned by non-American children. Likewise, the German children saw themselves as good, ambitious, wealthy, and intelligent, whereas many other groups of children, while agreeing that Germans are good, also saw them as aggressive and bad. Furthermore, the

[2] H. Fischer and U. P. Trier. *Das Verhältnis zwischen Deutschschweizer und Westschweizer: Eine sozialpsychologische Untersuchung.* Bern, Hans Huber, 1962; reviewed in H. C. Triandis. The influence of culture on cognitive processes. In L. Berkowitz, (Ed.), *Advances in experimental social psychology.* New York: Academic, 1964.

Brazilian children considered their own people to be good, intelligent, cultured, happy, and unambitious, whereas children from most other nations have no clear image at all of Brazilians. Taking into consideration the fact that the procedures of the two studies are quite different, still we found no evidence that heterostereotypes are more exaggerated than autostereotypes. In fact the content of the two types of stereotypes were often quite dissimilar; when they were alike, the autostereotypes were generallv more favorable than the heterostereotypes, and were more exaggerated in the sense that they did not have negative as well as favorable elements. It would be worthwhile to examine more extensively the autostereotypes and heterostereotypes of different national groups and of different ethnic groups within nations. Is there a general developmental trend for auto- and heterostereotypes to become more similar or more dissimilar with age, or do discrepancies occur mainly in those settings where the heterostereotypes are unfavorable or seen as exaggerated?

We compared children's views of their own group with their views of those foreign groups they particularly admired. This comparison, we felt, would throw some light on how satisfied or disenchanted they were with their own way of life. For instance, we noted that the French children were attracted to foreign peoples whom they saw as good, cultured, and interesting, that is foreign peoples who resembled their own group to a great extent. The American children also admired foreign peoples whom they perceived as essentially like themselves. Other groups of children, however, were apparently less content with their own national image. The German youngsters, for example, were attracted to good, wealthy, and peaceful nations, but since they failed to mention peaceful as a descriptive trait of their own group, its absence may have been a source of irritation for them. Similarly, the Brazilian and Japanese children characterized desirable nations as wealthy, a trait notably lacking in their descriptions of their own country. From this point of view, the Japanese children, especially the older ones, showed a good deal of cultural dissatisfaction in that the foreign peoples they admired were said to be good, wealthy, peaceful, cultured, and clean, whereas their own people were described as poor and bad, although intelligent.

It would be valuable to look more carefully into young people's satisfactions or dissatisfactions with their images of their homeland.

As members of the generation coming up, they could, if dissatisfied, sullenly dwell on and exaggerate any perceived shortcomings in their own way of life and transform their disenchantment and envy into aggression toward the "have" nations or toward institutions and groups at home who may be blamed for the inadequacies. On the other hand, they might use foreign nationalities they admire as models for change and work constructively toward improvements. They could, however, develop other strategies for reducing their feelings of dissatisfaction; they might, for example, choose different nationalities to admire, others that are more similar to their own in values and available opportunities.[3]

FOREIGN PEOPLES SEEN AS SIMILAR AND AS DIFFERENT

We had several reasons for asking the children to name foreign peoples they thought of as being similar to or different from themselves. First we were interested in the actual choices of each group of children, for, apart from their sheer interest value, one can often infer from such choices the criteria different national groups of children use in categorizing foreign peoples as similar or different. We were also interested to see if there were cross-nationally favorite choices since from these one might be able to isolate common criteria used by children from various national backgrounds. For example, the American children frequently chose the British as similar (this was their most popular choice) as well as the Canadians, the French, and the Italians, while they categorized the Russians, Chinese, Africans, and Japanese as different. This pattern of choices suggests that American children define "like us," in this context, in terms of similarities of historical or cultural origin, and geographical proximity, and "not like us" in terms of ideological differences, ethnicity, and geographical distance. As it turned out, certain national groups—the American, British, and French—were thought of as similar by many

[3] The investigation to be found in Appendix E was conducted with the same eleven national groups of children and is concerned with their occupational aspirations for the future. The findings presented there bring to light important variations in desires to maintain or change the established ways of life these children have come to know.

or most of the different groups of children, and others—the Chinese, African Negroes, Japanese, Russians, and Americans (again)—were popularly regarded as different. Considering the nominations of all eleven groups of children, foreign peoples may be categorized as similar or different for various reasons, the most prominent ones being: a Western versus an Oriental-African bias, historical ties or animosities, ethnic similarities or contrasts, geographical proximity or distance, and similarities or contrasts in customs, presumed personality traits, language, values, and beliefs. Further research that systematically analyzes the criteria children of various nations use in categorizing foreign peoples would be particularly valuable, for, as we shall argue later, children apparently develop their own national identity in part through the comparisons they make between their own people and those foreign groups they consider to be similar and different from themselves. Research on this question might make use of a modified *method of triads* wherein children would be asked to consider three nations, one being their own, and to tell which two are more alike. As they explain why they choose as they do, one could probe the meanings these explanatory terms have for children of various ages.

The cross-national tendency to view Western nations as similar suggests that children from various parts of the world may try to identify with American, British, and French people, possibly using them as models for appropriate behavior, just as the Eastern and African peoples may be used as bad models or negative reference groups. We uncovered a certain degree of ambivalence toward Americans, however, since sizable subgroups of children in Brazil, France, Germany, Japan, and Lebanon see Americans as similar while other subgroups see them as dissimilar. It would be of interest to look more carefully into the bases for these signs of ambivalence. One might well find conflicting social pressures in these societies pulling toward and away from cultural alignment with American ideas and customs. However, the question as to what motivates children's identification with foreign peoples is even more basic. Do they identify through envy, as John Whiting might suggest,[4] and is it possibly societal

---

[4] J. W. M. Whiting. Resource mediation and learning by identification. In I. Iscoe and H. Stevenson (Eds.), *Personality development in children.* Austin: Univer. of Texas Press, 1960.

variations in strength of envy that underlie the ambivalence noted toward Americans?

It intrigues us to think of the procedure used here as one that generates a sociometry of nations, based on similarity and difference. From this point of view, the Americans, British, and French are the sociometric "stars" and the Eastern and African nations are the "isolates." Of course, we have too few contributors to this pattern to generalize, and unrepresentative samples at that, but still from this limited analysis one can see how instructive it would be to gather this type of information from a larger number of national groups and trace out the various groupings and cleavages of nations. In doing so, we would be able to determine with more confidence which nations are widely used as positive and negative reference groups.

DESIRABLE AND UNDESIRABLE NATIONALITIES

The children were asked to name the nationalities they would most like to have and least like to have if they were not what they actually are, and to explain their choices. In doing this, they indirectly revealed the criteria they used in categorizing foreign countries as desirable or undesirable places to live. If they were not what they are, most groups of children said they would like to be Americans. In fact, American nationality is the first choice for nine of the eleven national groups of children, and, in general, its popularity increases at each successive age level. Although less popularly nominated, British and French nationalities are also desirable for many groups of children. These were the more generally favored choices, but there were, of course, distinctive patterns of nominations given by each national group of children.

The reasons given for their choices of desirable nationalities indicate that, in general, children see desirable countries as places where people with good personal qualities (the major characteristic), habits, and customs live; these places also have interesting languages and geographical settings. For some groups, they are desirable because they are similar to the children's own country, while in other instances, they are desirable precisely because they are different. In other words, some groups of children, for example the American, English-Canadian and Turkish, nominate countries as desirable places to live because they are "like home" in many respects, whereas other groups of children choose countries as desirable because, unlike home, they are, for example, wealthy (the case for the Bantu, Japanese, and Brazilian children), or because they are peaceful, a characteristic stressed by the German, Japanese, and French children—those whose homelands were ravaged by recent wars.

If they were not what they are, many groups of children say they would least like to be Russian, African, Chinese, or German, listed here in order of nomination. In general, countries are mentioned as undesirable because of the belief that aggressive and bad people live there, this being the major theme, and because they are perceived as uncultured, dominated, unintelligent, poor, and dirty. Some of these themes are common in the thinking of children from many national backgrounds, while some are specific to those from small clusters of nations. To illustrate, the aggressive and bad descriptive theme was found with all eleven groups of children, whereas "unintelligent" was an important characteristic of undesirable places for the Bantu, French, and Israeli children, while "dirty" was stressed by the Japanese and Bantu children only. These themes apparently reflect underlying cultural values that may be essential in shaping children's reactions to foreign peoples and nations.

Although there was a good deal of overlap in the children's conceptions of similar peoples and desirable nationalities on the one hand, and dissimilar peoples and undesirable nationalities on the other, still important distinctions were made. For example, the Bantu children mentioned most frequently that the Whites and the British were different from them and yet they would most like to be White or British if they were not Zulu or Sesotho. However, it is very often the case that the countries children think of as desirable places to live are populated by people who are "like us," even though the similarity, from the children's perspectives, could be even greater if, for example, their own nation were wealthier or more peaceful. It is of interest that more children from Japan, Lebanon, France, and Brazil see the American way of life as desirable than see the American people as similar. In contrast, greater proportions of children see the Russian nationality as undesirable than see the Russian people as dissimilar. These findings suggest that at least certain groups of children, in deciding about the desirability of foreign nations, place somewhat more importance on the way of life and the opportunities available than on the characteristics of the people who live there. The main point, however, is that the children's concepts of desirability and similarity as used in this context overlap to a great extent although important distinctions were made between attractive or unattractive places to live and the similarity or dissimilarity of the inhabitants. America turned out to be a particularly desirable nation, in fact a sociometric "star" in this sense, and Russia was an undesirable nation.

CONCEPTIONS OF THE STANDARD REFERENCE PEOPLES

In the interviews, the eleven national groups of children were given the opportunity to present all aspects of their views of seven supposedly well known peoples—Americans, Brazilians, Chinese, Germans, Indians from India, African Negroes, and Russians. When these views were compared, certain noteworthy cross-national regularities became apparent. In the first place, as we have already noted, the Americans are commonly seen as being "like us," whereas the Chinese, Indians from India, and African Negroes are typically categorized as "not like us." The children had more trouble categorizing the Brazilians, Germans, and Russians inasmuch as subgroups of children from many national settings thought of them as similar while others saw them as dissimilar. In describing the Chinese, Indians, and Negroes, most national groups of children stressed dissimilarities to a noteworthy extent, suggesting that they may be commonly used by parents and educators as outstanding examples of exotic or bizarre peoples, thereby helping children develop conceptions of what they are themselves by means of contrasts with selected others.

Although certain of the reference peoples were not as easily categorized as others with regard to their similarity or dissimilarity, still when one examines the evaluative descriptions given by the various groups of children, there is an unexpectedly large amount of agreement in views about these seven peoples. In other words, judging from the evaluative descriptions given by children from various parts of the world, these seven peoples project surprisingly consistent views of themselves. It was found that Americans were commonly seen as good, wealthy, intelligent, and aggressive;[5] although the children apparently knew little about Brazilians, they were referred to as good by a certain proportion of children from eight different nations; Chinese people were regarded as good, poor, aggressive, and bad; Germans were seen as good, aggressive, intelligent, and bad; Indians from India, good and poor; African Negroes, good, uncultured, unintelligent, dominated, poor, bad, and aggressive; and Russians, aggressive, good, intelligent, bad, and dominated. These purely evaluative traits usually occurred as minor descriptive themes in context with many non-evaluative, factual statements and general references to similarities and contrasts. Even so, it is clear that the 10-year-olds and especially the 14-year-olds were quite spontaneously beginning to make stereotyped judgments about foreign peoples. The nature of the stereotyping process at this stage of development is of special interest. In the first place, as groups, the children referred to both the good *and* bad qualities of foreign peoples; they did not picture them in totally favorable or unfavorable terms as one might expect genuinely biased subjects to do. Future research may find that more biased views do emerge at some later time, say in the mid teens, when young people in certain countries become particularly concerned about achieving consensus and conforming to group standards.[6] On the other hand, it may be that national stereotypes typically incorporate both the positive and negative features of the group in question, as the study that Reigrotski and Anderson[7] conducted with adults suggests. In the second place, the stereotyping process itself may develop rapidly when teen-age children learn that their views of foreign groups, perhaps never fully articulated before, are shared by others, including others from foreign lands. Thus, if children in one nation learn, through whatever source, that their personal views of a certain

[5] The traits are listed in their order of commonness, "common" meaning that two or more national groups of children used the same trait in their descriptions. In this instance, a certain proportion of children in *all* of the national samples referred to the good qualities of Americans, whereas references to their aggressiveness were noted in *two* national samples only.

[6] Pettigrew, in a very instructive study, found in the case of older subjects that conformity played an essential role in prejudiced and stereotyped thinking. See T. F. Pettigrew. Personality and sociocultural factors in intergroup attitudes: a cross-national comparison. *J. Conflict Resol.*, 1958. 2, 29-42.

[7] E. Reigrotski and N. Anderson. National stereotypes and foreign contact. *Publ. Opin. Quart.*, 1959-60, *23*, 515-528.

foreign group are shared by people living in other countries, they may then have the social justification they need for making their views explicit and public, as though, through social consensus, they had become "correct" views. This notion deserves further study because it is concerned with a potentially important aspect of stereotypes—they may very well be socially contagious, both within and across national boundaries.

There are also certain outstanding cross-national regularities in the way children feel about the standard reference peoples. Some groups of children, especially the Americans but also to a less pronounced degree the English and French Canadians, the French, and the Germans, typically expressed affection for most of the reference peoples, including those considerd to be dissimilar to their own groups. Not all national groups of children, however, were so ready to express affection for others; Turkish, Japanese, and Lebanese children generally aligned the affection they expressed for others with their conceptions of similarity, and their disaffection or indifference with their conceptions of dissimilarity. Furthermore, there is no general trend for all groups to express affection for those people considered as similar. For instance, although the Germans were fairly often regarded as similar by the older French and the Israeli children at all three ages, expressions of affection for Germans were much less common.

The children's views of foreign peoples changed with age in several noteworthy ways. In the first place the 6-year-olds responded less frequently than the older children when questioned and the responses they gave were typically non-evaluative descriptions of facts, or general references to the good or bad qualities of the peoples in question. With age, children demonstrated a larger repertoire of evaluative distinctions, referring to foreign groups as good, bad, intelligent, aggressive, poor, wealthy, peaceful, dominated, and ambitious. Striking concurrent changes were also apparent in the content of the descriptive statements made about foreign peoples. The descriptions of the younger children focused on physical features, clothing, language, and habits in contrast to the older children's preoccupation with personality traits, habits, politics, religion, and material possessions. These evaluative and content changes in children's views indicate that the stereotyping process, at least in regard to foreign peoples, is not much in evidence with the 6-year-olds, but becomes very apparent in the early teen years. Judging from the views they expressed, children apparently come to think about foreign peoples in an increasingly more stereotyped manner between 6 and 14 years. This developmental trend is presumed to be due to many factors: an increased conceptual and linguistic skill in describing peoples,[8] an increased interest in and understanding of the more subtle and complex features of their own emotional makeup as well as that of their social worlds, changes in the ways they view themselves and members of their own national group, changes in the standard information sources they use to learn about foreign peoples, and the fact that, as teen-agers, they may feel more social pressure to express themselves in general terms that are easily understood and accepted by their peer groups.

In general, boys and girls had essentially the same views of foreign peoples in the Bantu, French-Canadian, Israeli, and Japanese samples. In contrast, in the Turkish, American, Brazilian, English-Canadian, French, and German samples, boys and girls differed in the amount of affection expressed for foreign groups. In various national samples, boys, particularly at the 10-year level, were found to be more affectionate than girls. There were also boy-girl differences with regard to the information sources typically used: boys, especially the 10-year-olds, used television and movies as sources more frequently than girls did.

Similarly, social class differences affected the views of certain national groups of children (the American, English-Canadian, French-Canadian, Israeli, Japanese, and Lebanese) more than others (the Bantu, Turkish, French, and German), and again their effects were noted especially on the amounts of affection expressed for foreign peoples. Generally the children from middle-class homes were more likely to express affection than were those from lower- or working-class backgrounds. Although this was a fairly general trend, still in three instances (the 6-year-old German, the 14-year-old French-

8 S. M. Ervin and G. Foster (The development of meaning in children's descriptive terms. *J. abnorm. soc. Psychol.*, 1960, *61*, 271-275) demonstrated that 6-year-olds (first graders) lack the ability to make fine distinctions between attributes, using as interchangeable synonyms the terms "big," "strong," "heavy," in one case, and "good," "pretty," "happy" in another; 12-year-olds, in contrast, are much more capable of making the appropriate distinctions.

Canadian, and the 14-year-old Japanese) it was the lower-class children who were the more affectionate. Social class differences also affected the children's conceptions of the similarity or dissimilarity of foreign peoples, although this pattern is less pronounced. In the case of four national groups, the lower-class in contrast to the middle-class children saw more foreign peoples as similar; since these four groups also contributed to the differences in expressed affection just mentioned, it appears that the older American and Lebanese and the younger English-Canadian and French children of low social class standing viewed foreign peoples as similar at the same time as they expressed indifference to or dislike of them. Apparently these particular groups of children were showing a dissatisfaction with their own lower-class status in their reactions to foreigners. In other words, a feeling of social unrest among those in the lower social class may, in certain national settings, manifest itself in a dislike of foreign peoples.

Children from different national backgrounds use, or at least say they use, essentially the same sources of information to learn about foreign peoples. Thus, when one compares the sources of information mentioned by the different national groups of children to account for their views, there are few noteworthy differences. There are, however, national differences with regard to the *variety* of sources of information mentioned; the older children from Lebanon, Germany, Israel, and America appear to have at their disposal varied information sources in contrast to the Bantu and Brazilian children whose sources are comparatively restricted. The really significant cross-national trend has to do with age differences in sources of information about foreign peoples: typically, the 6-year-old children rely mainly on their parents, and on television and movies if these are available, whereas the 10- and 14-year-olds make hardly any references to people— parents, teachers, or friends—as direct information sources. They turn rather to the mass media and general reading material for their information about foreign groups. Although there are no indications from this study that the use of nonpersonal information sources or the availabality of varieties of sources contribute in any systematic way to the noticeable beginnings of stereotyped thinking among the older groups of children, still these findings make evident the responsibility that parents, educators, and those in charge of the mass media have when discussing, or failing to discuss, foreign nations and people.

While it is likely that the older children are influenced by the stereo-typed thinking of their parents and other people more than they re-alize, the very general tendency of the older groups to say they rely on impersonal sources such as the mass media may be important; these sources are more likely to make use of broad generalizatior *; that could, without the purposeful intervention of parents and teachers, encourage children to think that everyone, everywhere holds what often are stereotyped views, favorable or unfavorable, of par-ticular foreign groups.

DESCRIPTIVE DIVERSITY IN CHILDREN'S VIEWS OF FOREIGN PEOPLES

When the descriptions of foreign peoples given by whole groups of children are examined for their diversity, one finds interesting age-group and national differences. Descriptions were considered to be diversified if one group of children, relative to others, referred to a large number of different characteristics of the foreign people in question. A statistical index of descriptive diversity was used to ex-amine both the evaluative and the content features of each group's descriptions. Using this index, we found a general increase in descrip-tive diversity of *evaluative* statements from 6- to 10- to 14-year levels, reflecting the increase with age in the richness of evaluative descrip-tions already noted. This trend was not universal, however, since the Japanese children's descriptions showed no essential change with age, those of the Israeli children were least diversified at the 10-year level, and those of the Lebanese children did not change appreciably from the 10- to 14-year levels. In general, the evaluative features of the children's descriptions of Chinese and of Indians from India in particular lacked diversity; in addition, the descriptions of Negroes from Africa given by 6-year-olds were especially restricted as were those of 10-year-olds when describing Russians. Compared to other national groups, the Bantu, American, and English-Canadian chil-dren, in general, lacked diversity in their evaluative descriptions of foreign peoples, especially when compared to the Israeli and younger Japanese children.

Considering the *content* features of the children's descriptions, there was a universal increase in descriptive diversity from ages 6 to

10, but no consistent change from 10 to 14. The Bantu and, to a less marked degree, the Japanese children are relatively restricted in their use of content features in contrast to the American and English-Canadian (whose *evaluative* descriptions were least diversified), and French children, whose descriptions are more diversified in their content.

We looked into the possibility that descriptive diversity might be related to favorable attitudes toward foreign peoples, that is, that friendly groups of children might have diversified views and unfriendly groups restricted views of foreign peoples. To do so, we correlated group variations in the extent of affection expressed for foreign peoples with variations in extent of evaluative and content diversity. It turned out that the descriptions of foreign peoples given by the more affectionate or friendly groups of children were restricted in their evaluative features but diversified in their content, whereas those of the indifferent or unfriendly groups were diversified in their evaluative features but restricted in their content. The important idea here is that friendly and unfriendly groups of children, especially the 10-year-olds, have distinctively different modes of describing and, presumably, thinking about foreign peoples. The friendly groups make only a limited number of different evaluative distinctions while demonstrating a relatively broad and detailed understanding of foreign people, their ways of life, and their countries. Conversely, the unfriendly groups make a large number of different evaluative distinctions while restricting their attention to only a limited number of different characteristics of the peoples in question. From the findings of this investigation, it is not clear why these important differences in reaction are especially prominent with 10-year-olds nor how they get established in the first place. For example, we do not know whether children come to like foreign peoples as a consequence of acquiring diversified knowledge about them or whether, because they are attracted to them initially, they are prompted to learn a good deal about them.

Other potentially important research questions are also raised by these findings. Judging from the recent work of Johnson, Thompson, and Frincke,[9] it is possible that children may find it easier

[9] R. C. Johnson, C. W. Thompson, and G. Frincke. Word values, word frequency, and visual duration thresholds. *Psychol. Rev.*, 1960, *67*, 332-342.

to develop a more diversified vocabulary of unfavorable than of favorable evaluative terms. Johnson *et al.* found that good or pleasant words are used much more frequently than unpleasant ones in English, suggesting that at least in English, children may have a more diversified vocabulary of unpleasant or unfavorable descriptive terms at their disposal in contrast to a more limited or restricted set of repeatedly used favorable terms. Our findings suggest that the other languages used in this investigation may also establish a similar linguistic bias for diversified unfavorable and restricted favorable descriptions of foreign peoples.

CHILDREN'S ATTITUDES TOWARD FOREIGN PEOPLES

In the final chapter we examined three facets of children's attitudes toward foreign peoples: their tendency to regard various foreign groups as similar or different, their readiness to express affection or disaffection for them, and their general ethnocentrism. We compared national and age groups in terms of each of these factors and analyzed the patterns formed by the three attitude components for each national group of children.

Considering first their tendencies to view others as similar or different, it was found that the Brazilian, Japanese, and Bantu children seem to view the world as populated more by peoples who are dissimilar than by peoples who are similar; in other words, they have what we referred to as comparatively limited similarity outlooks in contrast to the Israeli, French, American, French-Canadian, English-Canadian, and Turkish children. We presume that these national differences in breadth of similarity outlooks reflect basic differences in ways of regarding foreign peoples that determine, in part at least, whether children in certain societies come to view themselves as members of distinctive or culturally isolated groups or as people basically similar to most others. We also found a nearly universal tendency for the 6-year-old children to have limited similarity outlooks in contrast to the 10- and 14-year-olds. That is, 6-year-olds characteristically viewed foreign peoples as different much more frequently than did 10-year-olds, who generally considered a much larger array of foreign peoples as similar. There was little change in similarity outlooks between 10 and 14. In the final section we shall try to explain this important cross-national difference between 6- and 10-year-olds.

With regard to their feelings for foreign peoples, children generally were more likely to express affection for people from foreign lands than they were to consider them as similar. Even so, there are large national differences in this regard; the Japanese, Turkish, and Israeli children expressed least affection while the American children expressed most affection for foreign peoples. Again, the 6-year-olds were the most reluctant to express affection; while there was a large increase at age 10, there was not much change from the 10- to 14-year levels, and in several instances, the 10-year level was the most affectionate of the three considered here. Thus 6-year-olds had relatively restricted similarity outlooks and were least prone to express affection for foreign peoples, whether these were thought of as similar or dissimilar. In contrast, the 10-year age period emerged as the most encouraging one, for at this age children were particularly ready to view foreign peoples as similar and were especially friendly toward them, even those viewed as dissimilar. Comparing the 10-year-olds and the less knowledgeable 6-year-olds, it seems very likely that ignorance contributes to the suspicion or even fear of the strange noted at the 6-year level. The 14-year-olds in general showed less openness and friendliness; in other words, the favorable orientation noted at age 10 did not hold up into the teen years. We have argued that these age changes are attributable in part to parallel changes in the way children of different ages define "like us" and "not like us." Typically, 6- and 10-year-olds rely on clearly observable features to categorize others as different, whereas 14-year-olds generally make their judgments according to contrasts in personalities and habits; thus it is more likely that the older children dislike those foreign groups they consider to be different. This explanation is not the whole story, however, since other factors, apparently cultural ones, play their role, too. For example, the 14-year-old American children had larger similarity outlooks and were more affectionate toward foreign peoples than were the 10-year-olds; in contrast, the French-Canadian and Japanese 10-year-olds were decidedly less friendly toward others than were the 14-year-olds. It is important cultural variations such as these that call for further investigation since, while limiting the generality of the overall age trends noted, they offer a possibility of explaining how age changes in certain cultural settings affect children's reactions to foreign peoples.

When national variations in ethnocentrism scores (available for the 14-year-olds only) were examined, we found the Bantu and Brazilian children to have the highest scores, indicating most ethnocentrism, and the American, English-Canadian, French-Canadian, Japanese, and French to have the lowest. The problem comes in interpreting these scores. The measure was originally standardized for American children and we realize it may be biased and inappropriate in certain ways for children in other cultural settings. However, from our examination of the items (see Chapter 10), the scale as a whole seemed appropriate, at least superficially so. Moreover, Pettigrew used a very similar measure in his comparative study of the attitudes of white students in America and South Africa and, after analyzing responses item by item, suggested with a degree of caution "that racial prejudice and its personality concomitants [apparently] take extremely similar forms in many parts of the Western world."[10] Even so, there is still need for caution since Pettigrew worked with white students in both cases, whereas we were dealing with children from very diverse cultural settings. Because of these reservations, we have considered the ethnocentrism scores as only one facet of children's attitudes toward foreign peoples, to be used along with the two others as a help in describing each group's overall attitudinal orientation.

Nevertheless, certain differences are important in their own right. It may well be that groups of American children are among the least ethnocentric in the world; this would be consistent with other aspects of their reaction to foreign peoples encountered in this study. Or it may be that they are only more sophisticated in concealing their prejudices. We do not, in other words, really know why the Brazilian and Bantu children score so high or why the American and Japanese children rank so low on this measure. Further cross-national and intranational research is clearly called for here; with such research, we could, in time, even develop genuinely cross-nationally valid measures of ethnocentrism and prejudice.

Our approach, then, was to consider similarity outlooks and expressions of affection as two essential components of attitudes that

[10] T. F. Pettigrew, 1958, *op. cit.*, 37.

determine in large part how friendly children will be toward foreign peoples. We noted great variation from one national group to another, some having very limited similarity outlooks while freely expressing affection for foreign groups, others having broad similarity outlooks while only reluctantly expressing affection, and others viewing a large sample of foreign groups as similar and liking them all. It became apparent that one can more adequately describe children's attitudes toward foreign peoples by considering both of these components along with the indices of ethnocentrism. Noting how the three factors form a pattern for each group, we found that the American, French, English-Canadian, and French-Canadian children held comparatively friendly attitudes toward foreign groups, in contrast to the Japanese, Brazilian, Turkish, and Israeli children whose orientations are more unfriendly.

Even though these patterns of reactions are important in their own right, we cannot, from this investigation, explain why certain national groups of children develop basically friendly or unfriendly orientations toward foreign peoples, nor do we understand yet what underlies the various differences found among age and national groups in their tendencies to see foreign groups as similar, their different degrees of affection for foreign peoples, and the degrees of ethnocentrism they display. These very important matters call for detailed investigations of the cultural, sociological, and psychological factors that contribute to the development of children's views of foreign peoples. A valuable start along these lines has already been made by Paul C. Rosenblatt in his theoretical analysis of the origins and effects of nationalistic and ethnocentric thinking.[11]

DEVELOPMENTAL CHANGES IN CHILDREN'S VIEWS OF FOREIGN PEOPLES: A THEORETICAL INTERPRETATION

How does a child come to make distinctions between his own group and others? This question intrigues the behavioral scientist because it touches on an extremely important aspect of cognitive development. Early theorists believed that this tendency was a natural

[11] P. C. Rosenblatt. Origins and effects of group ethnocentrism and nationalism. *J. Conflict Resol.*, 1964, *8*, 131-146.

outgrowth of an innate "consciousness of kind," but as more recent attempts have been made to describe, study, and explain its nature and development, the phenomenon has become less mysterious. Although we were not directly concerned with this question when planning our study, nevertheless our working assumptions and research approaches were greatly influenced by it. Consequently, it is very gratifying to be able to offer, as a conclusion to our study, several notions that may contribute in a modest way to the understanding of this critical feature of human thought.

Several people have seen very clearly the implications of the problem involved here. For example, Jean Piaget and Anne-Marie Weil wondered whether "the cognitive and affective attitudes associated with loyalty to the homeland and initial contacts with other countries may not be at the root of subsequent international maladjustments".[12] Nancy C. Morse and Floyd H. Allport made the same issue the focus of their interests in an important investigation. For them, "the whole question of what a nation, as a collective structure, is, what it means to the individual, how he is involved in it, and the conflicts to which he is prone because of his involvement, needs further careful investigation."[13] They stressed this point because in their comprehensive study of prejudice they found that an exaggerated loyalty to one's own group was by far the most important single cause of discrimination and exclusion. Gordon W. Allport has also recognized the relevance of this issue and made it the basis of what he called "the first stage in learning prejudice."[14] As an aid in learning "that human beings are clustered into groups—that there are important distinctions," the child makes use of "the logical generalizations of the sort that mature adults accept," for example, that certain groups are untrustworthy or uncultured when compared to his own. Allport believes that the child prepares himself for prejudice by learning these generalizations.

[12] J. Piaget and A. M. Weil. The development in children of the idea of the homeland and of relations with other countries. *Int. soc. sci. Bull.*, 1951, *3*, 561.
[13] N. C. Morse and F. H. Allport. The causation of anti-Semitism: An investigation of seven hypotheses. *J. Psychol.*, 1952, *34*, 225.
[14] G. W. Allport. *The nature of prejudice.* Boston: Beacon Press, 1954, 307–308.

We shall begin our developmental account as near to the actual beginning as we can. According to Piaget and Weil:

The feeling and the very idea of the homeland are by no means the first or even early elements in the child's makeup, but are a relatively late development in the normal child, who does not appear to be drawn inevitably towards patriotic sociocentricity. On the contrary, before he attains to a cognitive and affective awareness of his own country, the child must make a considerable effort toward "decentration" or broadening of his centres of interest (town, canton, etc.) and towards integration of his impressions (with surroundings other than his own) in the course of which he acquires an understanding of countries and points of view different from his own . . . The child begins with the assumption that the immediate attitudes arising out of his own special surroundings and activities are the only ones possible: this state of mind . . . is at first a stumbling-block both to the understanding of his own country and to the development of objective relationships with other countries. Furthermore, to overcome this egocentric attitude, it is necessary to train the faculty for cognitive and affective integration . . . a slow and laborious process, consisting mainly in efforts at "reciprocity."[15]

By "reciprocity," they mean an objective understanding of other peoples, comprising a realization that one's own people are foreigners in other countries, that foreigners are not foreign at home, and that they, too, have feelings of belonging in their homeland.

Two major ideas are touched on in this theoretical statement.[16]

[15] Piaget and Weil, 1951, *op. cit.*, 562.

[16] It seems to us that the views of Piaget and Weil, or at least the emphasis they give to their views, are limited in certain important respects. In the first place, they overstress the spontaneous changes that are presumed to take place in the child's mental development (a mysterious shift from egocentric to integrative thinking) to the neglect of socializational and instructional influences that may account in large degree for the changes they want to explain. Vygotsky was also extremely conscious of the child's "inner developmental processes," but he criticized what is apparently a bias in Piaget's thinking and argued that instruction, considered very generally, "is one of the principal sources of the school-child's concepts and is also a powerful force in directing their evolution; it determines the fate of his total mental development" (L. S. Vygotsky. *Thought and language.* Cambridge, Mass.: M.I.T. Press and New York: Wiley, 1962, 85). Piaget and Weil also fail to recognize and make use of well established learning principles that may more simply and accurately account for developmental changes, principles such as the admittedly vague but extremely valuable explanatory notion of transfer or generalization from past experiences. The work

First, at the same time as the preschool child is learning to interact with others within his home and immediate social environment, becoming aware of their distinctness and developing rudimentary skills in viewing events from their perspectives, he also learns, often painfully that the private feelings of attachment he has for his own familiar and comfortable settings are not necessarily shared by those who belong to various social subgroups within his own nation, and even less so by strangers or by people who live in foreign countries. He comes to realize that others, those at home as well as outsiders, have their own loyalties to particular places, people, and experiences. Second, he gradually develops a conception of homeland or own national group, in part, through comparisons or contrasts—largely vicarious ones, derived unsystematically from various information sources—with foreign peoples and places, and, in part, through generalizations from interpersonal experiences he has had with the strange and different in his own family and close social environment. An American child, in other words, will understand what it is to be American by having his own group compared and contrasted with other national groups and by learning to perceive and react to foreign groups as he has to certain others he has encountered who were different in some essential way from himself and those with whom he identifies.

At this point, one might conclude that these reactions are merely transient stages children pass through in getting to know about the social world, with little long-range significance. The research findings of Morse and F. H. Allport,[17] however, indicate that such a conclusion would be false. On the contrary, these early experiences may very likely establish basic predispostions toward one's own group and foreign peoples that will manifest themselves throughout life. In their investigation, using non-student, adult Americans as subjects, they tested the relative importance of seven factors, each of which had previously been found to be associated with or functioned as a cause of discrimination and prejudice. They discovered three factors

---

of Whiting & Child (J. W. M. Whiting and I. Child. *Child training and personality*. New Haven: Yale, 1953) is a clear example of how useful such principles are (see especially their chapter on "Origins of the fear of others"). Accordingly, we have tried to be more comprehensive in the account that follows.

[17] Morse and Allport, 1952, *op. cit.*

to be by far the most important determiners of discriminatory, exclusive, and aversive reactions toward minority group members: (a) "national involvement," meaning a close identification of one's own interests with national interests, a belief that the policies of one's own country are always right, and a reification and glorification of one's own country; (b) a belief in the "racial essence" of the minority group in question, who "have a common racial quality and are different by nature" from us; and (c) a "differential loyalty" to one's own people, that is, a "generalized in-group versus out-group feeling" that expresses itself in a differential willingness to help members of one's own national group but not foreigners when they are in trouble. Their results demonstrate clearly that the conceptions people develop of their own national group in relation to others may very likely have long-term consequences. These conceptions vary in form within a national setting and, as we shall argue, from nation to nation, ranging from an intense in-out differentiation to an objective outlook on the similarities that exist among peoples, coupled with an inquisitive attitude about whatever differences may be perceived. When the concept develops in its extreme form, it may prejudice a good deal of one's reactions to members of one's own group as well as to members of other groups.

Our findings suggest to us that the manner in which the concept of own group is taught to children and ultimately learned by them has important psychological consequences. In the first place, the process of establishing the concept apparently produces an exaggerated and caricatured view of one's own nation and people. Since the child's own group is repeatedly compared with various other groups, it becomes, we presume, the focal point of the developing conception and its salient characteristics are magnified and stereotyped. We make this inference from our own finding that the first signs of stereotyped thinking turned up in the descriptions children gave of their own group rather than of foreign peoples; even at the 6-year age level many different national groups of children made overgeneralized statements about the personality traits of their own group at the same time as they described foreign peoples in more factual, objective terms. Thus, the stereotyping process itself appears to get its start in the early conceptions children develop of their own group, and it is only much later, from 10 years of age on, that children start stereotyping foreign peoples. By the time they are 10 and 14, children apparently become concerned with foreign peoples as something more than comparison groups. Their conception of national groupings seems to have widened so that equal attention can be given to homeland and foreign groups, both of which can be thought of with a similar degree of objectivity. Although children have developed by this age period a larger repertoire of conceptual categories for thinking about people, have learned the appropriate distinctions among geographical units, including nations, as Piaget and Weil have found, and are better able to make precise and diversified differentiations in describing them, still they have also apparently modified their interests in people, shifting from comparisons of the observable and objective characteristics to the more subtle, subjective features such as personality traits and habits, and have turned to quite different sources of information—from people to the mass media—to learn about foreign groups. These important changes in interests and information sources are supplemented, we presume, by two other factors working toward a common effect: a heightened awareness of social pressures that stimulate young people to think and speak as others in their peer groups do, a variable of great importance for prejudiced behavior according to the research of Pettigrew;[18] and a growing realization on their part that they must also begin to take on more adult ways of thinking and communicating. These factors in combination appear to play important roles in the development of the teen-ager's stereotyped, adult-like views of foreign peoples.

In the second place, the early training in national contrasts appears to mark certain foreign groups as outstanding examples of peoples who are different. We noted a strong cross-national tendency for children, even the 6-year-olds, to refer spontaneously to the same foreign groups as peoples who are "not like us," suggesting that these particular peoples are used for the training in contrasts needed to develop a concept of homeland and one's own group. Our results suggest that the effects of this training persist at least into the teen ages, but the consequences are very likely more pervasive than we have been able to assess; judging from the work of Isaacs,[19] this early

[18] Pettigrew, 1958, *op. cit.*

[19] Harold R. Issacs. *Scratches on our minds: American images of China and India.* New York: John Day, 1958.

training may leave very durable "scratches on our minds" that color our reactions to certain foreign peoples throughout our lives.

Thirdly, the early training in contrasts appears to leave the impression with children that foreign peoples are different, strange, and unfriendly. We found that at the 6-year age level, in contrast to the 10 or 14, children stressed the differences of foreign peoples much more than the similarities, displayed particularly narrow similarity outlooks, and tended to withhold expressions of affection for foreign peoples, suggesting that their overall orientation was a suspicious one. This effect, however, seems to be less permanent than the one previously noted, since for most of the national groups studied the initial orientation became more friendly by the 10-year age level. In fact, fundamental changes take place in children's views of homeland and foreign groups between the ages of 6 and 10. There is strong cross-national evidence from our study that children are most inquisitive and friendly toward foreign peoples and most prone to see others as similar at the 10-year age level than at either the 6- or 14-year levels. This may be due in part to the fact that by 10, children have become relatively well adjusted to their conceptions of the social world but, in contrast to the teen-agers, are still comfortably within the protection of family and institutional groups, not yet preparing to move out and up as the next generation. Whatever the reasons, the 10-year age period is the most friendly one, relatively, and whether the favorable views are maintained into the teen ages appears to depend on distinctive socio-cultural events taking place within each national setting.

In the fourth place, the early training in national contrasts also affects the child's self-conception. Judging from their self-descriptions, children in certain national settings thought of themselves in racial, religious, or national terms, whereas those from other nations made no mention of these characteristics, emphasizing instead that they were persons, or boys or girls. In other words, the self-concepts of certain groups of children reflect what we presume to be the culturally significant criteria used in their training to make distinctions between their own group and others. Furthermore, there are some indications that these same criteria may become standardized dimensions for categorizing and evaluating people in general, foreigners as well as compatriots.

We have shown that children's attitudes toward foreign peoples vary from one national setting to another. These variations indicate that parents and educators use culturally distinctive ways of teaching their children to differentiate their own group from others. Following the theoretical scheme of Smith, Bruner, and White,[20] we presume that children develop their particular attitudes toward foreign peoples first as a means of understanding reality as it is defined in their own cultural group (the "object-appraisal" function of attitudes) and second to help them identify with particular reference groups (the "social-adjustment" function of attitudes). Thus, depending on the national setting, children may, as we have found, develop an inquisitive and friendly attitude toward foreign peoples, seeing them as essentially similar to their own people, or they may develop another view of the world, seeing it as populated mainly by groups who are basically different from themselves and feeling unfriendly toward foreign peoples and places. In certain instances—we believe we encountered one in our study, the case of Japan—the latter viewpoint may be so pervasive that children will have unfriendly orientations toward their own people, suggesting that in some cultural settings training in national contrasts may miss its target or backfire. This type of training can very easily generate different degrees of dissatisfaction with particular characteristics of the children's own ways of life, and promote invidious feelings toward foreign peoples who enjoy advantages they would like to enjoy themselves.

In the process of developing their views of foreign nations, children, we presume, do not restrict their thinking to distant and unknown places and peoples. In most if not all national settings they have experiences with distinctive ethnic and religious subgroups at home to draw on or to generalize from, and they are confronted with the problem of understanding these local subgroupings at about the same time as they start to learn who they are themselves. It is, therefore, important to conclude our interpretation of the development of children's views of foreign peoples with a description of how children learn to react to members of socially distinctive peoples within their own nation, since developmental changes in views of foreign peoples undoubtedly affect and are affected by changes in views of local sub-

[20] M. B. Smith, J. S. Bruner, and R. W. White. *Opinions and personality.* New York: Wiley, 1956.

groups. G. W. Allport's account of the early stages of learning to be prejudiced is especially instructive for our purpose.[21] He believes that by 6 years of age the child has "gone through the initial period of curiosity and interest in racial and ethnic differences" and is now "aware of group differences, though not yet clear concerning all the relevant cues." Illustrating with the case study of a 6-year-old girl, he explains:

She knows that group X (she knows neither its name nor its identity) is somehow hateworthy. She already has the emotional meaning. She seeks now to integrate the proper content with the emotion. She wishes to define her category so as to make her future behavior conform to her mother's desires. As soon as she has the linguistic tag at her command, she will be like the little Italian boy for whom "Polish" and "bad" were synonymous terms.

He calls this stage "the period of pregeneralized learning."

The term draws attention to the fact that the child has not yet generalized after the fashion of adults. He does not quite understand what a Jew is, what a Negro is, or what his attitude toward them should be. He does not know even what *he* is—in any consistent sense.

It is during this period of development that

the place of linguistic tags . . . is crucial. They stand for adult abstractions, for logical generalizations of the sort that mature adults accept. The child learns the tags before he is fully ready to apply them to the adult categories. They prepare him for prejudice . . . Only after much fumbling . . . will the proper categorization take place.

There are several important ideas touched on here that bear directly on the development of children's views of foreign peoples. It is made clear that parents and other significant people in the child's environment transfer their own emotionally-toned views of other peoples to the child by assigning specific attributes to members of particular groups during that very period of a cognitive development when he has not fully differentiated one group from another or his own

[21] G. W. Allport, 1954, *op. cit.*, 307.

group from others. By incorporating these views, he learns to distinguish his own group from those others who are said to be hateworthy, untrustworthy, and so forth. When the assignments are finally mastered, the child will be able to rationalize the generalizations that are commonly made either about minority groups at home or peoples in foreign lands, and will be able to use them autonomously.

Appendices

Appendix A
The Interview Schedule

(First establish rapport with each subject and reassure him that you merely want to ask some questions — a sort of question and answer game — which have no right or wrong answers; indicate clearly, however, that his personal opinions are of interest and importance. Please record all responses.)

1. What are you? . . . .   2. What else are you?. . . . .
3. What else are you? . . . .   4. Anything else? . . . .
5. (Ask only if no national reference is given spontaneously.) What country do we live in? . . . .
6. Are there other people from other countries who are *like* you or *similar* to you? (Record all names in order given.)
   1st. . . . . 2nd . . . .
7. Any others?   3rd . . . .   4th . . . .
8. Are there any others who are *like* you? 5th . . . .
9. Are there other people from other countries who are *not like* you or *different* from you?   1st . . . .   2nd. . . . .
10. Any others?   3rd . . . .   4th . . . .
11. Are there any others who are *not like* you?   5th. . . . .

Those people considered like you
   a. In what way are the . . . . (enter the *first* group mentioned) *like you* or *similar* to you? . . . .
   . . . .
   b. Tell me what else you know about (them) . . . .
   . . . .
   c. Do you like (them)? . . . .   d. Why do you say that? . . . .
   . . . .

e. How do you know about (them)? ....
(In each case, attempt to get details about the source of information, *e.g.*, who actually told the child about the peoples, what
type of book, or magazine; was it through movies, T.V., direct
contact with them, etc.)

a. In what way are the........ (enter the *second* group mentioned)
like you or *similar* to you? ....
....
b. Tell me what else you know about (them) ....
....
c. Do you like (them)? .... d. Why do you say that? ....
....
e. How do you know about (them)?...........................

a. In what way are the ....(enter the *third* group mentioned)
like you or *similar* to you? ....
....
b. Tell me what else you know about (them) ....
....
c. Do you like (them)? .... d. Why do you say that? ....
....
e. How do you know about (them)?...........................

a. In what way are the .... (enter the *fourth* group mentioned)
like you or *similar* to you? ....
....
b. Tell me what else you know about (them) ....
....
c. Do you like (them)? .... d. Why do you say that? ....
....
e. How do you know about (them)?...........................

a. In what way are the .... (enter the *fifth* group mentioned)
like you or *similar* to you? ....
....
b. Tell me what else you know about (them) ....
....
c. Do you like (them)? .... d. Why do you say that? ....
....
e. How do you know about (them)...........................

Those people considered not like you

a. In what way are the . . . . (enter the *first* group mentioned) *not like you* or *different* from you? . . . .
. . . .

b. Tell me what else you know about (them) . . . .
. . . .

c. Do you like (them)? . . . . d. Why do you say that? . . . .
. . . .

e. How do you know about (them)?. . . . .

a. In what way are the . . . . (enter the *second* group mentioned) *not like you* or *different* from you? . . . .
. . . .

b. Tell me what else you know about (them) . . . .
. . . .

c. Do you like (them)? . . . . d. Why do you say that? . . . .
. . . .

e. How do you know about (them)?. . . . .

a. In what way are the . . . . (enter the *third* group mentioned) *not like you* or *different* from you? . . . .
. . . .

b. Tell me what else you know about (them) . . . .
. . . .

c. Do you like (them)? . . . . d. Why do you say that? . . . .
. . . .

e. How do you know about (them)?. . . . .

a. In what way are the . . . . (enter the *fourth* group mentioned) *not like you* or *different* from you? . . . .
. . . .

b. Tell me what else you know about (them) . . . .
. . . .

c. Do you like (them)? . . . . d. Why do you say that? . . . .
. . . .

e. How do you know about (them)?. . . . .

a. In what way are the . . . . (enter the *fifth* group mentioned) *not like you* or *different* from you? . . . .
. . . .

b. Tell me what else you know about (them) . . . .
. . . .

c. Do you like (them)? . . . . d. Why do you say that? . . . .
. . . .
e. How do you know about (them)?. . . . .

(For purposes of cross-national comparisons, the interviewers will then ask the child the probing questions (*i.e.* a-e) about specific national groups. If any of these had been mentioned spontaneously by the child, the questions would not, of course, be repeated. The order of presentation of the following eight national groups should be haphazardly randomized from child to child.)

12. Now let us talk about some other people. The *Americans* from the U.S., for example. Are they *like you* or *not like you?*
   a. In what way are they *like you* or *not like you?* . . . .
   . . . .
   b. Tell me what else you know about them. . . . .
   . . . .
   c. Do you like them? . . . . d. Why do you say that? . . . .
   . . . .
   e. How do you know about them? . . . .

13. Now, are the *Russians like you* or *not like you?*
   a. In what way are they *like you*, or *not like you?* . . . .
   . . . .
   b. Tell me what else you know about them . . . .
   . . . .
   c. Do you like them? . . . . d. Why do you say that? . . . .
   . . . .
   e. How do you know about them? . . . .

14. Now, are the *Chinese like you* or *not like you?*
   a. In what way are they *like you* or *not like you?* . . . .
   . . . .
   b. Tell me what else you know about them . . . .
   . . . .
   c. Do you like them? . . . . d. Why do you say that? . . . .
   . . . .
   e. How do you know about them? . . . .

15. Now, are the *Negroes* from *Africa like you* or *not like you?*
   a. In what way are they *like you*, or *not like you?*. . . . .
   . . . .
   b. Tell me what else you know about them . . . .
   . . . .
   c. Do you like them? . . . . d. Why do you say that? . . . .
   . . . .

e. How do you know about them? ....

16. Now, are the *Germans like you* or *not like you?*

   a. In what way are they *like you*, or *not like you?* ....

   ....

   b. Tell me what else you know about them.......................

   ....

   c. Do you like them? .... d. Why do you say that? ....

   ....

   e. How do you know about them? ....

17. Now, are the *Indians* from *India like you* or *not like you?*

   a. In what way are they *like you*, or *not like you?* ....

   ....

   b. Tell me what else you know about them ....

   ....

   c. Do you like them? .... d. Why do you say that? ....

   ....

   e. How do you know about them? ....

18. Now, are the *Brazilians like you* or *not like you?*

   a. In what way are they *like you*, or *not like you?* ....

   ....

   b. Tell me what else you know about them ....

   ....

   c. Do you like them? .... d. Why do you say that? ....

   ....

   e. How do you know about them? ....

19. Now what are the .... (mention child's own national group) like? ....

   b. Tell me what else you know about them ....

   ....

   ....

20. Now, if you were not a .... (mention child's own national group) what would you *most* like to be? ....

21. Why? ....

   ....

22. If you were not a .... (mention child's own national group) what would you *least* like to be? ....

23. Why? ....

   ....

PERSONAL DATA

24. Subject's name ....

25. Age .... Sex .... Religion ....

26. Father's occupation . . . .
27. Estimate of amount of travel experience inside and outside own
    country . . . .
28. Child's occupational aspirations . . . .
    . . . .
29. Teacher's estimate of child's comparative intelligence:
    a. High   b. Average   c. Low   (encircle)
30. Teacher's estimate of socio-economic class of family:
    a. Upper   b. Middle   c. Low   (encircle)

ETHNOCENTRIC QUESTIONNAIRE*

(At the end of each interview the *14*-year-old children will be read
the following items and their responses recorded as *yes* or *no*. Each
child should be given a copy of the items to read as the interviewer
reads them to him.)

"Here are some questions which you can answer with 'yes' or 'no'.
There are no right or wrong answers, for everyone has his own way of
thinking about them. Tell me how you think about each one."

Yes   No   1. Do you think people of different races and religions
              would get along better if they visited each other and
              shared things?

Yes   No   2. Do you think our country is a lot better off because of
              the foreign races that live here?

Yes   No   3. Do you think that most of the other countries of the
              world are really against us, but are afraid to show it?

Yes   No   4. Do you think there will always be war, that it is part of
              human nature?

Yes   No   5. Do you think it is interesting to be friends with someone
              who thinks or feels differently from the way you do?

*These items are taken from Else Frenkel-Brunswik, "A study of prejudice
in children," in *Human Relations*, 1948, *1*, 295-306. Each child can be given an
ethnocentrism score as follows: a *maximum* ethnocentrism (prejudice) score of 13
if a child gives "no" (or disagreement) responses to #1, 2, 5, 7, and 9 and "yes"
responses to all other questions. A *minimum* ethnocentrism score (unprejudiced)
of zero is given a child who says "yes" to #1, 2, 5, 7, and 9 and "no" to all the
other items. Each child can be given a score between 13 and 0. Then comparisons can be made between average scores for the three age groups, between
the two socio-economic groups, as well as correlations between ethnocentrism
scores and other indices. The *raw scores* for ethnocentrism should be sent to
McGill, indicating the age group and the social class of the children.

Yes   No   6. Do you think girls should only learn things that are useful around the house?

Yes   No   7. Do you think weak people deserve as much consideration from others as do strong people?

Yes   No   8. Do you think that a person must watch out or else somebody will make a fool out of him?

Yes   No   9. Do you think teachers should try to find out what children want to do and not just tell them what to do?

Yes   No   10. Do you think there is only one right way to do anything?

Yes   No   11. Do you think that someday a flood or earthquake will destroy everybody in the whole world?

Yes   No   12. Do you think there are more contagious diseases nowadays than ever before?

Yes   No   13. Do you think you can protect yourself from bad luck by carrying a charm or good luck piece?

Appendix B
Instructions for Coding Responses

CODE 1: RESPONSES TO "WHAT ARE YOU?" QUESTIONS

No answer

Sex reference

National reference

City or regional reference
(Berliner, Montrealer, etc.)

Religious reference

"Racial" reference (Negro, White, Semitic, etc.)

Person or human being

Student

Child

Personal qualities (descriptive adjectives, e.g., nice, smart, kind*)

Other

*Whenever compound descriptive responses are given, such as "nice person," "good boy," "un enfant de Dieu," they should be categorized according to the noun of the phrase, e.g., (person), (boy), and (child).

CODE 2: EVALUATIVE ANALYSIS OF THE DESCRIPTIONS OF OTHER PEOPLES

Codes 2 and 3 are designed to categorize the descriptive statements given about other peoples. Code 2 emphasizes the evaluations inherent in the statements while code 3 emphasizes the *type of content* referred to in the child's descriptions of other peoples. In most cases you are to analyze the same descriptions given according to both codes 2 and 3 in order to reveal both the evaluation and the content. You will note that code 2 has three categories labeled *non*-evaluative (01, 02, 03) that function as an "others" category. Rather than place all non-evaluative descriptions in one category, we feel that the differences between non-

239

evaluative statements of similarities (01) and differences (02) should be kept separate for later analysis. But our main objective with code 2 is to capture the child's *evaluative* responses in meaningful categories.

The coder should first decide if a description given is evaluative or not by studying what we have classified as "favorable, unfavorable, and general" evaluative responses in the categories available. If the description is evaluative, it should fit into one of these categories, *e.g.*, "they are cultured like us" would be coded as 14, "intelligent" as 13, or (they are different from us because) "they are superstitious" as 50. Category 50 takes all evaluative descriptions which have no other special category allotted — we felt that they occurred too infrequently in the pilot study to require separate categories.

Non-evaluative descriptions can be placed in one of three categories. If the child actually states a similarity or difference in terms such as "they dress like us," "they have different habits," then they are categorized as 01 and 02 respectively. If a comparison is *implied* but not stated in terms such as "like us" or "different" they should also be placed in categories 01 and 02. These implied comparisons occur regularly following the question, "In what way are they like us (or not like us)?" If a child should answer "they live in jungles" to these questions, the implication is that they are different from us in their way and place of living and the statement goes into 02. If the child says "they live in jungles" to the question "What else do you know about them?" it would then be categorized as a general statement of fact, non-evaluative, and placed in 03. The coder should always keep in mind which question was asked whenever he is categorizing the child's response. Category 03 then is the "others" category of non-evaluative descriptions.

One final point, even though the child uses the words "like us" or "different" but then gives a description which fits into the evaluative categories, make sure that the description goes in a category from 10 to 44 or 50, *not* in a non-evaluative category.

No response given (00)   *i.e.*, no response available to classify.

Non-evaluative statement of similarities (01)	Makes non-evaluative comparisons with own group using words "like us" or "like ours" or equivalents, *e.g.*, dress like us, eat like us, are like us, same skin color, we talk the same language, or same type of country as ours.

Non-evaluative
statement of
differences (02)

Makes non-evaluative comparisons with own country using words "not like us," "different from us" or makes implication of differences.

Other *non*-evaluative
statements of fact (03)

References to historical, geographical, or cultural facts, climate, contemporary affairs, professions, hobbies, customs which are not evaluative in nature; includes "they send us rice," "my father is one," "they are Catholic," or "Communist," "they have big families."

Favorable Evaluative Descriptions

Good

Or: are friends, nice, kind, friendly, with us in war, welcoming, generous, truthful, sympathiques, simple (French), help one another, all right, are with us (*i.e.*, friendly); also dependable, prompt, proud, brave, honest, hardworking, likeable (including "I like that country," "I think I would like them if I knew them").

Peaceful

Unhappy because of war, want peace, mind their own business, don't harm others.

Ambitious

Like to study, try, willing, want to get ahead, competitive.

Intelligent (13)

Able, smart, prudent for future, clever, broadminded, great scientific developments, atomic knowledge or power, inventors, imaginative, inventive.

Cultured (14)

Modern, fashionable, refined, reserved, good manners, cultivated, civilized, well-behaved, quiet, polite, modest.

General Evaluative Descriptions

Wealthy

Including references to high standard of living, material or industrial wealth, having servants, nice clothing, have a lot of electricity.

Poor · | Including explicit references to low standard of living, material or industrial shortages; also, crowded country, old or torn clothes, looking for jobs, no ice boxes — if the implication is that they are poor, have a hard life.

Strong | Powerful, mighty (as a nation), husky (physically strong).

Happy | Gay, fun, jovial, humorous, lighthearted, funny (in humorous sense), colorful, lively.

Unhappy | Sad, afraid, submissive, they don't like their leaders.

Free | Democratic.

Dominated | Not free, forced to act, servile, they are slaves.

Religious |

Clean |

Dirty |

Patriotic |

Interesting | Exciting, offer adventure.

Educated | Including "good schools."

Uneducated | Including "poor schools," "few schools," "people don't go to school much."

Unfavorable Evaluative Descriptions

Bad | Wicked, unfriendly, selfish, grasping, conceited, liars, untruthful, live with others' money, hypocrites, traitors, mean, bad, haughty, dishonest, tricky, sly, secretive.

Aggressive | Warlike, rough, gangsters, bandits, bad-tempered, cruel, irascible, dangerous, trouble-makers, maltreat slaves, love war, make war, hostile, quarrelsome, domineering, attack countries, made war on others, want whole world, want power, like to be superior, persecuted others, quarrel among themselves, use electric chair, fighting, riots, bestial, imperious, disputatious, persecutors of church, still believe in Hitler.

Unambitious — Lazy, don't care, don't want to try.

Unintelligent — Dumb, narrow-minded, backward, unimaginative, easily led.

Uncultured — Boastful, loud, rude, crude, flashy, impolite, brutes, bad mannered, wild, extravagant.

Other evaluative descriptions (50) — Other evaluative statements which do not have special categories, such as strict, superstitious, atheist, emotional, old fashioned; also includes "some good, some bad".

CODE 3: CONTENT ANALYSIS OF DESCRIPTIONS OF STANDARD REFERENCE PEOPLES

Personal

Physical-racial descriptions: slanted eyes, yellow skin, white skin, strong (bodies), husky.

Personality traits or descriptions: nice people, warlike, aggressive, and any response categorizable in code 2 that refers to personality characteristics or personal states such as intelligent, happy.

Cultural-Material

Food: eat rice, etc.

Clothing

Housing and material possessions: have few schools, have electricity or cars, are poor, have hard life — in sense of being poor.

Cultural-Behavioral

Language

Religion and religious beliefs: includes such responses as "have witch doctors."

Occupation: including hunting, fishing, general reference to work.

Political reference or political beliefs: including "dominated," have freedoms.

Habits of living, or other customs:* includes such responses as: don't
go to school often, "celebrate Christmas," live in jungle, eat the
animals they kill, or reference to similarity of habits.

Geographical facts: hot climate, rainy, mountainous, jungle region.

Non-categorizable response: *e.g.*, "same type of country as ours" since
one is not certain if a reference is made to a geographical fact or
to habits of living; or no-response.

CODE 4: RESPONDENTS' AFFECTIVE EVALUATIONS OF THOSE CONSIDERED AS "LIKE US" AND AS "NOT LIKE US"

No answer given.

Likes them: includes "probably would like them if I knew them better".

Is indifferent to them.

Doesn't like them.

Doesn't generalize about them: "yes and no," and "it all depends,"
"some yes, some no."

CODE 5: SOURCES OF INFORMATION ABOUT OTHER PEOPLES

(If a double statement is given about a similar source, consider only the
first part, *e.g.*, "geography texts and story books," code only
"geography texts." If the child mentioned "geography texts and
teacher," then the two parts would be coded separately, one under
"school texts" and the other under "teacher".)

No answer, or no one "told me about them" or never "met one" or never
"read about them"

Parents and other family members

Friends (from child's own national group)

Teacher

Direct contact: including visits to their country, someone from there
visiting their own country, living among them, having as neighbors,
or having someone from that country in the family.

Radio   Non-school books: including library books

T.V. or movies   and encyclopedia

Course work   Magazines, newspapers, comics

School texts   Doesn't know

*Excluding references to food, clothing, etc., which would be classified
above in "food" or "clothing" categories. A description such as "eat frog legs"
would go in "food" category, but "sit on floor to eat" or "use chop sticks"
would go in "habits of living" category.

Appendix C
Information Tables for National Profiles

Table C.1

Peoples Similar To Own Group: American Children's Responses

Table entries are percentages	6-Year-Olds	Social Class		10-Year-Olds	Social Class		14-Year-Olds	Social Class	
	Total	Low	Middle	Total	Low	Middle	Total	Low	Middle
No Response	83	85	80	55	57	53	38	41	35
British	4	1	6	10	5	14	22	18	25
Canadians	2	2	1	5	5	4	7	5	9
French	1	–	2	3	3	3	7	7	7
Germans	2	1	2	4	4	5	4	4	4
Italians	1	1	–	4	5	3	6	11	1
Others	7	10	9	19	21	18	16	14	19
Total of Percentages	100	100	100	100	100	100	100	100	100
Total Number of Responses	300	150	150	300	150	150	300	150	150

Table C.2

Peoples Different From Own Group: American Children's Responses

Table entries are percentages	6-Year-Olds	Social Class		10-Year-Olds	Social Class		14-Year-Olds	Social Class	
	Total	Low	Middle	Total	Low	Middle	Total	Low	Middle
No Response	72	75	68	33	32	33	29	33	24
Africans	3	2	3	8	9	7	10	8	11
Chinese	6	5	6	10	9	9	11	10	11
Hindus	3	2	3	4	5	3	3	3	3
Japanese	4	2	5	6	5	7	5	4	5
Russians	2	2	2	10	10	9	17	16	17
Germans	1	–	1	5	5	3	4	2	5
Others	9	12	12	24	25	29	21	24	24
Total of Percentages	100	100	100	100	100	100	100	100	100
Total Number of Responses	300	150	150	300	150	150	300	150	150

Table C.3

Most Like To Be: American Children's Responses

Table entries are percentages	6-Year-Olds	Social Class		10-Year Olds	Social Class		14-Year Olds	Social Class	
	Total	Low	Middle	Total	Low	Middle	Total	Low	Middle
No Response	23	26	20	2	—	4	0	—	—
British	5	2	8	9	2	16	33	22	44
Italians	3	6	—	15	20	10	20	26	14
Canadians	3	6	—	9	16	2	12	16	8
Chinese	9	6	12	9	10	8	0	—	—
Irish	1	2	—	7	6	8	6	4	8
French	3	—	6	8	4	12	7	4	10
Spanish	1	—	2	6	10	2	1	2	—
Germans	7	6	8	1	—	2	0	—	—
Others	45	46	46	34	32	36	21	26	16
Total of Percentages	100	100	100	100	100	100	100	100	100
Total Number of Responses	100	50	50	100	50	50	100	50	50

248

Table C.4

Least Like To Be: American Children's Responses

Table entries are percentages	6-Year-Olds Social Class			10-Year-Olds Social Class			14-Year-Olds Social Class		
	Total	Low	Middle	Total	Low	Middle	Total	Low	Middle
No Response	23	24	22	3	—	6	—	—	—
Chinese	13	16	10	6	4	8	3	2	4
Africans	4	2	6	13	12	14	18	14	22
Germans	13	8	18	9	8	10	2	2	2
Hindus	12	10	14	4	4	4	3	—	6
Japanese	10	8	12	5	6	4	2	—	4
Russians	7	8	6	43	50	36	59	70	48
Others	18	24	12	17	16	18	13	12	14
Total of Percentages	100	100	100	100	100	100	100	100	100
Total Number of Responses	100	50	50	100	50	50	100	50	50

249

Table C.5

Peoples Similar To Own Group: Bantu Children's Responses

Table entries are percentages	6-Year-Olds Social Class			10-Year-Olds Social Class			14-Year-Olds Social Class		
	Total	Low	Middle	Total	Low	Middle	Total	Low	Middle
No Response	73	74	73	59	56	59	47	48	48
Union African Tribe	27	26	27	29	28	28	27	27	26
Federation African Tribe	—	—	—	7	8	6	7	4	8
Others	—	—	—	5	8	7	19	21	18
Total of Percentages	100	100	100	100	100	100	100	100	100
Total Number of Responses	300	156	144	300	120	180	300	150	150

Table C.6

Peoples Different From Own Group: Bantu Children's Responses

Table entries are percentages	6-Year-Olds			10-Year-Olds			14-Year-Olds		
		Social Class			Social Class			Social Class	
	Total	Low	Middle	Total	Low	Middle	Total	Low	Middle
No Response	73	72	73	19	17	19	20	18	23
British	2	1	2	13	16	10	11	11	11
Chinese	1	1	1	7	5	8	8	10	5
Hindus	1	1	2	14	11	15	10	13	7
Whites	11	11	11	13	8	15	16	16	15
Union African Tribe	8	9	5	5	6	4	2	1	3
Boers	2	2	2	11	17	7	11	7	14
Coloured	2	2	3	7	6	8	5	5	3
Others	—	1	1	11	14	14	17	19	19
Total of Percentages	100	100	100	100	100	100	100	100	100
Total Number of Responses	300	156	144	300	120	180	300	150	150

251

Table C.7

Most Like To Be: Bantu Children's Responses

Table entries are percentages	6-Year-Olds	Social Class		10-Year-Olds	Social Class		14-Year-Olds	Social Class	
	Total	Low	Middle	Total	Low	Middle	Total	Low	Middle
No Response	18	17	19	3	–	5	7	4	10
Americans	–	–	–	1	–	2	7	4	10
British	7	6	9	35	30	38	39	48	30
Whites	55	59	50	34	40	30	26	30	22
Union African Tribe	5	4	6	7	5	8	3	4	2
Boers	7	6	8	1	2	–	–	–	–
Others	8	8	8	19	23	17	18	10	26
Total of Percentages	100	100	100	100	100	100	100	100	100
Total Number of Responses	100	52	48	100	40	60	100	50	50

Table C.8

Least Like To Be: Bantu Children's Responses

Table entries are percentages	6-Year-Olds			10-Year-Olds			14-Year-Olds		
		Social Class			Social Class			Social Class	
	Total	Low	Middle	Total	Low	Middle	Total	Low	Middle
No Response	37	40	34	11	10	11	13	8	18
Africans	1	–	2	6	10	3	3	4	2
Chinese	1	2	–	6	5	7	3	6	–
Hindus	3	4	2	12	8	15	9	8	10
Union African Tribe	50	48	52	43	45	42	35	42	28
Boers	3	4	2	8	2	11	20	16	24
Others	5	2	8	14	20	11	17	16	18
Total of Percentages	100	100	100	100	100	100	100	100	100
Total Number of Responses	100	52	48	100	40	60	100	50	50

253

Table C.9

Peoples Similar To Own Group: Brazilian Children's Responses

Table entries are percentages	6-Year-Olds			10-Year-Olds			14-Year-Olds		
		Social Class			Social Class			Social Class	
	Total	Low	Middle	Total	Low	Middle	Total	Low	Middle
No Response	95	99	94	66	80	54	35	47	25
Americans	1	—	3	6	3	9	8	6	9
Portuguese	1	—	1	8	5	11	14	13	15
French	1	—	1	3	1	4	6	4	7
British	—	—	—	2	2	3	2	2	2
Italians	1	1	—	1	—	1	6	5	8
Argentinians	—	—	—	4	3	5	5	5	5
Chinese	—	—	—	1	1	1	—	—	—
Germans	—	—	—	3	2	5	3	4	3
Russians	—	—	—	—	1	—	1	1	1
Spanish	—	—	—	2	1	3	2	1	3
Others	1	—	1	4	1	4	18	12	22
Total of Percentages	100	100	100	100	100	100	100	100	100
Total Number of Responses	300	150	150	300	150	150	300	150	150

254

Table C.10

Peoples Different From Own Group: Brazilian Children's Responses

Table entries are percentages	6-Year-Olds Social Class			10-Year-Olds Social Class			14-Year Olds Social Class		
	Total	Low	Middle	Total	Low	Middle	Total	Low	Middle
No Response	90	99	83	50	64	37	25	35	17
Americans	–	–	1	5	6	3	5	2	7
Africans	–	–	–	5	3	7	4	6	3
British	1	–	3	4	–	7	5	2	7
Chinese	2	–	3	9	5	13	15	14	16
French	1	–	1	4	5	3	3	3	2
Germans	1	1	1	2	2	3	4	4	4
Italians	–	–	–	1	2	1	–	1	–
Japanese	2	–	3	7	5	9	13	14	13
Portuguese	1	–	2	3	5	2	–	1	–
Russians	1	–	1	2	–	5	12	8	15
Spanish	1	–	1	1	1	1	1	1	1
Others	–	–	1	7	2	9	13	9	15
Total of Percentages	100	100	100	100	100	100	100	100	100
Total Number of Responses	300	150	150	300	150	150	300	150	150

255

Table C.11

Most Like To Be: Brazilian Children's Responses

Table entries are percentages	6-Year-Olds	Social Class		10-Year-Olds	Social Class		14-Year-Olds	Social Class	
	Total	Low	Middle	Total	Low	Middle	Total	Low	Middle
No Response	80	92	68	43	58	28	17	18	16
Americans	8	2	14	22	16	28	31	30	32
Argentinians	1	2	–	3	4	2	4	4	4
British	2	2	2	2	–	4	3	4	2
Italians	2	2	2	2	–	4	7	10	4
Chinese	1	–	2	–	–	–	2	4	–
Germans	–	–	2	2	2	2	3	2	4
Japanese	1	–	2	2	2	2	1	2	–
Portuguese	2	–	4	13	6	20	10	6	14
Africans	–	–	–	1	2	–	–	–	–
French	–	–	–	6	6	6	13	10	16
Uruguayans	–	–	–	2	2	2	2	4	–
Others	2	–	4	2	2	2	7	6	8
Total of Percentages	100	100	100	100	100	100	100	100	100
Total Number of Responses	100	50	50	100	50	50	100	50	50

Table C.12

Least Like To Be: Brazilian Children's Responses

Table entries are percentages	6-Year-Olds	Social Class		10-Year-Olds	Social Class		14-Year-Olds	Social Class	
	Total	Low	Middle	Total	Low	Middle	Total	Low	Middle
No Response	84	98	70	23	34	12	10	16	4
Argentinians	1	–	2	4	4	4	–	–	–
Africans	2	–	4	17	12	22	17	20	14
Chinese	4	–	8	10	10	10	8	10	6
French	1	–	2	1	2	–	–	–	–
Japanese	3	–	6	5	2	8	8	8	8
Russians	3	–	6	19	12	26	36	24	48
Portuguese	1	–	2	1	2	–	3	2	4
Americans	–	–	–	6	10	2	3	2	4
Germans	–	–	–	3	2	4	2	4	–
Hindus	–	–	–	2	2	2	4	2	6
Others	1	2	–	9	8	10	9	12	6
Total of Percentages	100	100	100	100	100	100	100	100	100
Total Number of Responses	100	50	50	100	50	50	100	50	50

Table C.13

Peoples Similar To Own Group: English-Canadian Children's Responses

Table entries are percentages	6-Year-Olds			10-Year-Olds			14-Year-Olds		
		Social Class			Social Class			Social Class	
	Total	Low	Middle	Total	Low	Middle	Total	Low	Middle
No Response	82	87	77	37	42	31	15	22	12
Americans	5	2	7	16	14	19	26	22	29
British	4	3	5	16	14	19	24	16	30
Scottish	1	1	1	6	6	7	2	3	1
French (France)	1	–	1	4	4	4	–	–	–
Australians	–	–	–	1	1	–	10	6	11
Others	7	7	9	20	19	20	23	31	17
Total of Percentages	100	100	100	100	100	100	100	100	100
Total Number of Responses	300	150	150	300	180	120	300	101	199

258

Table C.14

Peoples Different From Own Group: English-Canadian Children's Responses

Table entries are percentages	6-Year-Olds Social Class			10-Year-Olds Social Class			14-Year-Olds Social Class		
	Total	Low	Middle	Total	Low	Middle	Total	Low	Middle
No Response	66	76	58	16	18	14	13	21	10
Africans	4	3	4	12	11	14	11	8	12
Chinese	5	5	6	14	10	11	17	14	19
Russians	1	1	1	6	4	10	15	11	17
Germans	2	1	3	4	5	3	4	3	4
Japanese	2	2	3	5	6	4	4	4	4
Eskimos	1	–	2	6	9	2	2	1	2
Others	19	12	23	37	37	52	34	38	32
Total of Percentages	100	100	100	100	100	100	100	100	100
Total Number of Responses	300	150	150	300	180	120	300	102	198

Table C.15

Most Like To Be: English-Canadian Children's Responses

Table entries are percentages	6-Year-Olds			10-Year-Olds			14-Year-Olds		
		Social Class			Social Class			Social Class	
	Total	Low	Middle	Total	Low	Middle	Total	Low	Middle
No Response	34	46	22	9	10	3	3	3	3
Americans	12	8	16	36	33	17	35	44	30
British	5	4	6	13	10	7	21	9	27
Scottish	2	2	2	4	3	2	6	6	6
Indians	6	0	12	1	2	0	2	6	0
Others	41	40	42	37	42	11	33	32	34
Total of Percentages	100	100	100	100	100	100	100	100	100
Total Number of Responses	100	50	50	100	60	40	100	34	66

Table C.16

Least Like To Be: English-Canadian Children's Responses

Table entries are percentages	6-Year-Olds			10-Year-Olds			14-Year-Olds		
		Social Class			Social Class			Social Class	
	Total	Low	Middle	Total	Low	Middle	Total	Low	Middle
No Response	38	52	24	13	12	15	6	3	8
Russians	5	2	8	15	8	25	50	38	56
Africans	8	8	8	11	10	13	6	6	6
Germans	12	6	18	14	19	8	8	17	3
Hindus	12	12	12	10	8	13	2	3	1
Others	25	20	30	37	43	26	28	33	26
Total of Percentages	100	100	100	100	100	100	100	100	100
Total Number of Responses	100	50	50	100	60	40	100	34	66

Table C.17

Peoples Similar To Own Group: French Children's Responses

Table entries are percentages	6-Year-Olds Social Class			10-Year-Olds Social Class			14-Year-Olds Social Class		
	Total	Low	Middle	Total	Low	Middle	Total	Low	Middle
No Response	86	88	84	20	23	19	15	11	21
British	2	2	2	14	14	14	15	13	16
Germans	2	2	1	13	13	13	14	15	11
Americans	2	2	2	10	10	10	9	10	8
Swiss	—	—	—	9	6	10	9	9	9
Italians	—	—	—	8	10	7	9	10	6
Belgians	—	—	1	5	4	6	11	10	12
Spanish	3	3	2	5	3	6	4	6	2
Others	5	3	8	16	17	15	14	16	15
Total of Percentages	100	100	100	100	100	100	100	100	100
Total Number of Responses	300	135	165	300	99	201	300	174	126

Table C.18

Peoples Different From Own Group: French Children's Responses

Table entries are percentages	6-Year-Olds Social Class			10-Year-Olds Social Class			14-Year-Olds Social Class		
	Total	*Low*	*Middle*	*Total*	*Low*	*Middle*	*Total*	*Low*	*Middle*
No Response	73	85	64	12	14	12	16	12	21
Africans	8	4	11	19	20	19	17	17	17
Chinese	3	2	4	16	14	17	16	18	12
Japanese	2	1	3	6	5	7	5	6	2
Americans	2	2	2	4	2	5	7	7	6
Russians	1	—	2	3	1	5	6	6	6
Hindus	—	—	—	7	4	7	5	4	6
Others	11	6	14	33	40	28	28	30	30
Total of Percentages	100	100	100	100	100	100	100	100	100
Total Number of Responses	300	135	165	300	99	201	300	174	126

Table C.19

Most Like To Be: French Children's Responses

Table entries are percentages	6-Year-Olds Social Class			10-Year-Olds Social Class			14-Year-Olds Social Class		
	Total	Low	Middle	Total	Low	Middle	Total	Low	Middle
No Response	33	40	27	4	3	4	7	5	10
Americans	6	9	4	14	19	12	21	20	22
British	9	7	11	13	12	14	12	5	22
Spanish	6	7	5	12	9	14	12	16	7
Swiss	2	2	2	10	6	12	13	12	14
Germans	2	–	4	–	–	–	9	9	10
Italians	4	2	5	5	3	5	8	14	–
Belgians	–	–	–	7	9	6	2	3	–
Others	38	33	42	35	39	33	16	16	15
Total of Percentages	100	100	100	100	100	100	100	100	100
Total Number of Responses	100	45	55	100	33	67	100	58	42

Table C.20

Least Like To Be: French Children's Responses

Table entries are percentages	6-Year-Olds Social Class			10-Year-Olds Social Class			14-Year-Olds Social Class		
	Total	Low	Middle	Total	Low	Middle	Total	Low	Middle
No Response	33	31	34	18	12	21	19	15	25
Africans	15	16	14	12	19	9	10	14	6
Chinese	7	11	4	6	6	6	11	10	12
Germans	8	11	5	13	15	12	6	5	7
Russians	3	–	5	11	3	15	10	9	12
Hindus	–	–	–	3	6	1	12	15	7
Americans	6	5	7	5	6	5	5	7	2
Others	28	26	31	32	33	31	27	25	29
Total of Percentages	100	100	100	100	100	100	100	100	100
Total Number of Responses	100	45	55	100	33	67	100	58	42

265

Table C.21

Peoples Similar To Own Group: French-Canadian Children's Responses

Table entries are percentages	6-Year-Olds			10-Year-Olds			14-Year-Olds		
	Total	Social Class		Total	Social Class		Total	Social Class	
		Low	Middle		Low	Middle		Low	Middle
No Response	84	88	.79	23	40	6	2	1	1
Americans	2	1	3	12	10	12	21	19	22
British	3	3	4	14	12	15	20	17	22
French	5	3	7	20	14	26	26	27	29
Italians	4	4	4	9	5	11	7	5	9
Spanish	1	—	1	4	5	2	5	5	4
Others	1	1	2	18	14	28	19	26	13
Total of Percentages	100	100	100	100	100	100	100	100	100
Total Number of Responses	300	147	153	300	144	156	300	150	150

Table C.22

Peoples Different From Own Group: French-Canadian Children's Responses

| Table entries are percentages | 6-Year-Olds | | | 10-Year Olds | | | 14-Year-Olds | | |
| | Social Class | | | Social Class | | | Social Class | | |
	Total	Low	Middle	Total	Low	Middle	Total	Low	Middle
No Response	70	75	66	16	26	8	1	2	1
Africans	7	5	10	14	12	15	16	14	18
Chinese	8	9	8	23	21	25	22	25	21
Germans	1	1	2	2	2	2	5	3	7
Japanese	2	1	4	14	10	18	17	20	13
Russians	1	—	1	4	3	4	11	8	14
Hindus	—	—	—	6	3	9	7	7	7
Others	11	9	9	21	23	19	21	21	19
Total of Percentages	100	100	100	100	100	100	100	100	100
Total Number of Responses	300	147	153	300	144	156	300	150	150

Table C.23

Most Like To Be: French-Canadian Children's Responses

Table entries are percentages	6-Year-Olds Social Class			10-Year-Olds Social Class			14-Year-Olds Social Class		
	Total	Low	Middle	Total	Low	Middle	Total	Low	Middle
No Response	28	33	24	2	4	—	—	—	—
Stay as I Am	33	47	20	6	12	—	4	2	6
Chinese	7	6	8	2	4	—	2	2	2
French	9	6	12	19	18	20	32	36	28
Americans	2	—	4	16	12	20	35	28	42
Africans	2	—	4	6	8	4	—	—	—
British	3	—	6	20	20	20	8	10	6
Spanish	3	4	2	6	10	2	5	4	6
Others	13	4	20	23	12	34	14	18	10
Total of Percentages	100	100	100	100	100	100	100	100	100
Total Number of Responses	100	49	51	100	48	52	100	50	50

268

Table C.24

Least Like To Be: French-Canadian Children's Responses

Table entries are percentages	6-Year-Olds			10-Year-Olds			14-Year-Olds		
		Social Class			Social Class			Social Class	
	Total	Low	Middle	Total	Low	Middle	Total	Low	Middle
No Response	54	68	42	4	6	2	2	–	4
Africans	16	12	20	19	9	30	20	20	20
Chinese	8	8	8	19	19	20	12	14	10
Germans	1	–	2	6	8	4	6	10	2
Hindus	4	–	8	12	19	6	7	10	4
Japanese	3	–	6	6	4	8	1	–	2
Russians	3	–	6	15	15	16	38	30	46
Others	11	12	8	19	20	14	14	16	12
Total of Percentages	100	100	100	100	100	100	100	100	100
Total Number of Responses	100	49	51	100	48	52	100	50	50

Table C.25

Peoples Similar To Own Group: German Children's Responses

Table entries are percentages	6-Year-Olds			10-Year-Olds			14-Year-Olds		
	Total	Social Class		Total	Social Class		Total	Social Class	
		Low	Middle		Low	Middle		Low	Middle
No Response	60	66	56	17	19	15	15	17	12
Americans	11	9	12	13	14	13	12	13	10
British	5	2	8	12	6	19	11	10	13
French	4	3	6	12	9	15	10	10	9
Russians	4	5	4	7	9	4	2	—	3
Austrians	1	1	1	5	4	6	7	6	9
Swiss	1	—	1	5	5	5	7	5	10
Swedes	2	3	1	4	4	4	8	7	8
Italians	2	1	3	5	5	5	3	3	3
Others	10	10	8	20	25	14	26	29	23
Total of Percentages	100	100	100	100	100	100	100	100	100
Total Number of Responses	300	150	150	300	150	150	300	150	150

Table C.26

Peoples Different From Own Group: German Children's Responses

Total entries are percentages	6-Year-Olds Social Class			10-Year-Olds Social Class			14-Year-Olds Social Class		
	Total	Low	Middle	Total	Low	Middle	Total	Low	Middle
No Response	48	50	46	15	24	7	14	19	10
Africans	19	19	19	20	18	23	20	21	19
Chinese	9	9	9	19	17	21	19	19	20
Japanese	2	1	3	10	9	10	5	5	2
Americans	5	5	4	4	5	4	2	2	2
Russians	3	1	4	3	3	2	7	7	7
Italians	2	3	2	2	1	2	6	3	9
Eskimos	1	1	1	5	2	7	2	3	1
Others	11	11	11	22	21	24	25	21	31
Total of Percentages	100	100	100	100	100	100	100	100	100
Total Number of Responses	300	150	150	300	150	150	300	150	150

271

Table C.27

Most Like To Be: German Children's Responses

Table entries are percentages	6-Year-Olds Social Class			10-Year-Olds Social Class			14-Year-Olds Social Class		
	Total	Low	Middle	Total	Low	Middle	Total	Low	Middle
No Response	11	12	10	–	–	–	3	6	–
Americans	29	18	40	40	34	46	54	54	54
Africans	13	12	14	9	10	8	–	–	–
British	8	10	6	10	16	4	4	4	4
Italians	2	2	2	7	8	6	6	4	8
Swedes	4	4	4	3	4	2	7	10	4
Swiss	1	2	–	3	2	4	8	8	8
Chinese	6	8	4	1	2	–	1	2	–
Dutch	1	2	–	5	4	6	1	–	2
French	6	8	4	–	–	–	1	–	2
Others	19	22	16	22	20	24	15	12	18
Total of Percentages	100	100	100	100	100	100	100	100	100
Total Number of Responses	100	50	50	100	50	50	100	50	50

272

Table C.28

Least Like To Be: German Children's Responses

Table entries are percentages	6-Year-Olds Social Class			10-Year-Olds Social Class			14-Year-Olds Social Class		
	Total	Low	Middle	Total	Low	Middle	Total	Low	Middle
No Response	12	14	10	—	—	—	—	—	—
Russians	37	34	40	54	58	50	35	34	36
Africans	21	24	18	12	10	14	16	16	16
Chinese	6	4	8	19	20	18	29	32	26
Hindus	4	—	8	3	4	2	7	6	8
Eskimos	1	—	2	5	4	6	4	4	4
Others	19	24	14	7	4	10	9	8	10
Total of Percentages	100	100	100	100	100	100	100	100	100
Total Number of Responses	100	50	50	100	50	50	100	50	50

Table C.29

Peoples Similar To Own Group: Israeli Children's Responses

Total entries are percentages	6-Year-Olds			10-Year-Olds			14-Year-Olds		
		Social Class			Social Class			Social Class	
	Total	Low	Middle	Total	Low	Middle	Total	Low	Middle
No Response	43	43	44	17	17	16	10	10	10
Americans	15	14	16	18	16	19	20	24	18
British	8	8	8	14	11	15	15	10	18
French	6	6	5	10	12	9	14	13	14
Germans	4	5	4	4	4	4	4	4	4
Poles	5	4	7	7	7	7	5	1	7
Russians	5	4	6	5	3	6	7	7	7
Others	14	16	10	25	30	24	25	31	22
Total of Percentages	100	100	100	100	100	100	100	100	100
Total Number of Responses	300	132	168	300	105	195	300	108	192

Table C.30

Peoples Different From Own Group: Israeli Children's Responses

Total entries are percentages	6-Year-Olds Social Class			10-Year-Olds Social Class			14-Year-Olds Social Class		
	Total	Low	Middle	Total	Low	Middle	Total	Low	Middle
No Response	48	46	50	21	29	18	11	13	10
Arabs	10	8	12	7	10	6	7	3	9
African Negros	15	16	15	18	14	21	20	21	20
Chinese	7	5	8	11	10	12	14	12	15
Hindus	2	3	2	3	1	4	12	15	10
Am. Indians	1	2	—	5	5	6	4	6	4
Japanese	1	2	—	5	7	3	5	2	6
Others	16	18	13	30	24	30	27	28	26
Total of Percentages	100	100	100	100	100	100	100	100	100
Total Number of Responses	300	132	168	300	105	195	300	108	192

275

Table C.31

Most Like To Be: Israeli Children's Responses

Total entries are percentages	6-Year-Olds			10-Year-Olds			14-Year-Olds		
		Social Class			Social Class			Social Class	
	Total	Low	Middle	Total	Low	Middle	Total	Low	Middle
No Response	31	26	36	10	15	8	7	8	6
Americans	30	28	32	33	35	32	34	43	30
British	5	9	2	11	3	15	19	17	21
French	3	–	5	18	12	21	18	17	19
Germans	4	6	4	–	–	–	–	–	–
Iraqi	2	–	4	3	6	2	–	–	–
Russians	4	4	4	2	3	2	2	–	3
Swiss	1	–	1	–	–	–	4	–	6
Others	19	27	12	23	26	20	16	15	15
Total of Percentages	100	100	100	100	100	100	100	100	100
Total Number of Responses	100	44	56	100	35	65	100	36	64

Table C.32

Least Like To Be: Israeli Children's Responses

Total entries are percentages	6-Year-Olds			10-Year-Olds			14-Year-Olds		
		Social Class			Social Class			Social Class	
	Total	Low	Middle	Total	Low	Middle	Total	Low	Middle
No Response	30	32	29	4	6	3	2	–	3
Arabs	27	26	29	28	30	27	31	22	37
Africans	7	7	7	17	15	18	14	17	13
Egyptians	8	9	7	21	23	20	9	11	8
Germans	8	9	7	6	2	8	19	20	19
Russians	2	–	4	4	9	2	9	6	11
Others	18	17	17	20	15	22	16	24	9
Total of Percentages	100	100	100	100	100	100	100	100	100
Total Number of Responses	100	44	56	100	35	65	100	36	64

277

Table C.33

Peoples Similar To Own Group: Japanese Children's Responses

| | 6-Year-Olds | | | 10-Year-Olds | | | 14-Year-Olds | | |
| | Social Class | | | Social Class | | | Social Class | | |
Table entries are percentages	Total	Low	Middle	Total	Low	Middle	Total	Low	Middle
No Response	85	87	84	42	45	37	28	29	27
French	—	1	—	3	3	4	2	1	2
Chinese	3	2	3	16	12	19	25	22	27
Americans	5	5	5	13	14	12	3	5	1
Koreans	2	1	3	10	9	12	23	24	21
British	2	2	1	4	5	3	1	1	1
Russians	1	1	2	3	3	3	—	—	1
Formosans	—	—	—	—	—	—	3	—	6
Others	2	1	2	9	9	10	15	18	14
Total of Percentages	100	100	100	100	100	100	100	100	100
Total Number of Responses	300	150	150	300	150	150	300	147	153

Table C.34

Peoples Different From Own Group: Japanese Children's Responses

Table entries are percentages	6-Year-Olds			10-Year-Olds			14-Year-Olds		
		Social Class			Social Class			Social Class	
	Total	Low	Middle	Total	Low	Middle	Total	Low	Middle
No Response	62	65	60	24	25	21	11	11	10
Americans	19	17	20	16	16	16	29	26	31
French	7	9	5	7	6	7	11	14	7
Hindus	3	3	3	14	13	13	6	5	6
Africans	2	2	3	7	7	7	10	13	7
British	2	1	3	11	6	15	18	16	19
Chinese	2	–	3	3	5	2	–	–	1
Germans	1	–	1	3	3	3	6	5	6
Russians	1	1	1	3	3	3	6	5	6
Swiss	–	–	–	2	1	3	2	–	2
Others	1	2	1	10	15	10	1	5	5
Total of Percentages	100	100	100	100	100	100	100	100	100
Total Number of Responses	300	150	150	300	150	150	300	147	153

279

Table C.35

Most Like To Be: Japanese Children's Responses

Table entries are percentages	6-Year-Olds			10-Year-Olds			14-Year-Olds		
		Social Class			Social Class			Social Class	
	Total	Low	Middle	Total	Low	Middle	Total	Low	Middle
No Response	20	28	12	3	6	—	1	1	—
Americans	40	36	44	65	78	52	52	67	37
British	5	8	2	6	6	6	3	2	4
Chinese	3	2	4	1	—	2	—	—	—
French	12	12	12	11	—	22	5	2	8
Russians	4	4	4	6	6	6	5	4	6
Hawaians	2	—	4	1	2	—	1	2	—
Hindus	2	—	4	1	2	—	1	2	—
Swiss	—	—	—	3	—	6	23	15	31
Germans	—	—	—	—	—	—	5	2	8
Others	12	10	14	4	—	6	4	3	6
Total of Percentages	100	100	100	100	100	100	100	100	100
Total Number of Responses	100	50	50	100	50	50	100	49	51

280

Table C.36

Least Like To Be: Japanese Children's Responses

Table entries are percentages	6-Year-Olds			10-Year-Olds			14-Year-Olds		
		Social Class			Social Class			Social Class	
	Total	Low	Middle	Total	Low	Middle	Total	Low	Middle
No Response	20	24	16	4	6	2	5	–	10
Americans	31	32	30	2	2	2	2	–	4
Africans	15	14	16	37	38	36	48	59	37
British	3	4	2	–	–	–	–	–	–
Chinese	8	8	8	14	10	18	1	2	–
Hindus	11	10	12	22	20	24	12	10	14
Koreans	1	2	–	6	12	–	7	10	4
Brazilians	1	–	2	4	4	4	–	–	–
Germans	4	–	8	2	2	2	1	–	2
Russians	2	–	4	2	–	4	18	13	23
Portuguese	–	–	–	2	2	–	–	–	–
Others	4	6	2	5	–	8	6	6	6
Total of Percentages	100	100	100	100	100	100	100	100	100
Total Number of Responses	100	50	50	100	50	50	100	49	51

281

Table C.37

Peoples Similar To Own Group: Lebanese Children's Responses

Table entries are percentages	6-Year-Olds			10-Year-Olds			14-Year-Olds		
		Social Class			Social Class			Social Class	
	Total	Low	Middle	Total	Low	Middle	Total	Low	Middle
No Response	94	97	92	42	60	25	21	29	14
Syrians	1	1	1	10	7	13	16	15	17
Egyptians	1	1	1	9	7	11	14	14	15
Americans	2	1	3	7	7	8	12	9	14
Iraqi	—	—	—	3	1	4	7	5	9
French	1	1	—	4	1	7	3	3	5
Jordanians	1	—	1	2	2	2	6	6	5
Arabs and North Africans	—	—	—	3	3	3	3	4	3
British	1	—	1	3	1	5	3	2	3
Others	1	—	2	17	13	22	14	13	15
Total of Percentages	102	101	101	100	102	100	99	100	100
Total Number of Responses	300	150	150	300	150	150	300	150	150

Table C.38

Peoples Different From Own Group: Lebanese Children's Responses

Table entries are percentages

	6-Year-Olds	Social Class		10-Year-Olds	Social Class		14-Year-Olds	Social Class	
	Total	Low	Middle	Total	Low	Middle	Total	Low	Middle
No Response	89	91	87	34	50	18	29	31	26
Americans	3	2	5	9	7	11	8	8	7
Africans	1	2	1	10	6	14	5	4	7
Chinese	1	1	1	5	3	8	6	8	5
French	1	1	1	5	5	5	5	3	7
Egyptians	1	1	1	3	4	3	5	7	3
British	–	–	–	3	3	3	5	3	7
Syrians	1	1	–	1	1	1	5	8	3
Others	3	1	5	29	21	37	32	28	35
Total of Percentages	100	100	101	99	100	100	100	100	100
Total Number of Responses	300	150	150	300	150	150	300	150	150

Table C.39

Most Like To Be: Lebanese Children's Responses

Table entries are percentages	6-Year-Olds			10-Year-Olds			14-Year-Olds		
		Social Class			Social Class			Social Class	
	Total	Low	Middle	Total	Low	Middle	Total	Low	Middle
No Response	–	–	–	–	–	–	–	–	–
Americans	17	10	24	29	26	32	31	30	32
Egyptians	15	16	14	24	24	24	22	20	24
Lebanese	11	4	18	8	8	8	8	10	6
Syrians and UAR	6	6	4	9	10	8	9	10	8
French	3	4	2	7	8	6	4	4	4
Arabs	–	–	–	1	–	2	8	6	10
Russians	2	2	2	5	8	2	2	4	–
No Answer and Others	46	58	36	17	16	18	16	16	16
Total of Percentages	100	100	100	100	100	100	100	100	100
Total Number of Responses	100	50	50	100	50	50	100	50	50

284

Table C.40

Least Like To Be: Lebanese Children's Responses

Table entries are percentages	6-Year-Olds Social Class			10-Year-Olds Social Class			14-Year-Olds Social Class		
	Total	Low	Middle	Total	Low	Middle	Total	Low	Middle
No Response	–	–	–	–	–	–	–	–	–
Africans	8	6	10	19	12	26	21	22	20
Americans	4	4	4	16	24	8	18	20	16
Israeli and Hebrew	4	2	6	6	6	6	14	14	14
Russians	1	–	2	12	8	16	18	12	24
Chinese	1	–	2	11	6	16	3	2	4
Syrians and UAR	10	12	8	5	2	8	1	2	–
Hindus	7	4	10	6	6	6	7	10	4
French	2	2	2	2	–	4	5	8	2
Egyptians	3	4	2	3	6	–	1	2	–
No Answer and Others	60	66	54	20	30	10	12	8	16
Total of Percentages	100	100	100	100	100	100	100	100	100
Total Number of Responses	100	50	50	100	50	50	100	50	50

285

Table C.41

Peoples Similar To Own Group: Turkish Children's Responses

Table entries are percentages	6-Year-Olds			10-Year-Olds			14-Year-Olds		
		Social Class			Social Class			Social Class	
	Total	Low	Middle	Total	Low	Middle	Total	Low	Middle
No Response	53	61	46	1	1	–	1	1	1
Americans	9	8	10	16	16	16	15	11	15
British	7	4	9	12	10	14	11	10	13
French	2	1	4	13	10	17	9	8	10
Germans	4	1	7	14	12	17	21	21	20
Italians	1	–	1	5	4	6	4	3	6
Persians	–	–	–	7	7	7	6	7	5
Greeks	5	6	5	3	3	3	1	1	1
Iraqi	–	–	–	3	2	4	4	4	4
Others	19	18	19	26	33	18	30	34	25
Total of Percentages	100	100	100	100	100	100	100	100	100
Total Number of Responses	300	156	144	300	159	141	300	147	153

Table C.42

Peoples Different From Own Group: Turkish Children's Responses

Table entries are percentages	6-Year-Olds Social Class			10-Year-Olds Social Class			14-Year-Olds Social Class		
	Total	Low	Middle	Total	Low	Middle	Total	Low	Middle
No Response	54	62	46	5	8	2	1	1	1
Africans	10	8	13	13	11	14	14	15	12
British	4	2	6	3	5	2	5	6	5
Chinese	3	3	3	18	16	20	18	18	18
Russians	4	3	6	8	10	6	14	14	14
Greeks	4	4	4	2	4	1	3	2	4
Japanese	1	1	1	13	10	16	13	12	14
Arabs	1	—	2	8	6	10	2	3	1
Hindus	1	—	1	6	3	8	4	3	6
Others	18	17	18	24	27	21	26	26	25
Total of Percentages	100	100	100	100	100	100	100	100	100
Total Number of Responses	300	156	144	300	159	141	300	147	153

287

Table C.43

Most Like To Be: Turkish Children's Responses

Table entries are percentages	6-Year-Olds			10-Year-Olds			14-Year-Olds		
	Total	Social Class		Total	Social Class		Total	Social Class	
		Low	Middle		Low	Middle		Low	Middle
No Response	11	14	8	1	2	–	1	–	2
Americans	23	14	32	43	41	44	37	40	34
British	7	4	10	2	3	2	6	4	8
French	4	4	4	3	–	6	1	–	2
Germans	9	8	10	11	10	12	34	34	34
Turks	38	46	30	22	23	20	2	4	–
Pakistanis	–	–	–	–	–	–	4	7	2
Others	8	10	6	18	21	16	15	11	18
Total of Percentages	100	100	100	100	100	100	100	100	100
Total Number of Responses	100	52	48	100	53	47	100	49	51

Table C.44

Least Like To Be: Turkish Children's Responses

Table entries are percentages	6-Year-Olds	Social Class		10-Year-Olds	Social Class		14-Year-Olds	Social Class	
	Total	Low	Middle	Total	Low	Middle	Total	Low	Middle
No Response	33	37	28	1	1	–	–	–	–
Americans	5	4	6	–	–	–	–	–	–
Africans	13	14	13	15	11	18	19	18	20
Chinese	1	1	–	11	10	13	6	6	6
Giavours	9	10	8	–	–	–	–	–	–
Russians	10	10	11	51	54	48	58	64	52
Greeks	9	10	9	6	10	2	5	2	8
Arabs	–	–	–	4	6	2	1	–	2
Others	20	14	25	12	8	17	11	10	12
Total of Percentages	100	100	100	100	100	100	100	100	100
Total Number of Responses	100	52	48	100	53	47	100	49	51

289

Appendix D
Variations in Children's Responsiveness to Questioning

For most national groups, the younger children did not answer the questions put to them as often as the older children did, and in certain cases the children of all ages were particularly unresponsive. There are many possible reasons why children fail to answer. They may, for example, be uninformed about the topic under discussion, or they may be reserved or reticent, possibly because they are unaccustomed to interacting verbally on a person-to-person basis with adults in interview settings. If they fail to respond to questions dealing more with opinions than facts, it could be that they are either unimaginative or, possibly, merely reflecting the training they received in their culture to keep silent unless they are very sure of their answers. The following analyses, although not adequate to help us decide between these alternative interpretations, direct attention to cross-national variations in children's responsiveness, thereby suggesting further research studies that could explain the phenomenon.

NATIONAL DIFFERENCES IN RESPONSIVENESS

To answer questions about seven reference groups, the children had to have at least some information, although they could, and often did, respond when they obviously had very limited knowledge of the people under discussion. We shall refer to these as *information questions*, distinguishing them from *opinion questions*, those asking mainly for personal feelings or opinions, such as: "What are you?", "What is your own group like?", "What would you most (and least) like to be if you weren't, say, American or Brazilian?", "Can you name some foreign peoples who are like us and some who are different from us?" The

average percentages of no-answer or "don't know" responses for each
of these two sets of questions were determined for the three age groups
of children from all eleven nations. These are presented in Table D.1.

Responses to Information-Type Questions

Considering first the children's responses to information-type questions, it will be noted that the range of percentage scores is large. At
one extreme, 77% of the Brazilian 6-year-olds failed to respond to these
questions; at the other, only 9% of the 14-year-old American and German
children failed to respond. In general, marked increases in responsiveness occur from one age group to another. Still, at each age level there
are substantial national differences. At the 6-year level, the most responsive are the German, American, Bantu, and Turkish children; on the
other hand, over 50% of the Brazilian, French-Canadian, Lebanese,
Israeli, and French children failed to respond to this set of questions.
For six national groups (the Bantu, French, English-Canadian, Japanese,
Turkish, and American), the 14-year-olds do not differ substantially from
the 10-year-olds in responsiveness. However, there are notable increases in responsiveness from the 10- to 14-year levels for the Brazilian, French-Canadian, and Lebanese children. Considering all three age
levels, the most responsive national groups, in general, are the American, German, Turkish, and Lebanese, in contrast to the Brazilian,
Israeli, Bantu, and Japanese children, who are relatively unresponsive.

A question arises as to the interpretation of these cultural and age
variations: Are the Brazilian and Israeli children less informed or less
imaginative than the American, German, and Turkish youngsters? Why
does the response rate level off at 10 and 14 years in some countries
and continue to increase in others? Are there cultural factors that determine how responsive children of certain age groups are when interacting with adults?

Reactions to Opinion-Type Questions

The same general trends are apparent when one considers the children's reactions to opinion-type questions. That is, there are progressive
age changes in responsiveness, from large percentages of failures to
respond at age 6 to relatively small ones among 14-year-old groups.
However, several noteworthy changes occur in the relative standings of
the various national groups. Some are generally unresponsive to both
opinion-type and information-type questions (the Brazilian, Bantu, and

Table D.1

National Differences in Failures to Respond*

	Information Questions			Opinion Questions		
	6 Years	10 Years	14 Years	6 Years	10 Years	14 Years
American	40	13	9	47	24	18
Bantu	45	26	24	51	26	23
Brazilian	77	45	24	77	39	19
English-Canadian	50	21	15	54	21	13
French	51	18	13	52	15	16
French-Canadian	65	24	8	56	16	8
German	35	15	9	33	10	11
Israeli	54	26	16	37	16	10
Japanese	48	24	18	49	23	17
Lebanese	56	21	8	70	25	17
Turkish	45	6	12	35	5	3

* Table entries are mean percentages of no-answers or "don't know" responses. The higher the percentage, the less responsive the group.

293

Japanese children) and others are responsive to both types (the German and Turkish children). On the other hand, the American and Lebanese children, when compared with the other groups, are *less* responsive to opinion-type than to information-type questions, whereas the Israeli and French-Canadian children are more responsive to opinion-type questions.

SOCIAL CLASS AND SEX DIFFERENCES IN RESPONSIVENESS

Comparisons were made between lower- and middle-class children (Table D.2) and between boys and girls (Table D.3) of each country. In these cases we examined all responses to the information-type questions and determined the proportion of times the lower-class children gave fewer responses than the middle-class (listed under L in Table D.2) and the proportion of times the middle-class children gave fewer responses than the lower-class children (listed under M in Table D.2). In this analysis, "fewer" does not refer to statistical significance, but simply "any amount less than." For instance, the first two entries in Table D.2 mean that the American 6-year-olds were asked 24 questions (four questions about six reference peoples) and to 25% of these the lower-class children made fewer responses than middle-class children, whereas in 71% of the cases the middle-class children had a greater number of no-response entries. These do not add to one hundred because of cases where there was no difference between the social class groups. The same procedure was followed for the set of opinion-type questions.

Social Class Differences

There are several noteworthy trends apparent in Table D.2. First, the 6-year-old, lower-class children from seven of the eleven national settings gave fewer responses than did middle-class children. The four exceptions were the American, French-Canadian, German, and Japanese samples, where the middle-class 6-year-olds were less responsive than the lower-class children.

At the 10-year age level, the lower-class children from *all* eleven nations are less responsive than the middle-class children. Furthermore, at the 14-year age level, the lower-class children from eight nations are also less responsive. The exceptions among the 14-year-old groups are not all the same as those noted at the 6-year level; in this instance the French, Israeli, and American middle-class groups respond less, especially so in the case of French and Israeli children. In general, then, the lower-class children at all ages are more prone to say they "don't

Table D.2

Social Class Comparisons of Failures to Respond

	Information Questions						Opinion Questions					
	6 Years		10 Years		14 Years		6 Years		10 Years		14 Years	
	L	M	L	M	L	M	L	M	L	M	L	M
American	25	71	54	33	38	46	100	0	33	67	33	17
Bantu	67	38	58	33	50	46	50	33	17	83	17	50
Brazilian	79	21	96	4	75	4	100	0	100	0	67	33
English-Canadian	86	14	79	14	79	18	100	0	67	33	67	33
French	93	4	54	32	25	64	83	17	50	50	17	83
French-Canadian	29	57	68	21	57	21	83	17	100	0	33	33
German	33	62	71	21	92	4	67	33	67	0	83	0
Israeli	75	25	79	18	36	61	33	67	67	17	33	50
Japanese	43	54	61	32	71	29	83	17	100	0	83	17
Lebanese	75	18	75	7	54	25	100	0	100	0	75	25
Turkish	64	29	93	4	58	18	100	0	83	17	0	50

L = Lower class, M = Middle class.
Information Questions are those concerning the standard reference peoples.
Opinion Questions are those concerning self, peoples similar and different, least and most like to be, and description of own group.
Entries are the proportion of times that the children in one category gave fewer responses than those in the alternate category.

Table D.3

Boy-Girl Comparisons of Failures to Respond

Information Questions

	6 Years		10 Years		14 Years	
	B	G	B	G	B	G
American	21	79	21	75	38	58
Bantu	71	33	42	58	46	50
Brazilian	4	96	67	21	50	42
English-Canadian	29	68	4	93	18	71
French	57	29	7	79	32	57
French-Canadian	29	50	50	32	32	39
German	21	71	12	75	8	88
Israeli	11	82	32	68	14	82
Japanese	14	79	7	75	18	75
Lebanese	14	82	0	100	14	64
Turkish	14	79	7	89	11	64

B = boys; G = girls.

know" or otherwise fail to respond to questions put to them. This is clearly the case for 10-year-olds from all nations and also for the Brazilian, English-Canadian, and Lebanese children at all ages. At 6 years the trend is not as clear because of the reversals in the case of American, French-Canadian, German, and Japanese children.

One might argue that lower-class children are less informed about foreign peoples than middle-class children because less information is available to them, particularly in their homes. But should a lack of information alone also make them less able or willing to answer questions dealing mainly with matters of opinion and feeling? When we compare the social class subgroups with regard to their failure to respond to opinion-type questions (Table D.2), a generally similar pattern of findings emerges. At the 6-year level, the lower-class children from all eleven nations are less responsive than middle-class children, and there are substantial differences except in the case of the Bantu children. At the 10-year level, the lower-class children from eight of the eleven nations are the less responsive. The exceptions are the American and Bantu children, while there are no social class differences for the French 10-year-olds. There is no trend, however, at the 14-year age level. At this age, the lower-class children from six nations are the less responsive (Brazilian, English-Canadian, German, Japanese, Lebanese, and American), whereas the middle-class are the less responsive in four cases (the Bantu, French, Israeli, and Turkish samples). For the 14-year-old French-Canadian children, there is no social class difference in this regard.

One might also intrepret these trends to mean that the 6- and 10-year-old lower-class children are either less informed or less imaginative than the middle-class children of the same ages, and are therefore less able to respond. This does not explain, however, why the middle-class American, French, and Israeli children are less responsive at certain age levels. An explanation in terms of the amount of information they have available or differences in imagination becomes more questionable as we examine boy-girl differences in responsiveness.

Boy-Girl Differences

The boy-girl comparisons are presented in Table D.3. Only responses to information-type questions were available since the opinion-type questions were not analyzed for sex differences in the individual studies. It will be noted that at all three age levels girls are generally less responsive than boys. The exceptions at 6 years are the Bantu and

French groups, where girls are the more responsive, and at 10 years the Brazilian and French-Canadian girls are more responsive than boys. At 14 years the Brazilian girls are somewhat more responsive than boys.

These findings make it less likely that a lack of information and imagination are the determining reasons for certain children's tendencies not to respond. It would be difficult, for instance, to argue that girls from so many countries are less informed or less imaginative than boys. Instead, these data suggest that failures to respond may be attributable to cultural variations in the degree of social reserve or reticence of children, or variations in values and norms of appropriate behavior for boys and girls or members of different social classes when they are in social interaction with adults. The importance of rapport between the young child and his examiner on verbal responsiveness has been noted and discussed by Pasamanick and Krobloch[1] in respect to American Negro children. The variations apparent in the present study suggest that further cross-national research on the social responsiveness of children would be extremely worthwhile.

[1] B. Pasamanick and Hilda Krobloch.   Early language behavior in Negro children and the testing of intelligence.   *J. abnorm. soc. Psychol*, 1955, *50*, 401-402.   See also: Ruth G. Matarazzo, J. D. Matarazzo, G. Saslow, and Jeanne S. Phillips. Psychological test and organismic correlates of interview interaction patterns. *J. abnorm soc. Psychol.*, 1958, *56*, 329-338.

Appendix E

Cross-National Comparisons of Boys' Occupational Aspirations and Achievement Orientations

The study presented below deals with the strivings and future-oriented aspirations of the boys from our various national samples.[1] Although it is not directly concerned with their views of foreign peoples, the study nevertheless serves as an important supplement because, by introducing the reader to the various modes of adjustment these children make to certain demands of their particular societies, it throws light on their evaluations of their own countries.

Recent advances in the study of motivation stem in large part from the use of a new approach, one that places emphasis both on the manifestations of a particular motive in various behavioral settings and on the various complex antecedent sources of influence that determine the motive's development. The work of McClelland, Atkinson, Clark and Lowell[2] on the achievement motive is an outstanding example of this new trend. In their studies, they compared various situational conditions with regard to their power of evoking the achievement motive. Later work[3] extended the scope of their analysis to include societal and cultural (including philosophical and religious) factors that affect the

[1]An earlier version of this study appeared as: W. E. Lambert and O. Klineberg. Cultural comparisons of boys' occupational aspirations. *Brit. J. soc. clin. Psychol.*, 1963, *2*, 56-65.

[2]D. C. McClelland, J. W. Atkinson, R. A. Clark, and E. L. Lowell. *The achievement motive.* New York: Appleton-Century-Crofts, 1953.

[3]D. C. McClelland. The psychology of mental content reconsidered. *Psychol. Rev.*, 1955, *62*, 297-303; D. C. McClelland (Ed.), *Studies in motivation.* New York: Appleton-Century-Crofts, 1955.

amount of achievement motivation likely to be found among members of various religious, social class, or cultural groups. The results of these investigations strongly support the hypothesis that achievement orientation, conceptualized as a stable personality disposition, is developed through particular socialization influences that, in turn, are affected by cultural and philosophical values. The stability of this disposition has been established in an important later study by Kagan and Moss,[4] who showed that achievement strivings noted at ages 6 to 10 are highly related to the achievement tendencies of the same individuals measured in adulthood.

In the same spirit, Rosen[5] has examined the interrelations of achievement motivation, cultural values relating to achievement, and the educational and occupational aspirations parents hold for their children. In view of the socio-cultural histories of various ethnic groups, Rosen believed that cultural backgrounds should play a strong role in determining the extent of achievement striving. Comparing second-generation Americans of different racial, religious, and ethnic backgrounds, Rosen's findings do not make clear whether cultural or religious backgrounds play the more important role in determining achievement motivation. But some very suggestive relations do exist between the stresses placed on achievement and independence training by mothers of different ethnic-religious backgrounds and the amounts of achievement motivation shown by their children. The present study, based on the behavior of members of cultural groups "at home" rather than as second-generation subgroups within the American cultural setting (the case for Rosen's study), throws further light on the nature of achievement motivation and its development. The results also lend support to McClelland's later work,[6] on the relation of achievement motivation and successful entrepreneurship in modern nations.

While interviewing our eleven national groups of children, we capitalized on the opportunity to make cultural comparisons of one particular aspect of their motivations. The boys were asked two questions, the responses to which provided a measure of this aspect. One dealt with the boy's occupational or vocational aspirations — what he wanted to do for his livelihood when be became an adult — and the other determined what his father actually did for his livelihood. The boys' aspirations

[4]J. Kagan and H. A. Moss. Stability and validity of achievement fantasy. *J. abnorm. soc. Psychol.*, 1959, *58*, 357-364.

[5]B. C. Rosen. Race, ethnicity, and the achievement syndrome. *Amer. sociol. Rev.*, 1959, *24*, 47-60.

[6]D. C. McClelland. *The achieving society*. Princeton: Van Nostrand, 1961.

and their fathers' occupations were compared in terms of their social class similarities. That is, the son might aspire to the same occupation as his father's or one judged as socio-economically equivalent for that culture, to one of a higher social class than that of the father, or to one lower in class. The occupational comparisons were made by those in charge of the national studies, all of whom were aware of the position of various occupations in that nation's economic class structure.

The purposes of the present study, then, were: (a) to compare the occupational aspirations of boys from a wide range of cultural settings, (b) to relate the boys' aspirations to the social status of their fathers' actual occupations and to examine age and cultural variations in this son-father comparison, and (c) to relate variations in these filial-aspiration indices to cultural measures of achievement motivation.

METHOD AND PROCEDURE

It will be recalled that the children included in the national sample had to live in a large city, have at least normal intelligence, and attend publically financed schools. The three age samples of 50 boys each were used for this analysis. Thus, 50 6-year-old, 50 10-year-old, and 50 14-year-old boys of normal intelligence, attending public schools in major cities, in each of eleven cultural settings were the subjects. Half the boys at each age level came from what were considered as lower- or working-class families for the particular cultural group involved, and half came from middle-class families. (The directors of the national studies collaborated with the local school administrators to decide which children came from homes of middle or lower socio-economic class and satisfied themselves that the final samples were representative of urban children with normal intelligence living in the particular cultural setting involved.)

The father's actual occupation was reported in as much detail as possible by the child himself, and his statements were checked against school records of family backgrounds if they seemed suspicious in any way. Somewhat later in the interview, the boy was asked what occupation he desired for himself when he became an adult. The research team for that nation compared the son's aspirations and the father's occupation, assigning a rating of 2 if the son aspired to an occupation which would be regarded indigenously as having the same general status significance as that of the father, a rating of 1 if the aspiration fell at a status level recognizably lower, or a 3 if it was at a status level recognizably above the father's occupation. The raters drew on their experience as social scientists and as residents of the country to determine if a child's aspiration would be typically recognized by others in the country as essentially at the same status level as the occupation of the father or whether it would be generally considered as higher or lower in status. This within-family occupational comparison will be referred to as a *filial-aspiration index*.

CULTURAL COMPARISONS OF BOYS' OCCUPATIONAL ASPIRATIONS

The more popular aspirations are presented in Table E.1. Only those that were given by at least two children from an age group of any particular culture are listed.

Although the samples are too small for normative comparisons, still several general statements can be made about trends. First, when one disregards age and class differences, there is a general similarity of occupational aspirations among cultural samples. That is, engineering, medicine, and mechanical occupations are popular aspirations in most of the cultures represented. Exceptions to these generally popular occupations are seen in the recurrent choices of the priesthood among the two younger age groups of French-Canadian boys, of teaching among the Bantu boys, of manual type occupations among German boys, and of employee or sales positions or baseball careers among the Japanese boys.

Secondly, distinctive social class variations do not, in general, show themselves in occupational choices. The lower- and middle-class boys appear to have very similar aspirations in most cultures represented. For example, the choices of engineering and medicine are generally as popular for lower- as for middle-class boys. Exceptions to this trend are noticeable in the older German and French samples, where the lower-class children more typically aspire to lower-class positions while the middle-class children mention middle-class aspirations.

Thirdly, no outstanding age variations appear in occupational aspirations. Although the younger children, comparatively, express attraction to the more glamorous and adventurous occupations (such as soldier, pilot, fireman, policeman, and, particularly, truck driver), still the more popular choices of the older boys in any particular culture are also apparent among the younger boys of that culture. There is the suggestion of a progressive age trend from more adventurous and glamorous occupations toward more serious and mature occupational aspirations.

The interesting fact is the similarities of occupational aspirations

Table E.1

Popular Occupational Aspirations for Boys from Eleven Cultural Settings by Age and Social Class

	6 Years		10 Years		14 Years	
	Low	Middle	Low	Middle	Low	Middle
Turkey	soldier 7 doctor 4 engineer 4 employee 2	engineer 8 sailor 3 pilot 3 architect 2 doctor 2	engineer 11 doctor 8 policeman 3	engineer 9 architect 4 policeman 3 doctor 2 pilot 2	engineer 11 doctor 3 lawyer 2	engineer 11 doctor 4 policeman 2
Lebanon	soldier 5 doctor 4 teacher 3	doctor 11 pilot 4 merchant 3 engineer 2	doctor 5 engineer 4 teacher 3 soldier 2 lawyer 2 mechanic 2	doctor 10 engineer 9 soldier 2 merchant 2 house 2 painter 2	engineer 12 doctor 5 teacher 3 merchant 2	engineer 10 doctor 6 pilot 3 soldier 2 teacher 2
French Canada	construction worker 9 priest 5 soldier 2	policeman 5 doctor 3 mechanic 3 priest 3	priest 4 carpenter 2 fireman 2 mechanic 2 painter 2 policeman 2	priest 6 doctor 3 farmer 3 policeman 3 reporter 3 accountant 2 pilot 2	clerk 5 accountant 3 architect 3 pilot 2 chemist 2	engineer 10 electronics worker 3 mechanic 2 printer 2 teacher 2

	6 Years		10 Years		14 Years	
	Low	*Middle*	*Low*	*Middle*	*Low*	*Middle*
Israel	engineer 4 pilot 4 driver 3 policeman 2 mechanic 2 carpenter 2	soldier 6 doctor 4 engineer 3 driver 2 pilot 2	pilot 4 mechanic 2 engineer 2	pilot 5 driver 3 soldier 2 sailor 2 mechanic 2 engineer 2	engineer 4 mechanic 4 soldier 3 clerk 3 plumber 2 teacher 2 farmer 2	engineer 8 doctor 2 lawyer 2 farmer 2
Bantu	teacher 12 doctor 3 driver 2	teacher 6 driver 6 doctor 5 clerk 4 builder 2	teacher 6 doctor 4 driver 3 carpenter 2	doctor 9 teacher 7 driver 4 clerk 3 policeman 3	teacher 7 doctor 4 clerk 3 driver 3 lawyer 2	clerk 6 teacher 6 doctor 3 lawyer 2
America	policeman 5 ballplayer 4 doctor 3 engineer 2 milkman 2 sailor 2	policeman 5 fireman 4 doctor 3 sailor 2 teacher 2	pilot 4 athlete 2 doctor 2 marine 2 priest 2	engineer 5 doctor 4 policeman 4 ballplayer 3 priest 2 scientist 2	engineer 6 electrician 2 mechanic 2 pilot 2 teacher 2	engineer 4 auto salesman 2 electronics worker 2 sailor 2

	6 Years		10 Years		14 Years	
	Low	Middle	Low	Middle	Low	Middle
Brazil	soldier 5 chauffeur 3 tailor 2 mechanic 2 doctor 2 dentist 2	doctor 8 engineer 4	doctor 5 engineer 4 mechanic 2 chauffeur 2	engineer 10 doctor 8	mechanic 9 engineer 8 typesetter 2	engineer 13 doctor 3 diplomat 2
English Canada	policeman 4 sailor 2 train engineer 2	doctor 6 engineer 4 policeman 4 pilot 2	engineer 6 pilot 4 scientist 2	engineer 3 soldier 2 lawyer 2 pilot 2	engineer 3 mechanic 3	engineer 8 doctor 4 lawyer 3
France	None of 2 each	fireman 3 barber 2 doctor 2 policeman 2	mechanic 3	engineer 10 doctor 7 pilot 2	mechanic 6 engineer 2 electronics worker 2 locksmith 2 metal worker 2 house painter 2 toolmaker 2	doctor 4 draftsman 2 machinist

Germany

	6 Years Low	6 Years Middle	10 Years Low	10 Years Middle	14 Years Low	14 Years Middle
	actor 2	policeman 4	butcher 2	train conductor 4	baker 4	electronics worker 5
	fireman 2	driver 3	engineer 2	policeman 3	mechanic 4	engineer 4
	mason 2	pilot 2	driver 2	engineer 2	civil servant 3	teacher 3
		soldier 2	worker 2		construction worker 2	architect 2
					engineer 2	doctor 2
					merchant 2	sailor 2
					telephone worker 2	

Japan

	6 Years Low	6 Years Middle	10 Years Low	10 Years Middle	14 Years Low	14 Years Middle
	driver 5	baseball player 4	clerk 6	baseball player 6	clerk 6	clerk 7
	engineer 4	clerk 3	baseball player 4	driver 4	merchant 5	salesman 3
	merchant 3	sales manager 3	sales manager 3	engineer 2	engineer 3	scholar 3
	clerk 3	driver 3	driver 2		iron worker 2	engineer 2
	metal worker 2	policeman 2	policeman 2			
	pilot 2	salesman 2				

noted among children of various ages, from different socio-economic backgrounds, and from cultures that vary in degree of economic development and standard of living. Apparently there is universal agreement among children, regardless of their backgrounds, as to which occupational roles are of interest.

CULTURAL COMPARISONS OF FILIAL-ASPIRATION INDICES

Cultural variations in mean filial-aspiration indices are presented in Table E.2, where cultures are ranked from high to low in this regard. For this analysis it was decided to combine the data for lower- and middle-class boys for several reasons. First, the filial-aspiration indices actually collected in the different cultural settings only permitted three degrees of variation: the son's occupational aspiration was categorized as being above, below, or at the same social class level as his father's occupation. More gradations of comparisons could, of course, be used in determining filial-aspiration indices, but in the present study it was not feasible to obtain more refined occupational comparisons. Consequently, the middle-class boys have less opportunity than lower-class boys of aspiring above their father's occupational level, and lower-class boys are similarly limited at the other extreme in that they have less opportunity of aspiring below their father's occupational level. Social class comparisons would have been affected by these limitations and were accordingly not made. Instead, attention is directed here to cultural and age variations based on samples of approximately equal numbers of lower- and middle-class boys at the three different age levels.

The differences among filial-aspiration indices were examined for statistical significance with an 11 (nations) x 3 (age groups) analysis of variance, presented in Table E.3. It will be noted that there are reliable differences among cultural and age groups of boys and that the age and cultural variations interact. The minimum cultural differences needed for significance (presented in Table E.2) indicate two clearly distinguishable cultural clusters. Those having high filial-aspiration indices are, starting with the highest: Turkey, Lebanon, French Canada, Israel, the Bantu sample, Brazil, and the United States. Turkey is reliably higher in this respect than all other cultural samples except Lebanon. The cultures with comparatively low filial-aspiration indices are, starting with the lowest: Japan, Germany, France, and English Canada.

Table E.2

Filial-Aspiration Indices for Boys from Eleven Cultural Settings

Culture	6 Years		10 Years		14 Years		Culture Means		Achievement Scores**	
	$\bar{X}$	N	$\bar{X}$	N	$\bar{X}$	N	$\bar{X}$	N	Means	Standard Scores
Turkey	2.44	45	2.75	48	2.81	48	2.67	141	3.62	2.16
Lebanon	2.45	42	2.46	56	2.68	59	2.54	157	2.71	.95
French-Canada	2.38	42	2.58	38	2.63	35	2.52	115	3.10	1.46
Israel	2.24	45	2.46	39	2.78	46	2.50	130	2.33	.44
Bantu	2.42	50	2.58	50	2.42	45	2.48	145	none available	
Brazil	2.24	45	2.59	46	2.43	46	2.42	137	none available	
America	2.26	43	2.49	43	2.50	40	2.41	126	2.24	.32
English-Canada	2.11	36	2.34	44	2.29	35	2.25	115	2.29	.39
France	2.03	34	2.43	42	2.17	42	2.22	118	2.38	.51
Germany	2.02	44	2.13	45	2.38	60	2.20	149	2.14	.19
Japan	1.83	47	2.07	45	2.48	44	2.12	136	1.29	−.95
Age Group Means	2.23	473	2.45	496	2.51	500				

Minimum mean age difference*: $P < .01 = .08$, $P < .05 = .07$.

Minimum mean cultural difference*: $P < .01 = .16$, $P < .05 = .15$.

*These minimum differences were obtained by following the techniques of Sheffe as presented in Edwards (A. L. Edwards. *Experimental design in psychological research.* New York: Rinehart, 1960, p. 154).

**Taken from McClelland (*op. cit.* 1961, pp. 461-463). McClelland had determined a score for Brazil, but it was decided not to use it for present purposes because McClelland noted that it was "not used in the main study, scored separately and open to coding bias" (p. 463). Three scores were given for Canada, one labelled "Canada" and which was used for the English-Canadian entry since it likely refers to readers used by Montreal's Protestant School Board and its system of schools, from which the English-Canadian children were chosen. Two other scores were given, an "English Catholic" and "French Catholic." Since training in English is started early (grade 4) in the Montreal French schools, and since school books must be approved by the Catholic School Board, it was decided to average the scores for the French and English Catholic readers since both are likely used in the training of the French-Canadian children. It was not possible to do the same for the English-Canadian sample, who also study French in the early grades, because McClelland had no score available for French Protestant readers. It is unlikely that Catholic books would be used in the Protestant schools of Montreal.

Table E.3

Variance Analysis for Culture and Age Variations in
Filial-Aspiration Indices*

Source of Variation	Sum of Squares	df	Mean Square	F	Significance
Culture	40.85	10	4.085	11.1216	< .01
Age	21.882	2	10.941	29.7876	< .01
Interaction	13.473	20	.6736	1.8339	< .05
Within	527.504	1436	.3673		
Total	603.71	1468			

*Because the N's varied from cell to cell, the methods for equating cell entries suggested by Ferguson (G. A. Ferguson, *Statistical analysis in psychology and education.* New York: McGraw-Hill, 1959, p. 259f.) were followed. The N's varied primarily because of children who gave no aspirations, i.e., did not know what they wanted to be when adults.

With regard to age differences, there is a marked increase in the magnitude of the indices from 6 to 10 years of age whereas the 10- to 14-year increase does not quite reach significance levels. Thus, the 6-year-old boys have lower filial-aspiration indices than the older boys do. The interaction is due to age trend differences from culture to culture. In six of the national samples (Turkey, French Canada, Israel, Germany, and Japan) there are step-wise increases from year to year in the indices, while in four samples (Bantu, Brazil, English Canada, and France) the highest indices are noted at age 10, with a decrease from 10 to 14 years.

The filial-aspiration index reflects the magnitude of discrepancy between a father's occupational achievement and his son's aspiration. In bringing these two elements into a ratio, it is assumed that the son sets his aspirational goals partly in terms of his father's actual occupation, in some cases lining up his goals with his father's achievement level, and in other cases departing from it by orienting above or below this parental reference point. Furthermore, we are placing emphasis on the average filial-aspiration index of groups of children from different cultural settings. It is assumed that these mean indices reflect variations in cultural orientations toward the next generation's getting ahead in relation to the present generation, as one extreme of the dimension, or staying close to the parental pattern and perpetuating the actual social class standing of the family. In other terms, it is presumed that the index reflects a cultural attitude toward the maintenance or rejection of established levels of family class status. If this attitude has culture-wide acceptance, one would expect that parents hold the attitude and try to pass it on to their children. On the other hand, the index could reflect a feeling of disappointment on the part of the younger generation toward the cultural achievements of the older generation, a sort of looking back one generation with chagrin if not with anger.

It may clarify these notions if we try to apply them in an interpretation of two trends apparent in Table E.2. The French samples show a reliable decrease in filial-aspiration indices for the 10- to 14-year-old groups ($t = 2.06$, $p < .05$) while Japanese, German, and Israeli boys show reliable increases in scores from 10 to 14 years ($t = 3.90$; $t = 2.50$; and $t = 2.39$ respectively). These trends could mean that transmitters of the French culture curtail any inappropriate aspirational ventures by the time a boy reaches his teens, whereas Japanese and German socializers possibly lose some type of control over their children's aspirations after the early years, since the teen-age boys in the Japanese and German samples seem no longer to keep their aspirations in line with their father's occupations, as was apparently the case at ages 6 and 10. Following the same logic, the Israeli boys would likely receive increasing amounts of social support for having high occupational aspirations inasmuch as the filial aspiration indices become progressively higher at each age level. These are speculations, of course, and further research is needed to adequately test the notion that socializers in various cultures differ systematically in their attitudes toward their children's desires to get ahead.

THE RELATION OF BOYS' ASPIRATIONS TO ACHIEVEMENT VALUES

McClelland has recently collected a large number of children's readers from various nations and analyzed their content for themes concerned with achievement.[7] Fortunately for us, nine of our eleven nations were included in McClelland's sample of nations and the readers selected were those in popular use in 1950, an especially appropriate time period for our purposes since all three age groups would probably have used readers of that vintage. Thus, it is possible for us to determine whether achievement needs, as reflected in children's readers, and filial aspirations are related. The means and standard scores for the achievement scores for the nine nations are presented in the right-hand section of Table E.2.

The datum of interest here is the correlation between average filial-aspiration indices and McClelland's achievement score: $rho = .87$, significant at beyond the .01 confidence level. This high correlation indicates that there is a strong relationship between children's desires to get ahead and the attitudes toward achievement dominant in their culture. Assuming that the popularity of the readers is a reflection of the culture-wide values which educators have chosen to stress, then we may consider this correlation to be supporting evidence for cultural variations in attitudes toward the maintenance or rejection of established levels of family class-status. The findings suggest that socializers in various cultural settings differ in the degree to which they encourage their children to get ahead in relation to the levels of achievement attained by the current adult group. The findings also suggest that achievement orientations may depend upon cultural variations in the freedom afforded children to modify established levels of the family's social standing.

[7] Ibid.

Index

(Numbers in italic type refer to tables.)